CULTURE AND CONTROL
IN COUNTER-REFORMATION
SPAIN

Hispanic Issues

HISPANIC ISSUES
VOLUME 7

CULTURE AND CONTROL IN COUNTER-REFORMATION SPAIN

ANNE J. CRUZ AND MARY ELIZABETH PERRY

◆

EDITORS

UNIVERSITY OF MINNESOTA PRESS

MINNEAPOLIS   OXFORD

The editors of this volume gratefully acknowledge assistance from the Program for Cultural Cooperation between Spain's Ministry of Culture and United States' Universities; the College of Liberal Arts and the Department of Spanish and Portuguese at the University of Minnesota; Occidental College; The UCLA Center for Medieval and Renaissance Studies; and the University of California at Irvine.

Published by the University of Minnesota Press
2037 University Avenue Southeast, Minneapolis, MN 55414.
Printed in the United States of America on acid-free paper.

Library of Congress Cataloging-in-Publication Data

Culture and control in counter-reformation Spain / Anne J. Cruz and Mary Elizabeth Perry, editors.
   p.   cm.
   Includes index.
   ISBN 0-8166-2025-3 (hard) : — ISBN 0-8166-2026-1 (pbk.) :
   1. Counter-Reformation—Spain.   2. Spain—Civilization—1516-1700.
3. Control (Psychology)—Religious aspects—Christianity.   I. Cruz,
Anne J., 1941-   .   II. Perry, Mary Elizabeth, 1937-   .
   BX1585.C84   1992
   306.6'8246'09031—dc20   91-19823
                                                                     CIP

A CIP catalog record for this book is available from the British Library.

The University of Minnesota is an
equal-opportunity educator and employer.

Hispanic Issues

Contents

◆ Introduction

Culture and Control in Counter-Reformation Spain

Anne J. Cruz and Mary Elizabeth Perry

> *To arrive at complete certainty, this is the mental attitude we*
> *should maintain: I will believe that the white object I see is black if*
> *that should be the decision of the hierarchical church.*
> —*Spiritual Exercises*, Ignatius of Loyola

Culture and control became issues of primary importance for public policy during the Counter-Reformation in Spain. From the reign of Ferdinand and Isabel through the sixteenth and seventeenth centuries, Spain experienced the exhilaration and anxiety of attempts to effect meaningful reform that pressed far beyond the confines of religion. The Counter-Reformation was an "order-seeking" period, in the words of historian A. G. Dickens, during which officials exerted greater efforts than before to define culture and set limits on how much cultural diversity would be tolerated.

'order seeking period'

Cultural formation, however, is not an internalized phenomenon, but responds to and influences a number of external factors, both political and economic. The consolidation of an empire that grew ever larger in the sixteenth century, for example, posed problems of unification and administration that a more homogeneous culture would have been able to ameliorate. Yet economic development, as the Spanish empire engaged in large-scale mercantile capitalism, produced class tensions that threatened the stability of any monolithic culture. The authors of this volume view culture as a social construct constantly in process. As anthropologist Clifford Geertz has argued, culture is best seen as a set of "control mechanisms," or systems of signification, that can assume different patterns. It is the accumulated totality of these patterns, he states, that governs human behavior and gives shape to human experience (45-46). Challenging traditional views that placed biological development before acculturation, Geertz considers culture central to human evolution, and its symbols prerequisites of social existence.

In stating that human beings are only "completed" or "finished" through highly particular forms of culture, Geertz's studies have been crucial to the rethinking of cultural development, particularly in moving away from the nature/nurture controversies and toward a view of symbolic structures as essential to cultural systems. According to Geertz, "Our ideas, our values, our acts, even our emotions, are, like our nervous system itself, cultural products—products manufactured, indeed, out of tendencies, capacities, and dispositions with which we were born, but manufactured nonetheless" (50). As an anthropologist, Geertz is mainly interested in the interpretation of culture, in discovering the conceptual structure that, he stresses, lies embedded in symbolic forms.

Yet, as Raymond Williams suggested more than a decade before Geertz, culture also involves issues of dominance and conflict. In order to reach an understanding of how individual societies form their members, we must study the nature and origin of the shaping process (312). In a dominant culture, he states, this happens through communication—not passively, but through the interactions of message, reception, and response (312-313). By historicizing cultural production, Williams reminds us that symbolic systems are not only inherited by one group, but equally as often are imposed by another. Culture, then, is a process by which humans construe significance for themselves and the world around them; in its response to external forces, it also represents alternative ideas of the nature of social relationships (325).

In the case of Counter-Reformation Spain, alternative means of coexistence were shaped both because of and despite the control imposed by the dominant social and religious groups. Supported by the Monarchy, and through the efforts of the Council of Trent and the Inquisition, the Catholic Church acted as an official organ of cultural production. In the first chapter of this volume, Jean Pierre Dedieu notes that the Church ensured religious instruction through its increasing catechization of the unlettered. Adherence to orthodox religious beliefs was then sought through such symbolic representations as the mass or, as Sara T. Nalle and Gwendolyn Barnes-Karol demonstrate, public devotions to saints and the theatrical rhetoric of religious oratory. The oral recital of prayers, as well as the aural and visual reception of sermons and spectacles, were effective means of impelling the members of society toward cultural and political integration.

The consequences of such an integration were complex and far-reaching. According to José Antonio Maravall, the reorganization of social hierarchies culminated in the restoration of seigneurial power through the revalorization of agrarian land ownership. He credits this process with granting new power to the upper classes, which he defines as including the nobility, the Church, wealthy commoners, and state bureaucrats (71-72). Because such social realignments were inherently unstable, however, they both proscribed a return to the earlier feudal system and resulted in a more strongly centralizing monarchy that required that order be imposed, as the continuing tensions between the dominant groups and marginalized subalterns constantly threatened to disrupt the tenuous social balance.

The marginalized groups were marked as different either through physical signs, as in the cases of *morisco* circumcision studied by Bernard Vincent, or metaphorically by the persistent conflicts within the social body, such as the clashes between New and Old Christians documented by Jaime Contreras. In studying gender repression, the chapters by Mary Elizabeth Perry, Anne J. Cruz, María Helena Sánchez Ortega, and Alison Weber illustrate the ways in which women endeavored to attend to their own spiritual and economic needs by challenging patriarchal control. John R. Beverley's chapter on the literary Baroque shows just how such paradoxes are contained and exploited within literature. He agrees with John Elliott, who warns against overestimating the passivity of Spanish society and exaggerating the dominant group's capacity to manipulate for its own ends since, as Elliott makes clear, "the works of Spain's Golden Age contain sufficient ambiguities to suggest that subversive subtexts are there for the reading" ("Concerto" 28).

The strife between social groups analyzed in the chapters of this volume forms part of a long record of gender, class, and ethnic struggles. From its early history, Spanish culture—its values, traditions, systems of signification, ideas, and institutions—has been heterogeneous and undiminishingly conflictive. Américo Castro often reminded us that Christians, Moslems, and Jews coexisted peaceably until the end of the fourteenth century; he dated the "conflictive age" to the span between that period and the total breakdown of caste relations in the seventeenth century (30-31, note 7). While opening the country to the modes of thought of other European countries, Spain's unification under the Catholic Monarchs ensured that only one of the three groups would predominate, dependent as the country was upon the dominance of Christianity and Castilian values over all others.

Although both nonconverted Jews and Muslims had recently been expelled from Spain, the sixteenth century's early decades ushered in a period of renewed vitality and intellectual freedom that encouraged the introduction of novel literary styles even as it created the climate for such political uprisings as the *comunero* rebellion of 1521 (Lynch 1: 51). The beginning years of Charles V's reign welcomed reform, in particular the humanistic revival advocated by such philosophers as Erasmus, whose writings were widely admired throughout Spain. The University of Alcalá de Henares, founded in 1498 by the Franciscan reformer and archbishop of Toledo, Francisco Ximénez de Cisneros, opened in 1508 and became one of the most renowned centers of learning in Europe.

Because of the rising dominance of the Catholic Church, this atmosphere of intellectual and religious openness was to be short-lived. By 1537, the Inquisition, soon to become the leading institution of the Spanish Counter-Reformation, had convicted of heresy both Alfonso de Valdés, Charles V's apologist for the sack of Rome, and Pedro de Lerma, the University of Alcalá's chancellor, who was condemned to recant his Erasmian preachings. Juan Luis Vives's letter to Erasmus decrying that "we can neither speak nor remain silent without danger," eloquently illustrated the difficult conditions under which these humanists soon found themselves, and nowhere was the situation more dangerous than in Spain (Lynch 1: 72-73). Prefiguring the Baroque vision of the "theater state," remarked upon by Beverley, with its entangling alliance of politics and art, Hernando de Acuña's sonnet heralding the age of "one monarch, one empire, one sword" in reality signaled an era increasingly intolerant and intent upon control.

One of the means utilized to program and delimit social behavior was the Inquisition. Originally established in 1478 to maintain religious unity within the Peninsula by exterminating apostasy among those Jews and Muslims who had converted to Christianity, this institution soon extended its jurisdiction to such diverse acts as bigamy, sodomy, and blasphemy. Virgilio Pinto has pointed out that heresy represented a complete breach with the Church, and was viewed as an intellectual crime in that it signified the point where freedom of thought became subject to punishment (304). The Inquisition's powers, therefore, eventually extended to deviant forms of private and public expression that threatened cultural homogeneity. Visually and ideologically similar to the public executions described by Michel Foucault in his study of the French penal system, the Inquisition's public exposure of the victim, paraded through the streets in *coroza* and *sanbenito*, and the dreaded *autos de fe* affirmed the power and superiority of the Church (Foucault 48-49).

The climate of fear created by the Inquisition preceded the Counter-Reformation, which was initially a movement begun by the Church to affirm dogma and discuss disciplinary reform so as to deter the encroachment of Protestantism. Religious reform had been attempted in Spain even before the Lutheran revolt; Ximénez de Cisneros's efforts were perhaps the most illustrious example of a movement that would include the Dominicans and Benedictines, as well as the Franciscan Observants, raising the standards of monasticism well before the Carmelite reform. By the beginning of the Council of Trent in 1545, theologians such as Francisco de Vitoria, Melchor Cano, and Domingo de Soto had strengthened the Catholic position, protecting Spain from

Protestant proselytizing (Lynch 1: 67). The Catholic Church applied its own rigorous programs of instruction through, among others, the catechistical and oratorical methods discussed by Dedieu and Barnes-Karol. Like the Inquisition, then, the reaches of the Counter-Reformation extended far beyond its intended purpose.

Meeting for some twenty-five sessions between 1545 and 1563, the Council of Trent reviewed in detail such issues of religious dogma as the constitution and function of the sacraments, consubstantiation, and the adequacy of the Latin Vulgate Bible, as well as those more directly affecting lay public attitudes such as the sacramental character of matrimony, purgatory, indulgences, and the veneration of relics, images, and saints. In an effort to counteract the Protestant Reformation, which rejected the veneration of saints, the Counter-Reformation especially promoted new cults, as Sara T. Nalle demonstrates in her chapter on Saint Julian. Yet the growing interest in spiritual matters became a threat to orthodox doctrine, and as religious occasions became intermingled with everyday concerns, social control depended on increasingly broader inquisitorial powers. If the Reformation left a legacy of political and religious division throughout Europe, Spain's Counter-Reformation would forever mark the country's spiritual, intellectual, and material development.

This volume focuses on the climate of repression fostered by the Counter-Reformation, and investigates the varying forms of social control exerted by Spanish institutions, both through the Inquisition and by less overt but equally powerful means. Religious as well as secular rhetoric, whether sermons or popular poetry, and ecclesiastical theater as much as the *comedia*, all contributed to a growing cultural homogenization. Indeed, all the chapters in this volume demonstrate that no one was entirely free from the strictures imposed by either Church or State, and several of the contributors focus on the diverse methods employed to maintain an atmosphere of conformity and fear. Yet they also recognize the paradoxical nature of these methods, which had to legitimize themselves while drawing precisely on the contingency of social authority. The analyses of the strategies of survival utilized by those minority groups—women, *conversos*, and *moriscos*—who suffered the greatest abuses from the institutions in power acknowledge the remarkable resilience of the heterogeneous cultures that had existed for so long on the Iberian Peninsula.

While the Inquisition pursued offenders, the Church was concerned with enforcing prescribed behavior through such normative means as prayers, sermons, and the promotion of religious cults. Even before the Council of Trent, the various synods had regulated Church doctrine, stipulating that children and adults learn the four basic prayers. Jean Pierre Dedieu relies on the Toledo synodal decrees in order to document the growing interest of the Church in the religious education of the people. By studying approximately 700 inquisitorial interrogatories, he demonstrates how the male population of New Castile learned the basic Catholic catechism and availed themselves of the sacraments. Dedieu concludes that by the beginning of the seventeenth century, Spain had reached a level of religious education surpassing that of France and Italy.

As we have seen, direct religious instruction was only one of several ways that the Church maintained control over its flock. Although literacy was increasing and religious texts flourished, oral and visual reminders of their beliefs helped sustain the people's faith. While Church officials encouraged the veneration of saints, Nalle states that they did so in a reversal of the traditional pattern in which popular enthusiasm for a local saint finally won official recognition. Studying the case of Cuenca, she points out that city government and cathedral chapter worked together to popularize Saint Julian, a medieval bishop whose cult had been all but forgotten. By moving his burial place, disinterring his body, and inviting the faithful to record miracles attributed to his relics, officials resurrected and revitalized his cult in order to strengthen the traditional faith. They held celebrations on his day that emphasized the hierarchy, visual decoration, and drama so essential to Counter-Reformation attempts to control and guide reception of public festivals. To Nalle, these celebrations were performed to impress the public as "baroque spectacles of power," rather than to permit participation in them.

This same hierarchy of power was evident in the religious oratory addressed to town audiences. The Council of Trent institutionalized preaching as a means of rhetorically controlling the people and of disseminating social propaganda that encouraged the status quo. In its attempt to regularize oratory, the Church formulated a religious discourse intended to instruct, entertain, and persuade, one that was delivered orally but that also availed itself of novel scriptural constructs. Gwendolyn Barnes-Karol demonstrates how the preachers' power to control public opinion depended upon both their linguistic ability and the dramatic appeal of the sermons. She analyzes the sermons not only for their rhetorical mastery, but also in relation to their semiotic function. Signs such as the preacher's voice, gestures, and dress combined with the theatrical settings of churches and convents—with their highly realistic images of the Crucifixion and saintly martyrs as backdrops—to manipulate the audience's reception of the total performance. Aiming for *admiratio* rather than rational consensus, preachers often became skilled actors, transforming their churches into "ecclesiastical theaters" with elaborate special effects. Barnes-Karol asserts that the parallel between the pulpit and the stage was frequently drawn for the purpose of instructing preachers, and she follows Maravall in her claim that the impact of live oratory, like that of secular theater, reaffirmed a past social reality. But in discussing the circulation of written sermons in collections called *sermonarios* (sermons that dealt insistingly with the stability of the written word), Barnes-Karol points to the same problematics of authority and entropy noted by Beverley. Because the written sermons were read aloud to groups, they encouraged attendance at oral sermons; the cycle of print to performance thus created a system that maintained Church conservatism.

Despite the efforts of the Church to impose religious homogeneity on the population, the various minority groups resisted change. Although nominally converted, as Bernard Vincent and Jaime Contreras explain, many *moriscos* and *conversos* held firmly to their preestablished practices. In many cases, persecution helped these groups rediscover the significance of their ethnic practices and actually encouraged new loyalties to the minority groups' origins. Vincent's chapter, "The *Moriscos* and Circumcision," deals specifically with the ceremony of circumcision in three townships. By tabulating the ages of circumcised and uncircumcised males, he is able to determine the responses of the *morisco* communities to religious control. As Vincent shows, the practice continued clandestinely: to elude inquisitorial persecution, the *moriscos* delayed circumcision until after infancy. The community proved admirably adept at dissimulating. When questioned by inquisitors, young males often blamed their deceased parents for their circumcision; others would deny any knowledge of the circumstances. Vincent makes clear how the practice of circumcision assumed significance to both Christians and *moriscos*. To the Inquisition, the visible sign meant an opportunity to implicate the individual further and thus extract a general confession; to the *morisco*, it offered an identity linking him to his community.

Like the *moriscos*, *conversos* were often the targets of inquisitorial persecution, inasmuch as the group was viewed as recalcitrant and subversive. In an impressive demonstration of historical detective work, Jaime Contreras goes beyond this perception to bring to light the intricate and hidden relations of power among Old and New Christians. The tensions between families who had previously coexisted peacefully escalated as municipal offices were increasingly relegated to the nobility. The decade of the 1560s witnessed the growing paranoia around the "purity of blood" issue, as *converso* efforts to purchase titles of nobility were blocked both by competing groups of commoners and by nobles. Piecing together clues of tightly interwoven lives of New Christians in the townships of Lorca and Murcia, Contreras uncovers the ways in which inquisitorial authority was often abused to marginalize New Christians from positions of power by accusing them of Judaizing. His case histories vividly illustrate that the climate of fear and hatred fomented by the Counter-Reformation against alleged crypto-Jews was exploited for political purposes as well.

Our efforts to address culture and control in Counter-Reformation Spain could hardly be complete if we ignored the repeated attempts to order and constrain women's lives. Unlike the religious minorities we have discussed, women posed different problems of control: crossing both class and ethnic lines, women were perceived in the Counter-Reformation as the most dangerous threat to Christian morality, yet they could not be totally separated from the majority, and indeed they were ever present, whether as wives, daughters, sisters, or mothers. Gender control, then, represents one of the most pervasive and complex of cultural mechanisms. During the Counter-Reformation, the Church and the State reinscribed misogyny by focusing on women's powers to lead men's souls to hell. While other minorities were condemned for their unorthodox beliefs and practices, only women as a group were viewed as inherently dangerous to men. Control of the female body was thus not only an economic strategy, but one of the most important means of ensuring men's salvation.

The chapters by Mary Elizabeth Perry, Anne J. Cruz, Alison Weber, and María Helena Sánchez Ortega discuss the significance of women's social roles both in the private and the public spheres, be they roles conforming to their accepted sexual and reproductive functions, or ones threatening social order. Either as Old Christians, *moriscas*, or *conversas*, women formed a gender subculture separate from other minority groups; rather than differentiated by ethnicity, religion, or class, women were distinguished by social expectations. As such, the primary behavior that had to be inculcated in them was sexual purity—not so much for their own social and moral good, but to protect male privilege.

For this purpose, chastity was the most exalted virtue for females, but given their "natural" weakness, it was also the most difficult to protect. Mary Elizabeth Perry reasons that while clerics urged parents to guard their daughters "as dragons," the very presence of unchaste women revealed the failure of the attempts to impose moral control over women. Officials feared that unchaste women threatened social order and the salvation of men's souls, yet their fear revealed an ambivalence: unchaste women could be seen either as Magdalens, victims of circumstances such as poverty and seduction, or they could be seen as Jezebels, agents of evil who seduced young boys and infected others with disease and debauchery. Disagreeing about the possibilities of redemption, officials nevertheless agreed that these women should be enclosed in the brothel, the Magdalen house, or the prison.

The forms of control over women's sexuality varied according to their own responses and others' needs. Many cities legalized prostitution as a means to protect the chastity of some women and the sexual privilege of men. Yet the appearance of the Sevillian syphilis epidemic gave real urgency to a growing debate over prostitution, calling both for stricter regulation of prostitutes and also, paradoxically, for their legal prohibition. Not surprisingly, the nun who proposed to Philip III a severe prison as punishment for recalcitrant women used disease as a metaphor to describe the contagion, both physical and moral, that female impurity could spread throughout his kingdom.

For those women whose chastity made them desirable brides, marriage represented yet another form of enclosure, and many were to lament their married state. Anne J. Cruz traces the ballad of *La bella malmaridada* from its lighthearted origins in French *chansons* to its increasingly darker Spanish variants, where the wife's unhappiness leads to adultery, then death at the husband's hands. Her chapter relates the attitudes expressed by literary texts—oral, cultured, and dramatic—to the growing strictures placed on Spanish women during the Counter-Reformation. By comparing literary genres, she studies the function of popular poetry and theater as oral and visual means of gender indoctrination.

Arguably less constrained during the medieval period, women's roles in the sixteenth century were privatized by the division of labor based on the sexes. When Lope de Vega glosses the poem in his play of the same title, both husband and wife exemplify Church teachings on marital behavior. Considered the most popular of popular songs, *La bella malmaridada*'s lament is staged by the Golden Age playwright as a lesson for the good wife. The woman's role never deviates from that of a caring mother and long-suffering wife whose love finally compels the husband to abandon his concubine and his gambling—a vice that had recently come under attack by Tridentine reformers. In its paradigm of Christian marriage, the play rewrites normatively the punitive lesson sung by the ballad's adulterous wife.

Yet no matter how normative, literary depictions sketch only a partial view of a very complex network of gender behavior. The enclosure of women, either through marriage or in convents, did not guarantee their control, whether real or fictional. The moralists' adjurations for cloistered women were increasingly losing ground, as more female labor was needed to contribute to the Hapsburg war economy. Perry comments that the urgency with which parents and clerics policed women implies the failure of the system to impose a homogenous moral order that would contribute to political stability. Enclosure, whether in the brothel, the Magdalen house, or the convent, often proved powerless in controlling women's behavior.

Religious women, for instance, often enjoyed more intellectual freedom without the domestic constraints imposed by husbands and children. The most striking example of how a religious vocation could offer women control over their own lives is Saint Teresa of Avila, whose writings demonstrate her indefatigable spirit as religious reformer, author, and mystic. Yet Saint Teresa's experiences were judged by her confessors as those of a religious woman, and as such, she was considered susceptible to diabolical illusions. Alison Weber's study of Teresa's works reveals her autobiography to be a dissenting demonological treatise that defines the nature and limits of diabolical power. Teresa's Devil never loses the grotesque appearance he had in medieval iconographic tradition, a characteristic that Weber suggests could be viewed as a strategic attempt to displace the more seductive Counter-Reformation Devil. Clearly preoccupied by the potential apparitions of demons to her nuns, Teresa attributed most demonic visions to physiological conditions brought on by excessive prayer and meditation, and refused to perpetuate the myth that women were the Devil's compliant sexual partners. In this, Weber tells us, as well as in her confidence in women's capacity for genuine mystical experience, Teresa dissented from the traditional view of women as pawns of the Devil.

Women's subversive tactics, within the convent or outside its walls, could not completely elude control; Teresa's experiences, for example, came under the careful scrutiny of her confessors. The gaze of her superiors carried with it apparent disciplinary power, what Foucault has called a "mechanism that coerces by means of observation" (170). By scrupulously obeying their orders, however, Teresa recast her submissive role into an active attitude of penitence, thereby reversing discipline to suit her own needs, rather than those of the Church.

Nonetheless, in the fervor of renewed ecclesiastical antifeminism, Teresa's skepticism toward demonic possession was uncommon and quite dangerous. The relationship between women and the Devil was increasingly affirmed through inquisitorial cases that intended to prove heretical behavior. Indeed, in daily life, women were as much feared as they were constrained; not only moralists, but society in general fostered strong beliefs regarding women's powers and viewed them as sources of evil. María Helena Sánchez Ortega studies Inquisition cases of women accused of sorcery, whose spells, she points out, gained a reputation as diverse and dangerous as the women who employed them. Most women who cast spells on livestock, crops, and their neighbors were not considered professional sorceresses, but many who practiced "love magic" took on a professional role and were sought by women abandoned by a lover. Men believed as fervently as women in the spells, and often would accuse the sorceresses to the Inquisition as a means of breaking their bonds. Men's testimonies demonstrate both their fascination with and their fear of these powerful women.

Although the Inquisition was generally more tolerant of the women accused than were their neighbors and relatives, when a case involved harm to a child, inquisitors often explained the events as a diabolical pact, effectively converting the women into witches. Older women, women who lived by themselves, and those whose lives were somehow different from others', increased people's suspicions and fears, and the transformation from sorceress to witch offered a way of controlling women by placing them more fully within the jurisdiction of the Inquisition.

The conversion of sorceress into witch is most evident in a literary source: Cervantes's description of Cañizares in his *El coloquio de los perros* (*The Dogs' Colloquy*). As a text of the Counter-Reformation, Cervantes's exemplary novel also exemplifies the cultural significance of Baroque literature. To John R. Beverley, the paradoxical quality of the Baroque may explain both the attempts and failures to control culture during the Counter-Reformation. A Janus that looked behind to the sunset of feudalism and ahead to the dawn of capitalism, this ambivalent phenomenon was the voice of both the absolutist state, with its small literate elite comprising the powerful aristocracy, and the growing commodification of literary production and distribution in nascent capitalism.

In the last chapter of this volume, Beverley traces the historical and social implications of Baroque literature as the "cultural form" of the Counter-Reformation. Emerging from the Renaissance genres that had been placed on the Index, this literature assigns itself the task of recontaining a subversive potential within Counter-Reformation orthodoxy. For the Jesuit Baltasar Gracián, for example, the art of literary conceits was indeed a prerequisite, not only for the "man of letters" but also for the *político*, the political man. Yet what Gracián recognizes is the irresolution between a rhetorical notion of power, and power as an innate quality that, as we have seen in Contreras's study of crypto-Jews and local power, was demanded by both the nobility and Counter-Reformation political theory.

Beverley therefore considers as overly monolithic Maravall's view of the homology of the Baroque as a cultural phenomenon with the absolutist monarchy as the very essence of aristocratic power. Instead, he sees the representation of the State, along with the authority of the Church, not as a reflection of its actual coherence, but as an imaginary concept, a projection of desire misconstruing the real. To Beverley, the Baroque literary forms that attack the emergent bourgeois and artisanal culture arise precisely from the forms that enhance a man as a "solitary individual." Baroque ambiguity is perhaps most evident in its representation of history as an apotheosis of empire, all the while acknowledging Spain's inexorable decline.

Pointing out the contradictory nature of Baroque literature, Beverley's chapter serves as a fitting conclusion to our volume. What he considers Baroque spiritualism's "paradoxical conjunction of the principle of submission to authority with the practical and theoretical ideal of the self-willed, independent individual" addresses as well the conflictive and conflicting values expounded by Counter-Reformation Spain. Yet not all groups could assume the individualism ascribed to them, as cultural identities often emerged from and depended upon communities. Rather, we have seen the ways in which many women, *con-*

versos, and *moriscos* relied upon each other in order to promote and maintain cultural difference. By isolating diverse instances of these social practices, as well as the normative means that intended to control them, the authors of this volume underline the cultural heterogeneity of a Spanish society made up of Old Christians, *conversos*, *moriscos*, women, and men. In doing so, they highlight both the methods of repression and control utilized to bring these minority groups into conformity with dominant patterns, and the alternative means of survival and subversion with which these groups responded.

Works Cited

Bataillón, Marcel. *Erasmo y España: Estudios sobre la historia espiritual del siglo XVI.* 2nd ed. México: Fondo de Cultura Económica, 1983.

Castro, Américo. *De la edad conflictiva: Crisis de la cultura española en el siglo XVII.* 3rd ed. Madrid: Taurus, 1972.

Dickens, A. G. *The Counter-Reformation.* London: Thames and Hudson, 1968.

Elliott, John H. *Imperial Spain: 1469-1716.* New York: New American Library, 1963.

———. "Concerto Barroco." *The New York Review of Books.* April 9, 1987: 26-29.

Foucault, Michel. *Discipline and Punish: The Birth of the Prison.* New York: Vintage Books, 1979.

Geertz, Clifford. *The Interpretation of Cultures: Selected Essays.* New York: Basic Books, Inc., 1973.

Lynch, John. *Spain under the Hapsburgs.* 2nd ed. 2 vols. Oxford: Basil Blackwell, 1981.

Maravall, José Antonio. *La cultura del barroco.* 2nd ed. Barcelona: Ariel, 1981.

Pinto, Virgilio. "Censorship: A System of Control and an Instrument of Action." *The Spanish Inquisition and the Inquisitorial Mind.* Ed. Angel Alcalá. Atlantic Studies on Society in Change. Boulder, Colo.: Social Science Monographs, 1987.

Williams, Raymond. *Culture and Society: 1780-1950.* New York: Columbia Univ. Press, 1960.

◆ Chapter 1

"Christianization" in New Castile Catechism, Communion, Mass, and Confirmation in the Toledo Archbishopric, 1540-1650

Jean Pierre Dedieu

(translated by Susan Isabel Stein)

And it is commonly observed that because of the defects of the teachers, neither children nor adults understand or learn what a Christian needs to know, and some of them are so ignorant that they are hardly worthy of being called Christians or human beings.

Unanimously agreed upon by the bishops of Toledo,
from 1480 until the end of the seventeenth century.
—José Sánchez Herrero

In 1975, Professor Delumeau, in his inaugural address at the College of France, presented a brilliant synthesis of the history of Christianity. According to him, during the Middle Ages an abyss separated an elite minority, who adhered to a set of established religious practices, from the masses, who believed in magic and ignored the most elemental Christian truths, in spite of the fact that they did indeed consider themselves Christians. During the sixteenth and seventeenth centuries, the Catholic and Protestant elite became aware of this fact, influenced both by the mendicant orders' attempts to awaken the religious spirit of the public and by the intellectual ferment of the Reformation and Counter-Reformation (Delumeau, "Déchristianisation" 3-20). They undertook the tremendous task of "Christianizing" the masses, an endeavor that reached its peak at the end of the seventeenth century.

Professor Delumeau believes that this effort achieved its objective. His project consists of quantifying the results and studying their geographical, sociological, and temporal aspects—a complex and impassioned undertaking. A scholar studying the twentieth century can at least evaluate external attitudes or analyze deeper levels expressed in public opinion polls (Michelat and Simon). The historian does not have the same resources.

The wealth of material available in the Spanish archives, nonetheless, converts the country into a veritable laboratory. Documents of inquisitorial trials offer rich sources of study (Dedieu, "The Archives" 158-189). Beginning with the case files of the Holy Office, we will study how a communal religious practice was created: how the Spanish people acquired a basic knowledge of theology, how they learned the fundamental prayers of the Church (the *Pater, Ave, Credo,* and *Salve*), how they fulfilled Church commandments (mass, confirmation, confession, and annual communion), and the extent to which they went even beyond that required of them. The documentation provides abundant sociological data allowing for various differential criteria such as age, cultural level, social category, and residence. The first part of this study analyzes the growing concerns of the ecclesiastical hierarchy with religious instruction of the masses and control over their religious practices. We will then examine the inquisitorial documents and compare them with results of the clergy's efforts.

The clergy's concerns are evident in their desire that everyone have a solid knowledge of basic Christian dogma and norms of behavior, what we today call the catechism. Let us examine measures taken between the fourteenth and the sixteenth centuries to institutionalize instruction in the Christian faith.[1]

Before 1473

Up to the late fifteenth century, the synods did not appear very concerned with catechesis. The acts of the 1323 synod contain a "Christian doctrine" in Latin, a text containing the Articles of Faith, God's Commandments with a commentary, and a list of the seven sacraments, vices, and virtues. Apparently ordered by the Cardinal of Santa Sabina, the Papal Legate, priests were to read the text to the public in the vernacular (Sánchez Herrero 173-176). The following ten synods and six councils did not mention the doctrine. It appeared once more at the 1356 synod, which included the 1323 measures and added the stipulation that the public readings take place during high mass at Christmas, Easter, Pentecost, Assumption, and on the first Sunday of Lent (Sánchez Herrero 224-226, 228). The 1379 synod made no reference to the doctrine.

From 1473 until Trent

The issue was revived at the end of the fifteenth century. The provincial council at Aranda ordered the priests to have a written copy of the Articles of Faith, the Commandments, and the list of sacraments, vices, and virtues in order to read them to parishioners every Sunday during Lent (Sánchez Herrero 285). While this order did not add anything new, Alonso Carrillo, who presided over the Alcalá synod in 1480, went much further. He ordered all priests to have, within three months, a parchment letter containing all the items required by the council at Aranda and including works of charity, the gifts of the Holy Spirit, the five corporal senses, and the list of the cases reserved for the Pope and the Bishop. This letter was to be posted in a public place and read to parishioners every Sunday of Lent. Furthermore, the synod publicly expressed for the first time its concerns about the religious instruction of the faithful (Sánchez Herrero 302-305). It requested that priests seek the assistance of a capable clergyman or sacristan in order to open a school and teach the parish children how to read, write, and sing. They were also taught the contents listed in the letter; priests encouraged parishioners to send their children to school. Thus, secular and religious education were to take place together. The Carrillo mandate was followed by all the assemblies until the end of the seventeenth century.[2]

The synods of reformist bishop Francisco Ximénez de Cisneros confirm these orders. In 1497, he instructed priests to ring the bells, calling to *Salve* and to sing the prayer solemnly every Sunday, after vespers and before nightfall. They were to teach children to make the sign of the cross,[3] and to recite the *Pater*, the *Ave María*, the *Credo*, the *Salve*, the Ten Commandments, and the General Confession; attendance at such sessions was mandatory. To induce the adults to attend, all present would receive forty days' indulgence (Sánchez Herrero 344-345). The 1498 synod published a text of the "doctrine" that priests were obliged to teach, which included the *Credo* in Latin, divided into twelve paragraphs, each one traditionally attributed to an apostle; the Articles of Faith; the Ten Commandments; the commandments of the Church; the works of charity and the capital sins, all in Castilian; as well as a final reminder of the two commandments to love God above all else and to love one's neighbor as oneself.

The 1536 synod led by Cardinal Tavera supported the effort to catechize. It did not publish any doctrine, but merely repeated, with some variations, the dispositions of its predecessors. It added that every Sunday at high mass, after the faithful were absolved of venial sins, the priest had to require them to recite a *Pater* or a *Credo* as penance and recite the prayers with them "in order to accustom the people to say them correctly" (Synod 1536, fol. 4r). The priest was to sing the *Credo* a capella, so as to facilitate better understanding of the words (Synod 1536, fol. 22r). Teachers were to instruct their pupils in Christian doctrine every day; couples who could not correctly recite the four basic prayers could not marry. Such a requirement at a key moment in life was significant: the synodal decisions were no longer abstract, but were to be carried out. This was the spirit of Trent *avant la lettre* (Synod 1536, fol. 3v).

Trent

The Council of Trent was not really concerned with catechism. It named a commission to compile an instruction manual for priests, but not for the public. It decreed that the bishops had to ensure early religious instruction in each parish, at least on Sundays and holidays (Session XXIV, Reformation Decree, Can. 4). The Spanish bishops showed more concern for catechesis than did the fathers of Trent. José Goñi Gaztambide has pointed out how obsessively the issue was dealt with during the Navarrese clerical visits beginning in 1540 (*Los navarros* 153-155). At the same time, many catechisms were being edited throughout Spain, earlier than in other Catholic countries (Guerrero 225-260); the French presses did not begin producing such books in large numbers before 1640, and the first mention of catechism in the synodal statutes of Autun occurred in 1652 (Delumeau, *Le catholicisme* 288, 290). Spain took the lead within Christendom, while within Spain Toledo led all other dioceses, if we may draw any conclusions from the Navarrese example.

In Toledo, the Council of Trent was but the continuation of a previous movement. The provincial council of 1565-1566 published the Tridentine decrees and ordered priests to teach the catechism on Sundays and days of obligation in the church or some other stipulated locale, after high mass, around noon (Council 1566, fols. 49v, 50r). Don Gómez Tello Girón, the diocese administrator during Carranza's captivity, added a canon at the 1566 synod that reiterated the dispositions of the provincial council (Synod 1568, fols. 20v-21r). He forbade communion to those who did not know the four prayers (Synod 1568, fol. 77v), a prohibition that turned catechism into a tool of social control for ensuring the fulfillment of the annual precept. We know that during the eighteenth century in Navarre, a similar measure obligated parishioners to obey the commands of the hierarchy; we will see that the same measures were efficient in Toledo (Goñi Gaztambide, "El cumplimiento pascual" 361-372). In this area as in others, Cardinal Quiroga suspended his predecessor's measures; Cardinal Rojas y Sandoval reinstated them. Returning to the Cisneros tradition, he published a complete "Christian doctrine": the *Credo* in Latin and a simplified version in Castilian, without dividing it into the apostolic paragraphs; the Articles of Faith in Castilian; the Ten Commandments in Latin and the vernacular; the Church commandments; the list of the sacraments, the works of corporal and spiritual charity, the virtues, the gifts of the Holy Spirit, the beatitudes, the mortal sins, the enemies of the body and the soul, the corporal senses, all in Castilian; the *Pater*, the *Ave*, the *Salve*, and formulas for making the sign of the cross in Latin and in Castilian; and various prayers for specific moments of the mass in Castilian.[4] Until the end of the seventeenth century, all synodal records would reiterate this "doctrine," discreetly expanding upon it. After Quiroga it was no longer published as an appendix, but at the beginning of the main text, constituting the most important part of the profession of faith that opened the text (Synod 1583, fol. 2r).[5]

At the 1601 synod, Cardinal Rojas incorporated learning the Ten Commandments and the commandments of the Church as prerequisite for marriage (Synod 1601, fol. 74r). He also published a canon that strongly recommended that the episcopal inspectors ensure catechism instruction (Synod 1601, fols. 97r-99r), and he changed the preamble to the "Christian doctrine" (Synod 1601, fols. 3r-3v). Cardinal Infante's constitutions again modified the same preamble (Synod 1622, fols. 1r-1v), and more important, introduced the obligation of knowing the Ten Commandments and the commandments of the Church in order to receive communion, as well as "all that is necessary for receiving the sacraments" (Synod 1622, fol. 85r). Later modifications were not quite so important.

In summary, the active interest shown by the Toledan hierarchy in catechism instruction began around 1480, according to synodal records. Archbishop Carrillo laid the groundwork, and each synod expanded upon it. In 1540 a stronger requirement than any called for by the Council of Trent was already in existence: during at least one moment in their lives—at the time of marriage—Christians must prove that they had learned the four prayers of the Church, a requirement constituting the clergy's maximum obligation in the mid-sixteenth century. Trent thus accelerated the movement, but did not create it. New details appeared: the Church commandments had to be fulfilled, and Christians were to be examined not only once during their entire lives, but rather every year. At the beginning of the seventeenth century, the minimum requisite became knowledge of the Ten Commandments and those of the Church.

We should note as well that the catechizing effort was not merely nor even principally directed at the young. In the schools, of course, instruction of the children was the main objective. However, the examinations, the most effective measures, affected the adults more. Christians were obliged to remember Church doctrine actively during their entire lifetimes, a fact that demonstrated its importance to the clergy.

What was the meaning of this immense effort? Why were the faithful obliged to memorize so many formulas? For the effort did indeed involve memorization and nothing more. There was no commentary, no hierarchization of the beliefs or the Commandments, no internal organization or governing principle in the doctrine, except for one formal category, singularly revealing, regarding "what one must believe," "what one must do," and "what one must ask."

Many did not understand what they were learning. The majority of the prisoners who appeared before the inquisitors for having believed that fornication was not a sin knew the Sixth Commandment and the meaning of the word "fornication"; they simply believed that prostitution was a special case, falling outside the divine prohibition. And despite the fact that Gabriel de Salazar knew that the Trinity was one God and three divinities, as he was taught according to the Articles of Faith, he also firmly believed that Christ was the Father, the Son, and the Holy Spirit (AHN, Inq. Leg. 205, Expd. 24). Was the Church laboring in vain?

Catechism must be understood within the context of the entire clerical project at that time. Memorization was only a principle; the preachers and confessors were responsible for commenting upon the "doctrine" and rendering it explicit.[6] Sermons developed, ordered, and gave meaning and feeling to bare doctrinal compendia. In reality, catechistical elements structured both sermons and confessions. The following instructions were given by all archbishops to priests beginning with the time of Cardinal Quiroga:

> We order that when the priests are preaching the gospel
> throughout the year, they be careful to include
> instruction of the articles of faith as well as the mandates
> and precepts of the Church, and . . . how to love God
> the Father, how to perform works of charity, how to
> avoid giving offense or committing moral sins; admonish
> the people to behave as good Christians, desirous of
> their salvation. (Synod 1536, fol. 4r; Synod 1622, fols.
> 7v-85r)

In other words, instruction had to be organized around the content of the "doctrines."

If we examine any "Art of Confession," we are presented with all the permissible forms of confession, an enumeration of the sins according to the Ten Commandments, the potentiality of the soul according to the Articles of Faith, the articles of the *Credo*, the corporal senses, and the demands of the *Pater* (*Arte para bien confesar*). Knowledge of the corresponding formulas, even in the form of rote memorization without any active comprehension, was indispensable for the clergy to be able to act. Inquisitors proceeded in the following manner when dealing with recalcitrant prisoners: they were ordered to say the *Credo* and the Ten Commandments or the Articles of Faith. When the pertinent point arose (the Sixth Commandment in the case of fornication), they were stopped and interrogated until they realized that they had explicitly or implicitly disobeyed one of the Ten Commandments or an Article of Faith by committing the sin. The effect was powerful: the prisoners experienced a profound emotional crisis (Bennassar 260-261). In order for this to occur, they had to have a knowledge of the Articles or the Commandments, and they must have assimilated the idea that without them, there could be no salvation. Without this, there could be no shock and consequent penitence. Memorizing formulas thus functioned as the bridge between the general will of the Old Christians to be good Catholics and, what was more difficult, the observance of the ecclesiastical institution's particular interpretations. This constituted a sign of identity, of being one of the faithful. It was, ultimately, a pedagogical technique appropriate for massive education of an illiterate society.

We will limit ourselves to a summary study of confession and communion. We must remember that these two sacraments were closely associated; before and after the Council of Trent, the hierarchy insisted that one could not receive communion without having confessed beforehand (Sánchez Herrero 165; Council of Trent, Session XIII, Can. 11). We must also remember that the essential dispositions dated from the Lateran Council IV (1215) and had not been modified since then; Christians had to confess at least once a year with the parish priest (not with another priest) and receive communion during Easter (Lateran Council IV, Can. 21). There was some resistance: the synods of 1323 and 1356, as well as the provincial council of 1339, were constrained to enforce this disposition (Sánchez Herrero 174-175, 203-204, 225).

After more than a century of silence, the issue was raised once more at the Carrillo synod in 1480. The synod did not allude to the precept, as it had undoubtedly become part of local custom earlier, but it did order that priests in towns with more than one hundred inhabitants be assisted by another priest at Easter and during epidemics, so that everyone could confess. Later synods repeated this constitution with minor variations. This marked the beginning of modern legislation on this issue (Sánchez Herrero 313).

Cardinal Tavera made a vital decision to institute an effective system of control. All the faithful of sound mind were to confess during Lent and receive communion between Palm Sunday and Quasimodo Sunday; in case they did not do so within a grace period of one week, they would be excommunicated ipso facto. The priests were responsible for drawing up a list of all parishioners and classifying them according to the head of each family; the names of the recalcitrants were to be sent to the archbishop's prosecutor. Since this occurred in 1536, it was a display of Tridentine spirit *avant la lettre* (Synod 1536, fol. 37v).[7]

The Council of Trent placed great importance on the Eucharist. Unlike the Protestants, the Council viewed this sacrament as defining Church doctrine and exalted its significance by various means. It insisted upon the annual communion as required by Church commandment and encouraged "frequent communion" (Session XIII, Cans. 9, 11). In Toledo, this decision gave rise to a series of decisions that made Tavera's mandates more effective. Don Gómez Tello Girón insisted that priests denounce publicly and by name all transgressors (Synod 1568, fol. 77v). He also ordered the construction of "the richest tabernacles that can be constructed," plated in gold or silver (Synod 1568, fol. 63r). He decreed that those who confessed to some priest other than their parish priest must present to the latter a proof of confession (Synod 1568, fol. 12r).[8]

In order that Christians could receive communion at times other than Easter, Cardinal Quiroga encouraged couples to take the sacrament at their wedding (Synod 1583, fol. 22v). He prohibited confession in private homes and ordered the use of the confessionaries (Synod 1583, fol. 12r). Extending previous measures against priests without benefice, he also prohibited confession without the permission of the parish priest (Synod 1583, fol. 11r). Confessors could not receive any remuneration or gifts from penitents (Synod 1583, fol. 11v).

Attending mass on Sundays and days of obligation was an ancient precept, so ensconced in religious practice that medieval synods hardly mentioned it. Cardinal Tavera's intense clerical concern led him, nonetheless, to take some additional measures. He emphasized that individuals were obligated to attend mass *in their own parishes* and encouraged priests to denounce recalcitrants (Synod 1536, fols. 13v, 7v).

The theology and celebration of the Holy Sacrifice were the focus of multiple decrees at the Council of Trent, and mass was one of the key points of Catholic reform. Thus, the Toledan synods made the ceremony more solemn and majestic. From the vantage of the clergy, the most important aspect was the attempt to elevate the parochial mass above private votive masses and convent masses. During high mass, Don Gómez Tello Girón wanted all stores closed, including all businesses of an essential nature (Synod 1568, fol. 33v). He recommended that family heads order their children and servants to attend (Synod 1568, fol. 34v). Those who gambled during the ceremony were to be fined. His successors did not introduce substantive changes to his mandate.

The Church had required confirmation for a very long time (Vacant and Mangenot, col. 1076). However, although the 1323 synod mentioned the topic, concrete measures were not taken until 1480. In that year one synod lamented the lack of public enthusiasm for the sacrament and ordered the priests to advertise it on the first Sunday of each month (Sánchez Herrero 318-319). There were no momentous decisions until the Council of Trent. The Tridentine fathers limited themselves to theological considerations and to the condemnation of Protestant doctrine (Session VII). However, the sacrament was revalorized through their interest: in Toledo, Cardinal Quiroga insisted on the necessity of making it a common practice (Synod 1583, fol. 8v). As we shall see, he need not have worried.

In concluding the first part of this study, we note the general precocity of the Toledo prelates' reformist tendencies.[9] The early desire to "Christianize" the masses is unmistakable. We may now begin to examine the results. Our investigation focuses on the inquisitors' first interrogation of prisoners. Fernando de Valdés describes the encounter in his 1561 *Instructions:*

After the interrogation concerning identity, the prisoner must declare his genealogy, as far back as possible. . . . Then he must be asked where he grew up, with whom, if he has ever studied in a school, whether he has ever left the country, and if so, with whom. . . . And he must be questioned about prayers and Christian doctrine, where and when he confessed, and with which confessors. (Jiménez Monteserín 205-206)

During the second half of the sixteenth century, Pablo García's *Order to Prosecute in the Holy Office* confirmed that this was a triple inquiry. It first asked about genealogy, then about Christian doctrine, specifically whether or not prisoners had been baptized and confirmed; if they attended mass, confessed, and received communion as ordered by the Church, specifying the time and place where they last did so, and with whom; if they knew how to make the sign of the cross; if they knew the *Pater,* the *Credo,* the *Ave María,* and the *Salve,* and in what language (Latin or vernacular); if they knew the "Christian doctrine"; if they could read and write, if they had studied, if they had ever left the country and with whom. Last, the prisoners had to tell their life stories: where they were born, where they grew up, and in chronological order, all the places they had lived, and what they did in each place (AHN, Inq. Leg. 199-211, 69-75, 31-48).

Focusing specifically on those questions concerning Christian doctrine, we have thoroughly investigated the cases preserved in the Toledo inquisitorial archive that deal with the following offenses: "scandalous words," "dishonesty," and "blasphemy." We have consulted a total of 1,286 case files from the years 1525 to 1650 (see Table 1). The vast majority of the prisoners are Old Christians. The inquisitors performed the interrogation regarding Christian doctrine in only 747 cases.

Luckily, Valdés's instructions covered an already familiar practice. The reader will note that inquisitorial concern about the level of religious instruction increased the Toledo clergy's concern with catechism. For this reason, it makes sense to study the history of the Inquisition within the framework of the general history of the Church (Bennassar 16-42). This parallel is even more noteworthy if we examine the kinds of questions

Table 1.

Year	Number of cases with doctrine interrogation	Percentage among cases consulted
Before 1540	8	3
1540-1550	69	27
1551-1555	134	60
1556-1560	82	79
1561-1565	64	84
1566-1570	79	95
1571-1650	280	97

asked. The oldest part of the questionnaire deals with the four Church prayers and the form of making the sign of the cross, and was present in 80 percent of the interrogations taking place before 1560 and in over 99 percent after 1574. These questions represented, coincidentally, the minimum religious instruction required by the Church from 1540 on. Prior to 1565, prisoners were rarely asked about the other formulas comprising "Christian doctrine" (Articles of Faith, general confession, the Commandments). After that date, the Ten Commandments alone acquired much more importance and were present in approximately 70 percent of the interrogations after 1574, foreshadowing their inclusion in the clergy's list of required knowledge at the beginning of the seventeenth century.

After 1550, in 75 percent of the cases it was asked whether the prisoner had confessed and received communion during the previous Lent. This question became standard after 1570 (in more than 95 percent of the cases) and appeared in all interrogations after 1574. At this time, the interest in identifying the officiating priest became evident. Finally, between the years 1565 and 1574 the inquisitors began to ask whether the prisoners could read and write. After 1575, this question became standard. In summary, the fundamental data were available after 1540, but not all issues mentioned by Pablo García can be studied before 1575.

The inquisitors evaluated the answers as good, fair, or bad; prisoners passed the test (for example, they recited the *Pater* correctly), passed it with a few errors (they made mistakes in a few words of the *Pater*), or they failed totally (they had no knowledge of the *Pater*). The prisoners' personal data concerning identity and "genealogy" were available from the interrogation: sex, age, occupation, place of birth, residence, "race," etc. The "story of a prisoner's life" allowed the geographical assessment of individuals on a nine-point scale.

The documents are extremely informative, yet also present serious problems. We must confront what we believe to be a false objection that the Inquisition trials concerned aberrant cases and the conclusions based on them cannot be applied to the population as a whole. In a previous article, I have concluded that this is not true. Yet the 747 prisoners whose case files we have examined do not constitute what a statistician would call a representative sample. First, women are almost completely absent from the sample, comprising less than 10 percent of the total; this small percentage prohibits any kind of differential study on the basis of sex.[10] Furthermore, we know very little of the geo-socioprofessional distribution of the population of New Castile. While manual laborers are poorly represented in the group, comprising one-third of the interrogated prisoners, city dwellers, especially those residing in the largest cities, are overrepresented. As a means of overcoming these defects, we need to study only the overall results for each subgroup.

Even more serious are the deviations resulting from the lack of homogeneity of the target population. We have noted the following, beginning with the most serious, a geographical deviation. Until approximately 1560, the target population represented the entire district. Later on, inquisitorial activities were concentrated in La Sagra, central La Mancha, and the region around Madrid and Alcalá, that is, the central and southern areas of the district. Second, there is a residential deviation (rural districts, city).[11] Third, we point out a deviation concerning migration patterns; while at first the migrants represent less than 20 percent of the cases, they comprise more than 50 percent at the end. Finally, we can detect other deviations that may have serious consequences for our investigation. We note that all the curves drop between 1585 and 1595, to rise again later. This is apparently because of the laborer subgroup's completely losing all knowledge of the catechism. Yet it is hard to believe that in only a few years the laborers had forgotten all the Church's prayers. In fact, at that time the Inquisition had changed its tactics to concentrate its efforts in the cities, not bothering with rural districts except in the most serious cases of poorly socialized individuals or in cases of subtle segregation not included in the total numbers. The drop thus appears to be deceptive.

With what criteria did the inquisitors evaluate the responses? Were the criteria stable or did they change over time? From 1540 until 1650, at least sixty judges presided over the Toledo tribunal. According to the documents kept by the inquisitor Diego Ramírez de Sedeño during his visit to the district in 1556, in the Henares region of Alcalá 85 percent of those questioned knew the four fundamental prayers perfectly. An examination of his colleagues' observations from the periods 1551-1555 and 1561-1565 reveals that the statistics are 41 and 53 percent, respectively. The percentage of responses classified as frankly "bad" does not vary substantially, however. We may conclude that Ramírez benevolently tabulated as "good" the stammerings his colleagues must have considered "fair," or that perhaps he limited himself to asking the prisoners if they knew the prayers without verifying their assertions.[12] Barring this, deviations in the system of notation could only indicate greater strictness; the changes traced in the first part of this study imply that this is indeed the case. This fact does not detract from our conclusions; rather, it strengthens them.

At any rate, Christianization is seen as gaining momentum. The global perspective from the documents is conclusive and confirms a striking homogeneity in each of the distinct subcategories that reflects on the conclusions of the whole.

The small number of cases obliged us to divide the material in seven blocks of unequal duration, thus compromising between constituting useful statistical unities and maintaining a precise chronological dimension. The divisions are shown in Table 2.[13] We have noted a universal indicator: individuals passed the test if they recited the four prayers correctly, and they failed if they were ignorant of one or more. Those who were familiar with all four without being able to recite them correctly were classified under the category of "fair."

Table 2.

Year	Number of interrogated individuals
Before 1550	77
1550-1554	134
1555-1564	146
1565-1574	131
1575-1584	77
1585-1599	67
1600-1650	93

Table 3.

					Rate of success			
Year	% Pater	% Ave	% Credo	% Salve	% Four prayers	% Ten Command	% Crossing oneself	% Sign of cross
Before 1550	70	86	45	49	37	–	78	92
1550-1554	73	85	49	54	39	–	84	91
1555-1564	85	89	69	70	59	–	77	90
1565-1574	90	93	78	71	69	40	85	99
1575-1584	97	97	83	77	72	40	96	98
1585-1599	90	90	83	70	68	68	89	95
1600-1650	93	92	88	84	82	77	94	93
					Rate of failure			
Before 1550	3	0	11	25	25	–	10	2
1550-1554	1	0	8	18	19	–	9	3
1555-1564	1	0	5	13	16	–	15	4
1565-1574	0	0	3	13	13	45	10	0
1575-1584	0	0	5	8	10	52	3	0
1585-1599	2	0	3	10	11	18	11	1
1600-1650	0	0	0	5	5	8	1	1

The results speak for themselves (see Table 3). The success rate is doubled between 1555 and 1575. This curve should be modified according to previous observations, however. The results would not change significantly: before 1550, 40 percent of males from New Castile passed the test on basic Christian doctrine, leaving the other half below the proficiency level required by the Church. Twenty years later, three out of four answered correctly and only one in ten failed completely. The beginning of the seventeenth century thus saw a total success rate for the tested population. If we remember that Inquisition prisoners were not among those who had best learned Church doctrine, it is probable that the above success rate is even higher for the population as a whole.

It is interesting that the progress between 1560 and 1570 was apparently due to efforts aimed more at adults than children. The individual's age had no influence on the response and corresponded to the above strategies utilized by clergy.

Table 4.

| Year | Success rate of four prayers by occupation | |
	Agriculture	Handicraft
Before 1540	17	42
1540-1550	21	48
1551-1555	50	71
1556-1560	65	69
1561-1565	78	82
1566-1570	50	77
1571-1650	74	91

The small number of cases obliges us to limit the occupational analysis to the two best represented groups: laborers and artisans. We note that both curves are similar; that they follow the general curve; and that artisans consistently achieved better results than laborers. This is to be expected for reasons impossible to elaborate on at the present time, but was perhaps due to greater literacy among artisans (Rodríguez and Bennassar). (See Table 4.) We note also the wide initial disparity followed by an increasing approximation; the progress of "Christianization" is the result not of the consolidation of former positions, but rather of the conquest of virgin territory. We must keep in mind that the drop in the number of laborers between 1585 and 1599 merely reflects a modification in the selection criteria of target individuals.

In studying the places of residence, we conclude that knowledge of the prayers varied in inverse proportion to the size of the township. The difference was minor, however, and the greater statistical importance of the cities at the end of the period undoubtedly distorts the results. Geographical mobility should be considered to be an explanatory factor. It is evident that (1) ignorance of the prayers was systematically greater among recently established populations; (2) the catechistical effort was successful in two phases—until 1565 among stable populations, and essentially between 1575 and 1585 among the migrant populations; (3) the Church was successful in *completely* eliminating ignorance of the basic formulas of the faith among settled populations, as well as substantially reducing ignorance among mobile populations.

It is important to point out the close relationship between literacy and the level of Christian culture. Between 1575 and 1650, 86 percent of literates successfully passed the test, as opposed to 73 percent of illiterates; 13 percent of the latter failed completely, as opposed to the former's 3 percent. Most likely the period's overwhelmingly positive results reduced the impact of illiteracy, and we encounter this problem again in more difficult tests, such as knowledge of the Commandments. The relation of instruction to literacy can be easily explained by methods used to teach reading; the "letters" containing the prayers were also used as textbooks in the elementary schools.

The level of familiarity with all four prayers was very different among the four, with the *Ave* and the *Pater* being the most familiar. By the mid-sixteenth century, there were few who could not at least stammer their way through the *Credo* in its simplified version. Yet, there were also few who could recite it correctly. In the seventeenth century, the percentage of those barely familiar with it is not above 10 percent. The results are the same with the *Salve*; in the seventeenth century only foreigners were unfamiliar with it.[14] In the mid-sixteenth century, however, the percentage of absolute failures was high, as was the percentage of those who knew the prayer well; few people had only partial knowledge of it. Some foreigners did not know how to cross themselves; this number diminished progressively, proving that the clergy reached even the most isolated groups. Ignorance of the sign of the cross soon became an aberration.

One-fourth of the cases specify the language in which the prisoner was to recite the prayers. The data, scarce before 1555, became more systematic after 1580, indicating greater accuracy on the part of the judges. Until 1585, they preferred the Latin version (appearing in half of the cases); afterward, the Castilian version was given preference.[15] Did this evolution correspond to a global change within the Church? If so, it would denote a trend toward interiorization and thus less insistence on the rote repetition of incomprehensible formulas.

In any case, we can generally conclude that until 1600, the male population of New Castile, after half a century's efforts by the clergy, possessed the minimum theological knowledge considered indispensable for salvation, and the seventeenth century was to see even more improvement. The Ten Commandments and the commandments of the Church became required knowledge at the beginning of the seventeenth century. Since 1570, the Inquisition had asked whether prisoners were familiar with the former. The success rate for this test remained approximately 40 percent for a long time, rising dramatically to 70 percent during the last fifteen years of the sixteenth century and slowly increasing. By 1595, the number of complete failures had fallen to 10 percent, regardless of age or place of residence.

Unfortunately, the inquisitorial documentation does not allow us to engage in a parallel study of other issues of "Christian doctrine." Questions on the Articles of Faith do not offer a basis for statistics; however, their importance appears equal to that of the Ten Commandments. During the second half of the sixteenth century, an increasing number of primarily urban prisoners could correctly recite "the entire Christian doctrine." In some cases, the inquisitors declared themselves satisfied or even impressed.

The study of the commandments of the Church regarding communion and confession presents no special difficulties. The percentage of recalcitrants, most notably before 1550, diminished rapidly; we cannot find a single case between 1575 and 1584. Except for extraordinary cases such as the refusal to forgive wrongs committed against another person—which barred one from absolution—and detainment in civil jails, by the end of the sixteenth century Old Christians fulfilled the obligations of confession and communion.[16]

It is noteworthy that if in the sixteenth century, detainment in civil jails was one of the most frequently alleged reasons for failing to fulfill the religious obligations, in the seventeenth century, prisoners in such jails (eleven cases in all) had all received communion on the last important holiday, thus surpassing Church requirements. This situation resulted from the intensive work carried out by the religious orders, especially the Jesuits, and confirms the fervor of the Counter-Reformation clergy.

In the sixteenth century, abstention from communion was due to several factors noted by statistics: to residence in large towns, a low level of Christian culture, unemployment and agriculture, and geographical mobility. Indeed, it may have been the result both of insufficient integration into the surrounding community, specifically with regard to the Church, and of the pressures of daily life that often eclipsed the Christian tenet of forgiving wrongs.

Since Valdés required that prisoners be questioned concerning their latest confession, it is possible to study and correlate the frequency of confession and communion. However, as the interrogations took place throughout the year with many occurring immediately after Holy Week, the phenomenon was undervalued. If people declared in April that they had received communion during Holy Week, this did not mean that they would not do so again for a year. Keeping in mind the dangers of reducing statistical data, the only solution is to isolate the interrogations that took place in January, February, and March, as shown in Table 5.

Table 5.

	1540-1554	1555-1574	1575-1599	1600-1650
Surpassing requirement	0%	10.5%	15.1%	50%
Cases studied	13	57	33	18

We can adjust the results presented in Table 5 by comparing them with the interrogations carried out between October and December, as shown in Table 6.

Table 6.

	1540-1554	1555-1574	1575-1599	1600-1650
Surpassing requirement	0%	3.3%	0%	35.3%
Cases studied	16	32	12	17

The data are consistent, as the strong increase of positive answers in January emphasized the role of Christmas as the date of the second annual communion. If we take all the dates into consideration, however, the granting of plenary indulgence (*jubileos*) was the most frequent reason for receiving communion, outside of Easter time.

The small number of the target group does not permit a differential analysis of frequent communicants. It seems that communion other than during Easter was systematically accompanied by confession to a confessor other than a priest. During the sixteenth century, chaplains and friars shared this responsibility; in the seventeenth century, the regular clergy appear to have had a true monopoly, perhaps due to their encouragement of the practice.[17]

While Spain evolved similarly to the rest of Catholic Europe as regards communion, confirmation was a different matter (Delumeau, *Le catholicisme* 282-284). In France, confirmation was implemented late and with difficulty; in the seventeenth century, a large part of the population was still not confirmed. In contrast, New Castile implemented this sacrament enthusiastically, and inquisitorial documents allow us to go back to approximately 1510. Almost all the prisoners acknowledged being confirmed at the age of fourteen; some of them declared a younger age. Almost all of them remembered the occasion, manifesting the importance this sacrament had for them. The ones who were not confirmed were three Frenchmen, one Italian, one Asturian, one Galician (these last two were still adolescents), one Moslem, and one Castilian, a very poor orphaned baker's apprentice. The concern of the clergy was quite intense. One Portuguese man said he had been confirmed twice, once in his hometown, and once at the beginning of the seventeenth century in Cuéllar by a priest who would not listen to his protests. Other indications reveal that the population was strongly attached to this sacrament.[18]

When studying attendance at mass, we must once again trust the prisoners' declarations, with an added difficulty: it is easier to lie about attending mass than it is about confirmation or meeting one's paschal obligation. Between 1560 and 1650, the total percentage of those who swore that they missed mass occasionally (no one confessed to never going) is less than 3 percent. In fact, absenteeism was stronger in some groups. Of the twenty-one cases that we know of, eight are artisans, five are shepherds, three muleteers, three servants, and only two laborers (one of whom lived in an isolated farmhouse). Three types of individuals did not attend mass: those who lived in isolated areas without a priest, travelers, and mountain people—muleteers, shepherds, transporters, merchants, coal burners, and servants. For these individuals, Sunday was a workday like any other, and if some artisans chose not to miss the opportunity to make money, others stated directly that they would not give up a card game or a day in the country with friends.[19] Local traditions limiting attendance to public services should also be taken into account; in La Mancha, for example, in the town of Daimiel, unmarried women did not attend mass except during Lent (AHN, Inq. Leg. 230, Expd. 5, fol. 60r).

Thus was the process of Christianization in New Castile. Does this mean that Charles V's subjects were not Christians? Obviously not, and the question would have surprised or even scandalized them: to be a Christian, to see oneself as one, was the center of their sense of identity (Bennassar 285). What we have observed, in fact, is a growing control exercised by the Christian elite over the masses who were no less Christian than they. Simply stated, a more intellectual conception of Christianity was imposed over another.

Can we speak accurately of "Christianization"? Certainly we can, if being a Christian meant manifesting by means of external signs one's belonging to a group, or if being a Christian meant practicing Christianity. Without a doubt the Spanish Church penetrated the center of the country as far as the conditions of the times permitted—at any rate, much farther than her French counterpart. No doubt her success was due to the Council of Trent, and the movement continued to grow after 1650. In later trials, the majority of Old Christian prisoners showed off their Christian culture, receiving communion several times during the year. In 1778, one of the prisoners declared that he wanted to confess in El Casar de Talamanca, a small town in the province of Guadalajara, but that he had been unable to do so because of the large number of penitents and the small number of confessors (AHN, Inq. Leg. 203, Expd. 5). Another prisoner responded to the inquisitor's questions "with certain depth" (AHN, Inq. Leg. 26, Expd. 11 [1718]), despite the fact that he was a journeyman from La Mancha who barely knew how to read.

What was obtained was much more than simple memorization; that aspect reflects the pedagogical phase. It is very possible that the deep structures of popular religiosity were modified by the new knowledge and practices. This is still a hypothesis to be either upheld or disproved by future studies. At any rate, the Church's actions appear increasingly as one of the determining factors in the evolution of religious mentalities. It would be of no use to study the latter without keeping this fact in mind (Russo clxxii-clxxxii).

Notes

An earlier version of this article was published as "Christianisation en Nouvelle Castille. Catéquisme, communion, messe et confirmation dans l'archeveché de Toléde, 1540-1650," in *Mélanges de la Casa de Velázquez* 15 (1979): 261-294. Professor Sara Nalle arrives at similar conclusions in her unpublished dissertation, "Religion and Reform in a Spanish Diocese. Cuenca, 1545-1650," Johns Hopkins University, 1983, based on the Cuenca Inquisition trials.

1. The synods and Toledan provincial councils of the fourteenth and fifteenth centuries have been published by José Sánchez Herrero. We will note others by the word "synod" or "council" followed by the year of publication and the page of the edition we have consulted. All documents are housed in the National Library, Madrid.

2. This synod, a forerunner of Trent, was also responsible for making essential decisions concerning marriage.

3. *Signarse* means the same as *persignarse:* to make the sign of the cross on the forehead, the mouth, and the chest, saying, "By the sign of the Holy Cross, from our enemies deliver us, our Lord God." Then the sign of the cross is made again, moving the fingers from the forehead to the umbilicus and from the left shoulder to the right, saying, "In the name of the Father, and of the Son, and of the Holy Ghost, Amen."

4. Cardinal Rojas added the Latin translation of these formulas to his "doctrine."

5. The priests were also to remind stepfathers that they are required to teach the doctrine to their stepchildren (Synod 1583, fol. 8r).

6. The catechistical value of preaching is evident. Usually, the value of confession is not stressed to the same extent. Between one-third and one-half of the prisoners appearing before the inquisitors discovered through the confessor that fornication was a sin, and when one prisoner alleged his ignorance, the judges invariably responded by saying that his confessor must have told him.

7. Cardinal Rojas includes a matriculation form in his synod (Synod 1601, fols. 83v-84r).

8. The case was frequent in Spain: the Cruzada Bull allowed the individual to choose freely his own confessor.

9. I agree with Casimiro Sánchez Aliseda's conclusions. We must remember, however, that there was a distance between the Church's will and its practice.

10. This fact diminishes the value of our study. The Inquisition archives, like all the judicial systems of the Hapsburg Regime, provide more data on men than they do on women, save the cases of New Christians.

11. We classify the populations in three categories, according to the number of inhabitants during the second half of the sixteenth century, the complexity of the socioprofessional structure, and the strength of the clergy's presence. We refer to Madrid, Toledo, Alcalá de Henares, Guadalajara, Talavera de la Reina, Ocaña, and Ciudad Real as "cities"; the "large towns" are Brihuega, Almagro, Mondéjar, etc.

12. Diego Ramírez de Sedeño (or de Haro, or de Fuenleal) was Inquisitor of Toledo from the end of 1555 until the end of 1562. When he died in 1573, he was the Bishop of Pamplona. His lack of seriousness led to a complaint by the prosecutor, directed to the Suprema in 1556 (AHN, Inq. Leg. 3067, Expd. 100). His character and his methods are studied by Sara Nalle, "Old Christians and the Inquisition: Blasphemy Trials in the Sixteenth-Century Tribunal of Toledo," unpublished paper presented at the Early Modern Seminar, Johns Hopkins University, 1977.

13. The period between 1555 and 1564 also has the advantage of including all the cases in which Ramírez intervened.

14. The Spanish Church was the only one requiring knowledge of the *Salve*.

15. This is the case if we exclude foreigners who do not speak Spanish and say the prayers in Latin. We have not included them in our statistics.

16. It was already evident, from the examples of the other regions, that Catholic reform had achieved unanimity in Spain.

17. Penitents who declare that they have confessed to Jesuits also declare that they have received communion outside of Easter time.

18. Communicated to me by Professor Christian Hermann.

19. The Spanish bishops came to the same conclusions; see Ayala.

Works Cited

Actiones Concilii provincialis toletanis. Alcalá, 1566.

Archivo Histórico Nacional (AHN). Various documents.

Arte para bien confesar; fecha por un devoto religioso de la Orden de San Hieronymo, ahora de nuevo corregida. Seville, 1537.

Ayala, Martín de. *Sínodo de la diócesis de Guadix y de Baza*. Alcalá de Henares, 1556.

Bennassar, Bartolomé. *L'Inquisition espagnole*. Paris: Hachette, 1979.

Dedieu, Jean Pierre. "Les archives de l'Inquisition, source pour une étude anthropologique des vieux-chrétiens. Un exemple et quelques reflexions." *La inquisición española. Nueva visión, nuevos horizontes.* Ed. Joaquín Pérez Villanueva. Madrid: Siglo XXI, 1980. 893-912.

————. "The Archives of the Holy Office of Toledo as a Source for Historical Anthropology." *The Inquisition in Early Modern Europe: Studies on Sources and Methods.* Ed. Gustav Hennigsen and John Tedeschi. DeKalb, Ill.: Northern Illinois Univ. Press, 1986. 158-189.

Delumeau, Jean. *Le catholicisme entre Luther et Voltaire.* Paris, 1971.

————. "Déchristianisation ou nouveau modéle de christianism?" *Archives de sciences sociales des religions* 45 (1975): 3-20.

García, Pablo. *Orden que comunmente se guarda en el Santo Oficio acerca del procesar en las causas de fe.* Madrid, 1622.

Goñi Gaztambide, José. *Los navarros en el Concilio y la reforma tridentina en la diócesis de Pamplona.* Pamplona, 1947.

————. "El cumplimiento pascual en la diócesis de Pamplona en 1801." *Hispania sacra* 26 (1973): 361-372.

Guerrero, José Ramón. "Catecismos de autores españoles en la primera mitad del siglo XVI (1500-1559)." *Repertorio de historia de las ciencias eclesiásticas en España* II, 1971.

Infante, Cardenal Fernando. *Constituciones sinodales.* Madrid, 1622.

Jiménez Monteserín, Miguel. *Introducción a la Inquisición española.* Madrid: Editora Nacional, 1981.

Michelat, Guy, and Michel Simon. *Classe, religion et comportement politique.* Paris: Presses de la Fondation Nationale des Sciences Politiques, 1977.

Nalle, Sara T. "Old Christians and the Inquisition: Blasphemy Trials in the Sixteenth-Century Tribunal of Toledo." Unpublished paper presented at the Early Modern Seminar, Johns Hopkins University, 1977.

————. "Religion and Reform in a Spanish Diocese. Cuenca, 1545-1650." Diss. Johns Hopkins University, 1983.

Quiroga, Gaspar de. *Constituciones sinodales.* Madrid, 1583.

Rodríguez, Marie-Christine, and Bartolomé Bennassar. "Signatures et niveau culturel des témoins et accusés dans les procès d'inquisition du ressort du tribunal de Tolède (1524-1817) et du ressort du tribunal de Cordoue." *Cahiers du monde hispanique et luso-brésilien* 31 (1978): 19-46.

Rojas y Sandoval, Bernardo. *Constituciones sinodales hechas a 13 de junio de 1601.* Toledo, 1601.

Russo, Carla. *Società, Chiesa e vita religiosa nell' Ancien Régime.* Naples: Guida, 1976.

Sánchez Aliseda, Casimiro. "Precedentes toledanos de la reforma tridentina." *Revista española de derecho canónico* 3 (1948): 457-495.

Sánchez Herrero, José. *Concilios provinciales y sínodos toledanos de los siglos XIV y XV. La religiosidad cristiana del clero y pueblo.* La Laguna: Universidad, Secretariado de Publicaciones, 1976.

Tavera, Juan. *Constituciones sinodales del Arzobispado de Toledo.* Alcalá, 1536.

Tello Girón, Gómez. *Constituciones sinodales del Arzobispado de Toledo, año de 1566.* Toledo, 1568.

Vacant, Alfred, and Eugene Mangenot. *Dictionnaire de théologie catholique.* Paris: Letouzey et Ane, 1938.

◆ Chapter 2
A Saint for All Seasons
The Cult of San Julián

Sara T. Nalle

While much of the focus of the Counter-Reformation was on the suppression of heterodoxy, enormous effort was also directed toward creating new cults that would carry forward the emerging Tridentine ethic. Particularly favored were cults that explicitly defended points of doctrine legitimating the religious regime that the Protestants hoped to overthrow. The Protestants cast doubt on the validity of the sacraments of penance and the Eucharist as the center of Christian faith. In addition, they denied the authority of priests, held images to be idolatrous, and attacked the cult of the saints as superstition. Each of these attacks on Catholic belief was countered not only in the famous decrees of the Council of Trent but also through the promotion of Tridentine cults for the people. Late-sixteenth-century Spain witnessed the creation of countless new holy days, pieces of artwork, and religious brotherhoods dedicated to celebrating cults of the Eucharist, souls in purgatory, the Holy Family, and the saints in heaven.[1]

Spanish Church officials especially wanted to promote new cults of the saints. In 1566 rioting Calvinists in the Netherlands smashed images of the saints and destroyed their relics. Philip II ordered the rescue of Flemish relics (most notably San Eugenio and Santa Leocadia) which were brought back to Castile and installed in El Escorial and the Cathedral of Toledo.[2] But the times demanded more than the rescue of saints endangered on foreign soil; militant, native exemplars of sanctity had to be put before the people to lead them in faith and succor them in times of hardship. In addition to new saints such as Diego de Alcalá, Ignatius Loyola, or Teresa de Avila, during the Counter-Reformation numerous older Spanish miracle workers were called up from reserve and put on active duty in the defense of their cities. Avila invented the cult of San Segundo while nearby Segovia rediscovered San Frutos. León turned to San Froylán, Madrid found San Isidro Labrador, Toledo celebrated Santa Leocadia, and Cuenca resurrected San Julián, the city's second bishop.[3]

Efforts to canonize the bishop of Cuenca and propagate his cult actually were begun in 1518, long before the Council of Trent, and continued throughout the sixteenth and seventeenth centuries. Because of the unusual amount of publicity generated by the lengthy fight to canonize the saint and win privileges for his cult, Julián's case effectively illustrates some of the aspects of cultural control at work during the Counter-Reformation. For nearly two centuries the saint was prominent in the public's eye, and as the religious and social environment changed, new generations found different meanings in the saint's life and works. The history of the cult reveals in striking detail how Church and city authorities came to see in the obscure medieval bishop a saint for their own times, a saint whose cult, if successfully promoted, would help to restore faith in the Church's threatened credibility.[4]

Unlike many of the saints whose cults were revived during the sixteenth century, there is little disagreement in the sources over the known details of Julián's life or the provenance of his relics. Julián was born circa 1128 in the city of Burgos. Oddly, despite the fact that he eventually became archdeacon of Toledo and bishop of Cuenca, his last name is not known. He left Burgos to study philosophy and theology in Palencia and also taught there for a number of years. When his parents died, Julián, now middle-aged, returned to Burgos where he retired to a small house next to the Monastery of San Agustín.[5] There he dedicated himself to prayer, giving lessons, and preaching to the Christians and Moors of the city. Preaching became his passion: he took holy orders and, accompanied by one companion, San Lesmes, he left the city to go on several evangelical missions among the Islamic and Jewish populations of Castile. In 1192 he became archdeacon of the Cathedral of Toledo and in 1196, at age 68, bishop of Cuenca, which had been reconquered only nineteen years before, in 1177. Shortly after his arrival in the diocese, Cuenca was attacked by a plague. Julián is credited with saving the diocese from the pestilence through his prayers. He died in the odor of sanctity on January 28, 1208, and was buried in a tomb close by the western entrance to the cathedral. According to one tradition, he was canonized by the Fourth Lateran Council in 1215; another tradition holds that he was canonized at the Council of Constance in 1414. Be that as it may, no record of any medieval canonization survives. In the late sixteenth century Clement VIII reconfirmed his sainthood and cult.

Despite his legendary beatification Julián's cult enjoyed little popularity in Cuenca during the Middle Ages. Even his own cathedral was slow to accord him honor. The earliest record of a mass in San Julián's memory is found in 1371, some 160 years after the saint's presumed canonization (Sanchiz Catalán 7). As late as 1531, his feast day was not part of the diocese's calendar of holy days (Ramírez, fol. 11v). Outside the realm of liturgical observance, there are other signs that the medieval cult was weak. For example, popular tradition in the seventeenth century held that San Julián had instituted the city's charity box, which dowered orphan girls. The records show, however, that the box was founded in 1478 by the cathedral chapter, which made no mention of the saint as the one establishing the charity (ACC, Estatutos, fol. 181v).[6] In the city hall's records there is no indication that Cuenca paid any public homage to the saint before 1550. Finally, if name-giving is taken as something of a barometer of the popularity of saints (Christian, *Person and God* 88-93; Wilson 46) Julián had no credit at all with the people of fifteenth-century Cuenca. In the city censuses of 1442 and 1502, which list a total of 1,350 citizens, the name "Julián/a" appears just once (AMC, Leg. 1503: 2, 9).

In 1516 the cathedral chapter decided to move Julián's resting place from the west entrance to a spot close to the high altar (ACC, Actas 1516, fol. 33r). The "translation" of a saint's body to a raised, prominent tomb is a critical moment in the growth of a cult, acknowledging the existence of popular veneration for the holy person. Had a cult in fact grown up around the bishop's burial spot? Late in the sixteenth century, Padre Escudero, a Jesuit who had access to the cathedral's records, wrote that perhaps the chapter had made the decision because relic seekers had damaged the saint's tomb. According to Escudero,

> The people had mistreated the sepulchre where it was, making holes in it with knives and other things so large that through one of [the holes] one could see the box where the saint was. By scraping the stone, collecting the dust and earth, and cutting slivers from the box and drinking them with water or wearing them around the neck like an amulet, the sick were cured of fevers and other illnesses, not only in Cuenca but in other places, as happened to some sick from Toledo. (Escudero, ms., fol. 18r)[7]

This is the first indication that Julián's cult had popular acceptance in Cuenca. However, Escudero was not an impartial chronicler of the saint's life nor was the chapter an innocent bystander in the translation of the saint's body. Normally a translation is ordered by the bishop, but in 1516 no bishop had set foot in Cuenca for twenty-three years.[8] Possibly the chapter orchestrated the move in order to promote its own authority in the neglected bishopric. In anticipation of the translation, the chapter approved plans to clean the high altar and grille and arranged for the sale of indulgences, a spiritual concession that would surely promote devotion to the saint (ACC, Actas 1516, fol. 33r).

The decision to move Julián's resting place turned out to be crucial. While uncovering the sepulchre in the presence of witnesses and notaries, the presiding canons and inquisitors decided to peek inside the coffin, just to make sure that Julián's compatriots from Burgos had not made off with the corpse.[9] At ten o'clock at night, January 7, 1518, the master stonemason cracked open the lid. A "celestial fragrance" escaped from the coffin, and by the torchlight of the workmen, the officials discovered that Julián's body, clothing, and jewels all rested in a perfect state of preservation. A palm frond, still green, lay by his side. Profoundly impressed by these miracles, the prelates removed a ring and one finger of the saint and resealed the coffin.[10]

The cathedral chapter knew that the fact that San Julián's body remained intact was an irrefutable sign of the bishop's favor with God, and it moved immediately to take advantage of the event.[11] First, news of the miracle had to be spread and the people given a chance to see the incorrupt body for themselves. The chapter called the parish clergy of the entire bishopric to Cuenca and hired musicians from Guadalajara to join in a triumphal procession of the body around town (ACC, Actas 1518, fol. 137v). The city streets were clogged with people and some even fought with one another to grab a bit of earth from the saint's grave (Escudero, ms., fol. 22). Anyone who came to view the body in the cathedral sacristy during the first few months after its transfer received a forty-day indulgence. The severed finger was put into a reliquary so it could be shown to the sick—and they were cured![12] Examples of the cures follow:

> Baltasar de Villapaña, a youth from Talavera, was in danger of losing his life to scrofula on his neck. They touched him with San Julián's finger and he was cured.
>
> Doña Inés de Barrientos, wife of the illustrious knight Luis Carrillo, lord of Colmenar de Oreja, was pronounced incurable by her doctors. She visited the body and was cured.
>
> Francisco de Peñalver, a citizen of Tortola, had a broken arm. He put it inside the saint's coffin and then his arm gave a crack, felt hot and was cured.
>
> Juana de Alarcón, from Cuenca, had an incurable breast cancer. She offered herself to Julián and they put a cloth on her which had touched the saint. She was cured with a great amount of heat and sweat. (Escudero, ms., fols. 36r-42v)

In all, that year Canon Eustachio Muñoz and a public notary collected sworn testimony to 300 miracles that proved the full range of the saint's intercessory powers and the healing ability of the relics. News of the saint's powers spread rapidly to out- lying towns, where parents sought to place their children under Julián's protection by naming them for the saint. In Buenache de Alarcón, sixty kilometers to the south, nearly half of the male children baptized in 1519 were christened "Julián," and several girls were baptized "Juliana" (see Table 1).

Table 1. Baptisms of "Julián/a" in Buenache de Alarcón, 1518-1528
(ADC, P-555. Year 1523 missing)

Year	Julián/a	Total baptisms
1518	3	14
1519	8	19
1520	4	31
1521	2	18
1522	3	31
1524	1	34
1525	1	16
1526	2	38
1527	0	25
1528	0	32

The events of 1518 convinced the chapter that Julián was a powerful saint, yet there was no solid evidence that the bishop had been canonized. With the miracles that Julián had facilitated that year, the chapter voted to start a modern inquiry that would win the saint formal recognition from Rome. Canon Muñoz, who had been present at the exhumation of the body, was put in charge of the campaign, which he began by making a memorial of the miracles referred to above (Escudero, ms., fol. 30r). Yet nothing came of Muñoz's commission. In 1532 the chapter en- listed Charles V's help with the case and the Emperor promised to intervene for the chapter in Rome (ACC, Leg. 1036: 8). Eight years later, in 1540, Pope Paul III agreed to another investiga- tion, which again led to nothing (ACC, Leg. 1036: 1). The chap- ter did not realize that as a result of Protestant attacks on the cult of saints, Rome had placed a moratorium on all canonizations until further notice.[13] Finally, in the late 1540s, thirty years after the discovery of the saint's incorrupt body, a second power, city hall, became interested in promoting the saint.

From the letters that city officials wrote on behalf of Julián and his cult, it appears that the municipal officials of Cuenca decided that the saint could be used as good publicity for the city. City hall contacted influential Conquenses at the imperial court and in Rome—Licenciado Hurtado de Mendoza, Canon Juan del Pozo, and the Cardinal of Coria—and reminded them of their patriotic duty to support and honor their hometown (*patria*) and its name (AMC, Leg. 1497: 59).[14] The city proposed changing the saint's feast day from the middle of winter, when travel was difficult and supplies scarce, to September 5, the date of the annual fair. The city's logic is clear: Julián's cult would benefit from the fair, and if the saint became popular enough, the fair would benefit from Julián. In anticipation of the Pope's approval of the change of dates, in 1550 the city bought two bulls for 11,522 *maravedís* for the September holiday, and the next year, when the holiday was approved, the city bought two more bulls costing 13,500 *maravedís*. The city's largesse, however, did not extend to a third year, when it felt obligated to spend only 2,253 *maravedís* on the saint whose holiday it had sworn to celebrate. As holy days went in Cuenca, Julián was worth far less than the highly secular midsummer celebrations for San Juan (22,806 *maravedís* in 1551) and slightly more than Corpus Christi, which had not yet become the religious holiday par excellence of the Counter-Reformation (AMC, Accounts Leg. 145).[15]

More than thirty years after the discovery of Julián's miraculously incorrupt body, the local church's efforts to propagate the cult had met with limited success. True, Rome had given permission to celebrate Julián's cult in September, which meant de facto acceptance of his saintly status. During the 1550s, members of the cathedral chapter gave money in Julián's name to various charities (Sanchiz Catalán 221). Yet no laymen gave money and the city government backed off from underwriting expensive holiday celebrations for the saint. The city's self-serving transfer of the holiday to September 5 precipitated a rash of "Julián" christenings in Cuenca during the first few years following the change; the number of christenings soon diminished. In fact, some laymen and local priests were openly skeptical of the cult. In 1556, a Genoese merchant residing in Cuenca fell into an argument with a priest and follower of Julián. The priest contended that one sure sign of Julián's sanctity was the celestial odor that had been in the saint's coffin. The Genoan replied, "They must have put on some fragrance that would smell and it could be that they embalmed the body" (ADC, Inq. 238: 3081). Some years later, a parish priest refused to honor San Julián, stating that "if [San Julián] is not canonized, then we don't have to believe anything about him or honor his feast day and if [the holiday] falls during my week [to celebrate mass] I won't hold him for a saint" (ADC, Inq. 240: 3120). Why, despite all the classic signs of sanctity, did many Conquenses remain skeptical of Julián's cult?

The normal sequence in the genesis of a cult, particularly in the Middle Ages, was popular veneration first, then episcopal acceptance, and finally, though not always, papal approval. In Julián's case, the evidence of a popular cult before 1518 is weak. In its deliberations to move the saint's tomb, the chapter made no mention of popular sentiment, and in 1543, in one of the first published accounts of San Julián's life, no cult is mentioned in association with the translation (Venero, fol. 93v).[16] In other words, the chapter had reversed the usual order of things and was attempting to spread Julián's cult *downward*. A second difficulty was that the chapter saw in Julián a model of sainthood that was being attacked by both Protestants and educated Catholics. Medieval saint cults centered on incorruptibility and relics, often without much concern for the historical reality of the saint's life. The chapter rested its arguments for recanonization not on the details of Julián's life, but on the modern miracles caused by Julián's relics. This tactic was ill-chosen. Led by Erasmus of Rotterdam, who had a large following in Spain during the second quarter of the sixteenth century, many Catholics came to see relic worship as an embarrassing superstition. (Protestants of course denied the existence of saints altogether.) At the highest level of the Church, unsure of how to proceed, Rome refused to grant Julián formal recognition. Locally, many remained aloof from the new cult.

At midcentury, while the cult of San Julián was at a standstill, the Council of Trent hammered out reforms of the Catholic faith that would soon engulf the diocese.[17] Toward the end of the sixteenth century Cuenca's cathedral and bishops resumed their crusade to canonize Julián and spread his cult. The intervening years served to transform the priests' way of thinking about God's army of saints. When Bishop Gómez Zapata reopened Julián's case in the 1580s, the saint's clerical supporters all but abandoned the medieval model of sanctity and instead tailored Julián's image to fit the ideals of the Catholic Reformation.

The Council of Trent placed a premium on the role of bishops in the reformed Church. The ideal bishop resided in his diocese, personally oversaw its administration, taught good doctrine, administered charity, and was an exemplar of chaste, devout behavior.[18] At the same time, Trent reaffirmed the place of saints and their relics in the Church but acknowledged that abuses in their cult had occurred. To protect the cult of saints from criticism, after Trent many saints whose existence was dubious were dropped from the Roman calendar and no new saints were admitted to the Roman martyrology until 1588. After that date, new saints had to pass a battery of tests carried out by the Sacred Congregation of Rites; these tests determined the quality of the saint's writings, heroic virtues, miracles, and if applicable, his or her martyrdom (Delooz 202-212). Through its power to canonize, over the years the Congregation established that the ideal saint of the Counter-Reformation had to be a real person, preferably a priest, or even better, a member of a religious order. During his career on earth, the Catholic hero ideally had either founded a new religious order, conducted missionary work, given charity, administered a diocese, or performed feats of mysticism (Burke 50-51).

When Julián made his third debut on the canonization circuit in the 1580s, it was as the exemplary bishop, who after death had been extraordinarily favored by God. Behind the new campaign were Bishop Gómez Zapata, the Jesuits of Cuenca, and the cathedral chapter. Their campaigns on behalf of the saint took shape as a three-pronged effort. The bishop would enforce what liturgical observance of the cult was allowed, while through diplomatic channels, he and the cathedral would apply once more for canonical recognition of the saint. Finally, through the printing press, ambitious authors would refashion and popularize the saint's public image.

Gómez Zapata began his campaign in 1584 with the foundation of the diocese's new conciliar seminary, where the future priests of the Counter-Reformation era would be trained. As patron of the seminary, he chose the diocese's most exemplary priest, San Julián (Nalle, "Religion and Reform" 173). The following year he sent out a circular addressed to the bishopric's clergy. In it he complained that some churches, monasteries, and private persons had stopped observing San Julián's holidays as they were obligated to do, and he ordered them to resume saying the *officio duplex* as required (Sanchiz Catalán 371-372). Gómez's last act, in cooperation with the cathedral chapter, was to initiate another trial to have Julián inserted correctly into the Roman calendar. Julián had survived Pius V's purging of the breviaries in 1568, but only on September 5, a date that was not connected to the saint's life. Gómez did not live to see his victory; in 1589 the January 28 holiday was restored in Baronius's new edition of the *Roman Martyrology* (RAH, Salazar y Castro 7: 289).

For the bishops and canons of Cuenca the privilege of inclusion in the *Martyrology* was not enough honor for their saint. They fought to have the Congregation, established in 1588, grant Julián modern status as a saint and give the cult its own service with lessons taken from the saint's life. To everyone's great joy, these privileges were granted in 1594, but the Church of Cuenca still was not satisfied. In 1613 it won for Julián his own service with *octave* and a special holiday mass. Later in the century the chapter thought it could do even better by the saint and in 1642 applied to have his service extended throughout Spain. Thirty years later the papacy granted its request. A modern historian of Julián's cult concludes that at the close of the seventeenth century Cuenca had taken its saint from obscurity to national prominence, second only to Santiago, the national patron saint, in liturgical dignity and importance (Sanchiz Catalán 75).

To aid in the work of popularizing the saint's image, between 1520 and 1700 local clergymen penned nine biographies of San Julián, five of which were published. The dates of these hagiographies and their success with the public are instructive. Canon Eustachio Muñoz, who figured so prominently in the cathedral's early efforts to recanonize the saint, wrote the first life of the saint sometime before 1550. The manuscript was never published and has since been lost (González 1: 445). A string of hagiographies accompanied the most intense period of the cathedral's fight for ritual acceptance of the saint by Rome. Four works were written between 1569 and 1613, three of which were published, one even going into second and third editions. Then followed a gap until the 1640s, when members of the chapter penned two new lives to substantiate its claims for the extension of Julián's cult. Neither of these efforts saw print. Two more lives came out at the end of the seventeenth century; the last one went into several editions and became the standard source for all subsequent writers.[19]

These new works were built around the scanty information available about Julián in such pre-Tridentine books as the *Catálogo de los santos de España*, *Enchiridion de los tiempos*, and the *Libro de las grandezas de España*. Lorenzo de Padilla's catalogue of saints, published in 1538, granted Julián just one paragraph and mistakenly recorded his feast day as January 17. San Lesmes, Julián's servant, is absent altogether. Padilla mentioned Julián's birth in Burgos, his studies, preaching, almsgiving, and recent arrival as a saint: "In our own times many visiting his sepulchre are cured of fever: by virtue of them he was put on the list of saints." Padilla also included a few miracle stories about the saint. One was that God gave a sign of Julián's sainthood to his mother while she was pregnant. She dreamt that she gave birth to a white puppy that breathed flames—a standard image from medieval hagiographies, including that of Julián's compatriot and contemporary, Saint Dominic (Weinstein and Weinstein, Chap. 1; Voragine 413). Also, at his baptism a child appeared wearing a miter and carrying a crozier and declared that the saint's name was to be Julián (Padilla, fol. 43).

Five years after the publication of Padilla's catalogue, Fray Alonso de Venero included Julián in his *Enchiridion de los tiempos*, a list of memorable things about Spain. Venero, a native of Burgos, recorded one of the most popular details of Julián's life, which was that he wove baskets for a living so he could give all of his stipend to the poor. Venero included several miraculous stories that would become standard parts of Julián's hagiography. In one, Christ came as a poor man to dine at the bishop's table. In another, the poor came to beg for bread and Julián ordered his almoner to fetch some to hand out. The almoner said there wasn't enough, but when he went to look, he found the bishop's granaries overflowing. In another famine, grain could not be found anywhere, but once Julián began to pray, there appeared many pack animals loaded down with wheat. They went directly to the bishop's residence without muleteers to guide them. When Julián felt his death was near, he put on his coarsest hair shirt and stretched out on a bed strewn with ashes. Finally, Venero described the discovery of Julián's incorrupt body in 1518 and briefly recorded some of the miracles associated with that event (*Enchiridion*, fols. 92r-94r).[20]

From these accounts alone as inspiration for his biographers, Julián's life blossomed in the fertile imaginations of his post-Tridentine promoters. The first published biography of the saint was written in 1569 by Padre Escudero, who comments that his superior ordered him to compose the life, perhaps on account of Philip II's visit to the saint's tomb in 1564.[21] He put the finishing touches on the biography in 1583 and it finally saw print in 1589, the year that Julián's original feast day was reinstated in the Roman calendar. In this biography, essentially a gloss of Venero's life, Julián the man shone with the qualities of a bishop of the Counter-Reformation. He personally looked after his flock and was especially stern with the wicked and lazy. He inspected the diocese at every moment and preached every week. He would not allow any of his clergy to be ignorant. Earning his living by weaving baskets, Julián gave all of his income to the poor. If that were not enough, he found time for contemplation and prayer, and the strength to fast, sleep on the floor, and resist all unchaste thoughts (Escudero, ms., Chap. 4).

Most important, since Julián's canonization was disputed at the time that Escudero was writing, the latter wanted to make it clear that Julián was a saint who from birth had enjoyed special favors from God and exhibited untold heroic virtues.[22] The Jesuit livened up the hagiography by claiming that Julián's birth had been accompanied by several portents of a holy calling. Many of the stories recall incidents from the Gospels and medieval legends about the Christ child. According to Escudero, Julián's parents (like Abraham and Sarah or the parents of John the Baptist) were a poor couple who prayed for a child for twenty years before Julián was conceived. In keeping with the renewed patriarchalism of the times, Julián's father received the sign that an extraordinary child would be born.[23] The future bishop was born in a humble dwelling outside Burgos, and at birth the child sat up to bless his parents in the manner of a bishop and made the sign of the cross. At his christening, angels sang and a child carrying a bishop's miter and crozier appeared and indicated that the boy's name was to be Julián. Reflecting the Jesuits' concern for the teaching of the catechism, Escudero added that Julián's pious parents taught him the elements of faith at a young age (Escudero, Vida y milagros, fols. 3r-4v).[24]

Escudero also slightly modified and added to Venero's accounts of miracles that occurred during the saint's tenure as bishop of Cuenca. As no saint's life is complete without overcoming temptation, Escudero invented two stories. Once while Julián was fasting, the Devil tempted him with a succulent three-pound trout, for which Cuenca is famous. Another time the Devil tempted Julián with a beautiful girl just rescued from the Moors (Escudero, ms., fols. 12r, 14v). The almoner who thought there was no bread became Julián's devoted, sainted companion, San Lesmes.[25] When he felt his death was near, Julián put on a hair shirt, lay down on the hard floor (again strewn with ashes), and received last rites dressed in his episcopal robes, i.e., as Escudero wished him to be remembered, the ideal bishop. The Virgin came surrounded by angels and awarded him a palm, a symbol of virginity.[26] When Julián died, those present saw a white dove (the Holy Spirit) fly out of his mouth straight to heaven. Finally, to round off the life, Escudero included an account of the discovery of the incorrupt body in 1518 and summarized at length thirty of the miracles from Canon Muñoz's inquiry.

Other authors relied heavily on Escudero's life of Julián, though the process of remodeling the image of the saint to fit the times continued. Fray Bartolomé de Segura put Escudero's story into twenty cantos in honor of the saint. Segura was not interested in Julián's learning, but in the example of his chastity, which he used as a pretext to praise the merits of virginity and

Christian marriage, subjects close to the heart of the Tridentine Church (Segura, ms., fols. 37-45).[27] Mártir Rizo and Santa María compared their saintly predecessor to the notable post-Tridentine bishops of Cuenca, Gaspar de Quiroga (future archbishop, Inquisitor General, and cardinal) and Enrique Pimentel, who turned down promotion to the archbishopric of Seville. The last biographer, Padre Alcázar, chronicled Julián's pastoral work as bishop of Cuenca, expanding Escudero's one chapter on the subject to a total of five; these dealt with Julián's reforms of customs, his "healthy doctrine," preaching, visitations, and the like. After a century of plagues in Cuenca, Alcázar was careful to include a chapter describing Julián's effectiveness against disease and famine.

The new currents brought by the Counter-Reformation also affected the city of Cuenca's response to Julián. During the second half of the sixteenth century, city authorities became increasingly involved in promoting the grandiose holidays for which the Counter-Reformation is known. The city's annual outlays for Corpus Christi mounted higher each year as the pageant became more elaborate, growing from homespun dances and skits to full-scale professional theater. In 1581 the city adopted a new holiday altogether, Saint Matthew's Day, to celebrate the reconquest of Cuenca from the Muslims on that day in 1177 (Nalle, "Religion and Reform" 251-254). When Julián was granted his own service in 1594, the city was eager to participate in the celebrations marking the event.

With a remarkable degree of amiability, city hall worked closely with the cathedral in arranging a spectacular week of festivities, solemn processions, and services. Once the papal brief arrived in late 1594, the bishop and chapter wrote to Philip II to inform him of the news and ask permission to mount a large celebration patterned after that given by Toledo for Santa Leocadia's translation (RAH, Salazar y Castro 7: 289). Permission was granted and the city and chapter set to work. By the middle of July 1595, the city was deeply involved in organizing the provisioning of the town for several weeks in September; supervising the rents charged for windows on the Plaza Mayor and Campo de San Francisco; setting up firework displays; orchestrating the bullfights, tourneys, and jousts; and settling disputes over the order in which laymen would march in Julián's procession (AMC, Actas, Leg. 262, fols. 58-71).

Meanwhile, Bishop Vadillo and the chapter were preparing to render Julián the most magnificent *dulia* the saint had ever received. Church politics and the defense of the faith aside, it had taken the chapter three-quarters of a century to get to this point and the canons meant to make the most of their opportunity. Bishop Vadillo gave one hundred expensive wax torches for the processions and masses. He also gave 1,000 ducats in dowries to twenty orphaned maidens (BNM, *Raros*, ms. 18654/1).[28] The chapter, which had always regarded Julián as *its* saint, outdid itself in honoring the venerable bishop.[29] First, the main chapel, where the saint's coffin was placed on view, was hung with brocade drapes three stories high. All of the central nave of the cathedral was hung with more drapes and decorated with paper banners. The Jesuits took charge of making these banners, which displayed epigrams, Latin verses, sonnets, and songs in Spanish, hieroglyphs, and ciphers.

The centerpiece of the decorations was a huge triumphal arch that the chapter had constructed at its own expense in the city's Plaza Mayor.[30] The arch, ninety feet long and sixty-three feet high, symbolized the cooperation between the highest levels of the Church and State that made Julián's cult possible. No reference was made here to popular veneration; the saint existed only within this mighty edifice of militant centralized authority. The obverse side of the arch, facing the cathedral, celebrated the popes who had given Julián's cult legitimacy. The reverse side of the arch faced down the hill toward city hall and honored the kings of Castile and the Holy Roman Emperor, whose wife was cured by one of Julián's baskets. Within the framework of the central and lateral arches, flanked by these figures of authority, hung paintings depicting scenes from Julián's life and more Latin verses contributed by the Jesuits.

Now that the cathedral and arch were ready, the celebrations began. On Monday afternoon, September 4, the royal governor, city councillors, the canons, and as many people who could find standing room crowded into the cathedral to hear the vespers service, which was accompanied by musicians and singers from Cuenca, Toledo, and Madrid. Afterward dances lasted until five o'clock, when matins began, followed by more music and caroling until eight o'clock. That night the city mounted its fireworks display. All of the surrounding hills were lit by bonfires, while in the Plaza Mayor and Campo de San Francisco figures of castles, lions, and serpents burned.[31] All night long, the narrow stone streets reverberated to the joyous racket of musicians blowing on their trumpets and shawms, and beating their kettledrums.

The next day was the saint's day, September 5, which was given over to a solemn, triumphant procession of Julián's body through the city. All of the villages within six leagues of Cuenca were ordered to participate with their pennants, crosses, clergy, and brotherhoods. To maximize the procession's solemn impact, the royal governor ordered everyone off the city streets for the duration of the parade. The cathedral's bells began to ring at 4:30 that morning. At 5:30 mass was sung while the procession waited in the cloister. Then they all filed out, parish pennants and crosses first, next the city's friars, clergy, and finally the canons and city councillors, who carried Julián's float among them. The procession passed under the triumphal arch and circled the city for six hours in complete silence, while people watched from their windows. By turn each constituency of the priesthood—canons, prebendaries, the city's parish priests, and the diocesan archpriests and clergy—carried the saint through the empty streets. At two o'clock in the afternoon, the saint was returned to the cathedral and vespers was sung as it had been the day before.

On Wednesday the games, bullfights, and jousting began, and went on until nightfall. The next morning the theater company of Salzedo and Ríos was to put on an original play of the saint's life, but the performance was postponed until Friday because they had not finished building the stage and theater.[32] The chronicler of these events noted that the *auto* was of "such spiritual joy, devotion, and tenderness that there could be no one so hard-hearted that he did not accompany the action with his tears." After vespers, the nobility paraded in full livery on their horses. The parades continued into Saturday and Sunday, when the week of celebrations ended. The chronicler concluded with satisfaction that visitors to the city declared that the festival was the best of its kind they had ever seen.

With Clement VIII's brief granting to Julián his own service and with the 1595 holiday, the saint's cult was secured for the two elite groups that had promoted it, the cathedral canons and the city councillors, who were tied together by the bonds of common interest and kinship. In contrast to the freewheeling, popular parade of 1518, the late-sixteenth-century celebrations were a baroque spectacle of power in which the people, banned from the streets, were not allowed to participate. Their role was that of spectators.[33] A few years later, the city hall and the chapter further established the aristocratic nature of the cult of a poor man whose lineage, ironically, was unknown.[34] The trend may be seen in their patronage of a new brotherhood dedicated to San Julián, which was to admit 200 "prominent" men and women in equal numbers and sixty priests. Members could not practice a so-called mechanical trade or be the children of those who had. Even if the brotherhood were full, any ranking member of the nobility, cathedral, or Inquisition, or a nun, could join at any time. Membership cost ten ducats for men and two ducats for women, plus a one-pound wax candle. The cathedral's records show that the exclusive brotherhood quickly attracted a large membership consisting of local notables (ACC, Leg. 1035: 7).

At the end of the century Julián's cult seems to have gained favor with Cuenca's upper classes who, like other elites in Spain, now stood squarely behind the Counter-Reformation's programs. For the lower classes the story was different. During the sixteenth century, Julián's cult gained acceptance among the people very slowly. Interest in the saint continually had to be supported by the Church hierarchy. Over the century there were three surges in the popularity of the saint, all in direct response to clerical initiatives: in the 1520s, following the translation of the body; in the 1550s, following the success of the second feast day; and in the 1590s, after Julián won his own service. After the first two initiatives, interest in the cult, such as it can be measured by baptisms, soon fell off, and the saint was never as popular in the countryside as he was in the city.

Instead, religious popularity, as indicated by foundations, brotherhoods, charitable donations, christenings, and faith healing, did not come until after 1595. In both the diocesan visitations of the 1580s and the text of Padre Escudero, published in 1589, there is hardly a trace of a sixteenth-century cult of San Julián, even though one visitation specifically listed the important church ornaments, foundations, and brotherhoods in each village (ADC, Leg. 204). One hundred ten years later, Padre Alcázar could list about one hundred foundations in the diocese as well as outside of it, many of which were maintained by brotherhoods. All of the fourteen parish churches of the city of Cuenca possessed a chapel, statue, or painting, and in the bishopric there were at least five other chapels and five rural shrines dedicated solely to Julián, in addition to the various paintings and statues scattered throughout the diocese (Alcázar 455-472). Following the baptismal records throughout the seventeenth century, the pattern of name-giving becomes quite different from that of the previous century. With the exception of a few years, the overall incidence of the name "Julián/a," even at its lowest points, attained higher levels than in the sixteenth century. Biographies of the saint rapidly went into second editions and sold out. The saint even turned up in the sorcerer's bag of tricks. In 1601 the Inquisition of Cuenca, trying a local priest for sorcery, presented as evidence a booklet of charms, one of which invoked San Julián: "Sancte Juliane que feciste sortes almaras e deas y acepisti e de precorte per tuam suntitatem et meam virginitatem me muestres" (the charm was declared unintelligible) (ADC, Inq. Leg. 351: 4992). The saint's reputation for effectiveness in white magic spread: in 1650, the Toledan inquisitors found in the house of a famous witch some earth from Julián's tomb, which was used to cure fevers (Cirac Estopañán 42).

For seventy-five years Julián's cult had barely survived in spite of constant ecclesiastical nursing, and then suddenly it found popular acceptance. Were the people of Cuenca swayed by the Church's propaganda or was another force at work? The manner in which Julián's cult spread to other bishoprics in the seventeenth century provides the answer. In 1637 the plague devastated Málaga. The bishop of that city, Fray Antonio Pimentel, brother of the bishop of Cuenca, asked for a painting of the saint to be sent to Málaga to aid the town. Miraculously, the plague ceased upon the painting's arrival and the grateful citizens erected a chapel in honor of San Julián (Alcázar 461). In 1648 at Murcia the experience was repeated and Cuenca was spared from that epidemic (Alcázar 471). During the plague years of the early 1600s in Cuenca, the average percentage of children baptized "Julián/a" was twice as high as it had been in 1590. In the course of the century, the saint's body was carried in processions in the city of Cuenca ten times to bring an end to droughts, heavy snows, and other natural disasters (Alcázar 473-475). So many villages in the bishopric were saved by Julián's intercession that the saint's biographer, Alcázar, listed them in a separate chapter of his book. The lean years of the seventeenth century finally gave Julián, guardian against plague, drought, and famine, ample room to prove his ability to protect those who could not protect themselves.

In the end Julián found two sets of clients and two identities. His first supporters were the canons of the cathedral church, later joined by the city government, the bishop, and the city's elites. At first the canons who discovered the incorrupt body of the bishop cast Julián in the role of a medieval saint who worked miracles through his healing relics. Although this approach found some short-lived favor with the people, it fell flat in Rome where the Reformation's attacks on the cult of saints had thrown officials into a crisis of conscience. Two centuries earlier, papal approval would not have mattered locally, but now the canons saw that legitimacy for Julián could come only from Rome. They struggled to win official recognition for their saint. This came late in the sixteenth century after Rome reaffirmed the cult of saints under more rigorous conditions and Julián's image was reworked to meet these conditions. Julián became a saint because he had been an exemplary bishop during an earlier age's struggles with the infidel. The man represented the power of the militant Church; his miracle-working incorrupt body defied the claims of the relic-burning Protestants. During the second half of the century, Cuenca's elites lined up to pledge their loyalty to the Holy Mother Church. They demonstrated their faith by embracing the new Tridentine cults and holidays, supporting the Inquisition, founding new monasteries, and accepting Julián as their patron saint.[35]

Julián's second set of clients was made up of the people of Cuenca. The vast majority had always believed in the saints; only rarely did the Inquisition discover a true skeptic. Conquenses, however, were shrewd shoppers for their saints. Villages would adopt one set and when those saints failed them, find another. During a bout of plague during the early sixteenth century, many villages made vows to Saint Roch, a new plague saint, and at midcentury, when several locust plagues swept La Mancha, other villages swore to Saint Gregory. Because of the unending variety of misfortunes, personal or collective, to which Conquenses were subject, they were always on the lookout for new, more powerful saints (Christian, *Local Religion*, Chap. 2). For example, in 1603 an especially devout lay brother from the house of Franciscan conventuals in Cuenca died while on visit to his sister in Tebar. The villagers, convinced that Fray Martín would become a saint, were determined to keep the body for the local monastery even if armed force were needed. The city of Cuenca recommended retrieving the corpse because given the life Martín had led, "the body is bound to shine" (AMC, Leg. 265, fol. 327).[36] For Julián to become a popular saint, his worth had to be proved to very knowledgeable consumers. The seventeenth century, the worst period in Spain for plague since 1348, gave the bishop his chance. Elites celebrated Julián's virtuous qualities as bishop and patron saint of Cuenca, while among the people, Julián represented what saints had always meant to them: powerful advocates for the poor and sick of this world in God's celestial court. The success of the Counter-Reformation was to accommodate these potentially conflicting identities and clients so that Julián became the versatile saint of a revitalized Church, exemplary bishop, miracle worker, and defender of the poor.

Notes

1. Spanish saints have received much attention from folklorists, anthropologists, and religious writers, but virtually none from historians. Some of the best-known studies of saints are by the anthropologist William Christian, whose work focuses on the fifteenth through the twentieth centuries.

2. Christian (*Local Religion* 141) also notes the revival and invention of saints in the late sixteenth century, but does not link the trend to the Counter-Reformation. A contemporary account of Santa Leocadia is M. Hernández, *Vida, martyrio y traslación de . . . Santa Leocadia desde Flandes a Toledo* (Toledo: P. Rodríguez, 1591). Philip II was a devoted follower of the saints and collector of their relics.

3. See the following contemporary accounts of the revival of these saints: for Madrid, Alonso de Villegas; for Avila, Antonio de Cianca (my thanks to Jodi Bilinkoff for pointing out the parallels between Segundo and Julián); for León, Anthanasio de Lobrera; for Segovia, J. de Horche. For many other accounts dating from the first years of the seventeenth century, see J. Simón Díaz.

4. Historians and sociologists agree that saints are good cultural indicators for both the time in which they lived and the one in which they are venerated. Like much of culture during the age of absolutism, during the Counter-Reformation the cult of the saints came under the direct control of a central authority, the pope himself; formerly, veneration of saints was decentralized and relatively informal (Burke 45).

5. An anonymous book on the cult of the Holy Cross in Burgos records that Julián's shack was later consecrated as a chapel and fell into ruins about 1530. At the time of publication, 1554, the author had not yet heard about the translation of Julián's body in 1518 (*Hystoria . . . del sancto Crucifixo*, fol. 15v). My thanks to William Christian for this reference.

6. In 1527, the city wrote to Charles V about the charity, which it claimed "fue ynstituyda . . . por vezinos della para dar cada dia a quantos pobres vienen a la yglesya mayor. . . ." (AMC, Leg. 865: 7). One hundred years later, Mártir Rizo (112) wrote in his history of the city that "ay tradición, que procede su primera institución del bienauenturado san Iulián. . . ."

7. Another reason for moving the location of the tomb, Escudero adds, was that one day during a procession one of the canons inadvertently spat on the bishop's grave!

8. The bishop at the time was Rafael Galeote Riario, nephew of Sixtus IV. He had been bishop since 1493, but never once visited the diocese. The chapter did obtain his permission for the translation.

9. During the Middle Ages, theft of relics was common; see Patrick J. Geary.

10. Escudero, ms., fols. 17v-18v; Sanchiz Catalán 373-378, 440-446. A 1556 inquisitorial trial confirms that these signs were to become common knowledge (ADC, Inq. Leg. 238: 3081). Saints' bodies typically gave off a powerful, sweet odor (see Weinsteins' quantification of saintly characteristics). Julián's odor was so strong that the inquisitor's servants smelled it on his robes when he came home.

11. On the subject of incorruptibility, see Joan C. Cruz.

12. In 1583, Escudero noted that the severed finger "now moves about on its own" ("ahora anda por sí") (fol. 18v). A legend about the missing finger quickly sprang up. It explained that in the procession of 1518, an overzealous *hidalgo* had bitten off the finger and carried the relic away, but returned it within a matter of hours when his own finger was bitten off in a brawl (López 1: 199-200). This story apparently was in circulation by the time Philip II visited San Julián's tomb

in 1564. The monarch wished to have a relic of the saint for his collection, but when told of the *hidalgo's* mishap, he changed his mind, saying he had not come in search of miracles (Sanchiz Catalán 379, taken from Poza). In 1605 the cathedral chapter and bishop noticed that the saint's body was deteriorating, and, anxious to preserve it entire and in good condition, they resolved to seal the coffin forever. Pressure to see the relic was too much, however; Philip IV insisted on viewing it in 1642 (he declared it was the best preserved relic he had ever seen). At that date the chapter observed that the saint was missing a few more odds and ends (Sanchiz Catalán 121, 383). The relic was burned in 1936.

13. See Burke 46. No saints were canonized between 1523 and 1588. Burke comments, "[i]t does not seem unreasonable to explain this hiatus in terms of a failure of nerve and to speak of a 'crisis of canonization' at a time when . . . the very idea of a saint was under fire."

14. Hurtado was at the imperial court while Pozo and Coria (Francisco de Mendoza y Bobadilla) were in Rome. The city wrote to Licenciado Hurtado de Mendoza, "and your excellency has the same obligation as does His Most Reverent Lordship of favoring and honoring your country and the name of the same" ("pues v.m. tiene la misma obligación que su Señoría Reverendísimo de favorescer y honrrar su patria y nombre della"). If there were any trouble in procuring the hoped-for indulgences and pardons, the city was sure that "your excellency would abolish it with your prudence, industry, and authority" ("v.m. con su prudencia, yndustria y auctoridad . . . la quitaría").

15. Before 1550, the city had vowed to honor Corpus Christi, Nuestra Señora de las Nieves, San Juan, San Bernabé, Nuestra Señora de las Candelas, San Abdón, San Senén, and Santa Ana.

16. Predating the first hagiography dedicated to Julián (published in 1589), I have found four sixteenth-century accounts of the saint; two mention the translation and two do not. In the two early accounts of the translation, both authors (Venero and Medina) state that the reason for moving the tomb was that the saint was buried in "un lugar muy baxo" (which can mean either a low or an unworthy place) and the chapter wished to give him a more honorable resting place.

17. On the Tridentine reforms in Cuenca, see Nalle, "Religion and Reform."

18. The "ideal bishop" has been the subject of at least two books, by H. Jedin and J. Tellechea.

19. The nine works in order of appearance are Muñoz (before 1550); Escudero (1589, 1595, 1601); Segura (1599); Valenzuela Velázquez (1611); Porreño (1613); Pineiro y Osorio (1642); Poza (1646); Santa María (1686); and Alcázar (1692). See Works Cited for full references.

20. Medina's *Libro de grandezas de España*, also a popular book, repeats most of the information in Venero's account of San Julián.

21. Escudero, ms., "Prólogo del autor." Escudero lists his sources for the hagiography as Venero, Padilla, and Medina.

22. Escudero even wrote a chapter titled, "On how one should not think less of Saint Julian for not being canonized, and on the doubt that exists if he is, and on the brief of Pope Julius III to pray to him on September fifth" ("De como no se ha de tener San Julián en menos por no estar canonizado y de la dubda que ay

si lo está y del breve del papa Julio terzero para rezar del a zinco de septiembre").

23. The father dreamed that he saw his wife surrounded by a white light. Apparently the medieval portent (a flame-breathing puppy) had gone out of favor.

24. The Jesuits' first college in the diocese was founded in the city of Cuenca in 1554. Members of that college as well as the others in the diocese concentrated on catechismal instruction (Nalle, "Religion and Reform" 168-169).

25. The cult of Lesmes also grew during the sixteenth century, although it seems to have been more specifically a devotion based in the city of Burgos. In fact, Burgos honors two saints by that name, a cause for some confusion. One Lesmes was a French Benedictine who was abbot of Casa Dei and died in Burgos in 1097. In the fourteenth century he became patron saint of the city, which he remains to this day. The other Lesmes, Julián's grainkeeper, is first mentioned in Venero's *Enchiridion*, although Venero made no effort to distinguish between the two men. Perhaps Venero dispelled the confusion in a later book, *La vida y milagros del bien aventurado confesor santo Lesmes*, a work apparently now lost. Despite all the publicity, the anonymous author of the *Hystoria del sancto Crucifixo* (1554) failed to link Julián to Lesmes. Later in the century Escudero wrote that Lesmes was sought by persons suffering from kidney illnesses, who would rub their backs against his tomb and pray to Lesmes to ask for Julián's intercession (ms. 9/2601, fol. 9v). Earlier in the twentieth century the tomb was still frequented by old women (Albarellos 29). The diocese also honors both of Julián's days, January 28 and September 5, and a seventeenth-century monument to the saint may be observed near the southern gate of the old city wall.

26. These latter two stories helped to explain the presence of a green palm frond in Julián's coffin—palm trees do not grow in the region—and why the bishop was found dressed in his vestments.

27. On marriage in Counter-Reformation Spain, see A. Redondo.

28. This, and the description of the triumphal arch and the holidays that follows, are taken from an account of the celebrations written by the chapter on September 16, 1595. The author of the account apparently had access to the original designs for the arch, as his detailed description of it coincides with the conditions set down in the building contract (see note 30). Bishop Vadillo's participation in the holidays was cut short by his death on September 1. The chapter scarcely noticed.

29. According to Mártir Rizo, Canon Pedro de Mendoza, son of the Marquis of Cañete and brother of the Viceroy of Peru, gave in excess of 10,000 ducats for the festival (148).

30. Further research in the city's notarial archives has uncovered the original contract (dated June 3, 1595) between the chapter and the arch's builders, sculptor-architect Diego de Villadiego and painter Bartolomé Matarana. Villadiego and Matarana agreed to build the arch according to a design drawn by Alonso Serrano. Serrano received 14 ducats for the design, Villadiego 768 ducats for the arch (he got to keep most of the materials that went into it except eight paintings, which are now in the Diocesan Museum), and Matarana was paid 382 ducats to paint the entire arch in watercolors and execute the paintings. The arch had to be ready by August 31 (AHPC, P-383, fols. 685r-689r).

31. Possibly the fireworks represented the kingdoms of Castile and León in combat with the Devil.

32. On September 14, Nicolás de los Ríos and Mateo de Salzedo accepted payment of 4,400 *reales* for their presentation of San Julián's play (AHPC, P-384, fols. 150v-151r). In 1603 Ríos became one of eight persons in Castile allowed to run a royally licensed theater company (Rennert 215). A company consisted of about fifteen players plus props and costumes.

33. José Antonio Maravall's work, *The Culture of the Baroque*, is a thoughtful study of the political implications of the baroque style, the most important aspect of which was the use of propaganda in defense of the Church and State.

34. The canons and city councillors may have been attracted to that aspect of Julián's life, since many of them had Jewish ancestry, which they preferred to forget.

35. In the seventeenth century, while still not common, more individuals began to choose personal patron saints other than Mary, whom they would name in their last testaments. Favorites were Julián, the Archangel Michael, Santiago, and the Guardian Angel. The practice appears mostly in upper-class, male testators.

36. This friar became a local celebrity, inspiring the book *La vida y muerte santa de Fr. Martín de Carrascosa sepultado en S. Francisco de Cuenca*, by Fray Melchor de Huélamo, a native of Cuenca.

Works Cited

Albarellos, Juan. *Efemerides burgalesas (apuntes históricos)*. 2nd ed. Burgos: Diario de Burgos, 1964.

Alcázar, Bartolomé. *Vida, virtudes y milagros de San Julián, segundo obispo de Cuenca*. Madrid: J. García Infanzón, 1692.

Archivo Catedralicio de Cuenca (ACC). Various documents.

Archivo Diocesano de Cuenca (ADC). Various documents.

Archivo Histórico Provincial de Cuenca (AHPC). Various documents.

Archivo Municipal de Cuenca (AMC). Various documents.

Biblioteca Nacional, Madrid (BNM). Ms. 18654.

Burke, Peter. "How to be a Counter-Reformation Saint." *Religion and Society in Early Modern Europe, 1500-1800*. Ed. Kaspar von Greyerz. Boston: Allen & Unwin, 1984. 45-55.

Christian, William A. *Apparitions in Late Medieval and Renaissance Spain*. Princeton: Princeton Univ. Press, 1981.

———. *Local Religion in Sixteenth-Century Spain*. Princeton: Princeton Univ. Press, 1981, 1988.

———. *Person and God in a Spanish Valley*. Rev. ed. Princeton: Princeton Univ. Press, 1989.

Cianca, Antonio de. *Historia de la vida, invención, milagros y translación de San Segundo, primero obispo de Avila*. Madrid: Luis Sánchez, 1595.

Cirac Estopañán, Sebastián. *Los procesos de hechicerías en la Inquisición de Castilla la Nueva (Tribunales de Toledo y Cuenca)*. Madrid: Consejo Superior de Investigaciones Científicas, 1942.

Cruz, Joan C. *The Incorruptibles: A Study of the Incorruption of the Bodies of Various Catholic Saints and Beati.* Rockford, Ill.: Tan Books, 1977.

Delooz, Pierre. "Towards a sociological study of canonized sainthood in the Catholic Church." *Saints and Their Cults: Studies in Religious Sociology, Folklore and History.* Ed. Stephen Wilson. New York: Cambridge Univ. Press, 1983. 189-216.

Escudero, Francisco. *Comiença la vida y glorioso fin, translación, y milagros del Bien auenturado San Julián, segundo obispo de Cuenca.* RAH, ms. 9/2199.

————. *Vida y milagros del glorioso confesor San Iulián, segundo obispo de Cuenca.* Toledo: P. Rodríguez, 1589; Cuenca: I. Massellin, 1595; Cuenca: C. Bordán, 1601.

Geary, Patrick J. *Furta Sacra: Thefts of Relics in the Central Middle Ages.* Princeton: Princeton Univ. Press, 1978.

González Dávila, G. *Teatro eclesiástico de las iglesias metropolitanas y catedrales de las dos Castillas.* 4 vols. Madrid: F. Martínez, 1645.

Horche, J. de. *Historia de la vida del glorioso San Frutos, patrón de la Ciudad de Segovia y de sus hermanos San Valentín y Santa Engracia.* Valladolid: C. Lasso Vaca, 1610.

Huélamo, Fr. Melchor de. *La vida y muerte santa de Fr. Martín de Carrascosa sepultado en S. Francisco de Cuenca.* Cuenca: M. de la Iglesia, 1617.

Hystoria de cómo fue hallada la ymage[n] del sancto Crucifixo, q[ue] está en el monesterio de sancto Augustín de Burgos. Burgos: Juan de Junta, 1554.

Jedin, Hubert. *Il tipo ideale di vescovo secondo la riforma cattolica.* Brescia: Morcelliana, 1950.

Lobrera, Anthanasio de. *Historia de . . . León y de su obispo y patrón sant Froylán, con las del glorioso San Atilano . . .* Valladolid: D. Fernández de Cordoua, 1596.

López, Mateo. *Memorias históricas de Cuenca y su obispado.* 2 vols. Madrid: CSIC, 1949.

Maravall, José Antonio. *The Culture of the Baroque.* Trans. Terry Cochran. Minneapolis: Univ. of Minnesota Press, 1986.

Mártir Rizo, P. *Historia de la muy noble y leal ciudad de Cuenca.* Madrid: Herederos de la Viuda de P. de Madrigal, 1629. Rpt. Barcelona: Ediciones "El Albir," 1979.

Medina, Pedro de. *Libro de grandezas y cosas memorables de España.* Seville: D. de Robertis, 1549. Ed. Angel González Palacios. Madrid: Consejo Superior de Investigaciones Científicas, 1944.

Nalle, Sara T. "Religion and Reform in a Spanish Diocese. Cuenca, 1545-1650." Unpublished diss. Baltimore: Johns Hopkins Univ., 1983.

Officium Sancti Juliani Episcopi Conchensis. . . . Barcelona: Lacavalleria, 1672, 1675; Madrid: D. de Villa-Diego, 1673.

Padilla, Lorenzo de. *Catálogo de los santos de España.* Toledo: F. de Santa Catalina, 1538.

Pineiro y Osorio, J. *Vida de San Julián.* ACC ms., ca. 1642.

Porreño, Baltasar. *Historia de San Julián.* ACC ms., 1613.

Poza, Juan Bautista de. *Vida de San Julián.* ACC ms., 1646.

Ramírez, Diego de. *Constituciones synodales del obispado de Cuenca.* Cuenca: F. de Alfaro, 1531.

Real Academia de Historia (RAH). Various documents.

Redondo, Augustín, ed. *Amours légitimes, amours illégitimes en Espagne (XVIe siécles)*. Paris: La Sorbonne, 1985.

Rennert, Hugo Albert. *The Spanish Stage in the Time of Lope de Vega*. New York: Hispanic Society of America, 1909. Rpt. New York: Dover, 1963.

Sanchiz Catalán, R. *Noticia del culto tributado a San Julián*. Cuenca: Imprenta Madina, 1909.

Santa María, A. de. *Vida de San Julián, obispo y patrón de Cuenca*. . . . Alcalá de Henares: F. García de Hernández, 1686.

Segura, Bartolomé de. *Del nacimiento, vida y muerte, con algunos particulares milagros del milagroso confesor San Julián, segundo obispo de Cuenca*. Cuenca: Miguel Serrano, 1599.

_____ . *Quaderno primero del nacimiento, vida y muerte de San Julián, segundo obispo de Cuenca*. RAH, ms. 9/2601.

Simón Díaz, José. *Bibliografía regional y local de España. I. Impresos localizados (siglos XV-XVII)*. Madrid: Consejo Superior de Investigaciones Científicas, 1976.

Tellechea, José Ignacio. *El obispo ideal en el siglo de la Reforma*. Rome: Iglesia Nacional de España, 1963.

Valenzuela Velázquez, J. B. *Discurso en comprobación de la santidad de vida y milagros del Glorioso San Julián*. Cuenca: B. de Selma, 1611.

Venero, Alonso de. *Enchiridion de los tiempos*. Salamanca: Juan de Junta, 1543.

_____ . *La vida y milagros del bien aventurado confesor santo Lesmes*. Burgos: Pedro de Junta, 1563.

Villegas, Alonso de. *Vida de Isidro Labrador, cuyo cuerpo está en la iglesia parroquial de San Andrés de Madrid*. Madrid: Luis Sánchez, 1592.

Voragine, Jacobus de. *The Golden Legend of Jacobus de Voragine*. Trans. adapted from the Latin by Granger Ryan and Helmut Ripperger. New York: Longmans, Green and Co., 1948.

Weinstein, Donald and Rudolph M. *Saints and Society: The Two Worlds of Western Christendom, 1000-1700*. Chicago: Univ. of Chicago Press, 1982.

Wilson, Stephen, ed. *Saints and Their Cults: Studies in Religious Sociology, Folklore and History*. New York: Cambridge Univ. Press, 1983.

◆ Chapter 3

Religious Oratory in a Culture of Control

Gwendolyn Barnes-Karol

The culture of Counter-Reformation Spain is often analyzed in terms of ideological control. Along these lines, literary and cultural historians usually highlight the religious, social, and political intimidation and repression of the Inquisition; the opulent *fiestas* and public festivals designed to inspire awe in spectators; and the propagandistic power of the new comedy (*comedia nueva*) to engender respect for the values of the traditional monarchical-seigneurial order. Less attention has been paid to religious oratory, which was perhaps one of the most effective agents of the Counter-Reformation culture of control. Because of the frequency of sermons, their accessibility to all sectors of Spanish society, and, above all, the substantial impact of live performances on audiences, they were useful tools of ideological manipulation. This essay will deal with this genre, focusing on religious oratory as oral performance and as printed text and on its role within the culture of control of Counter-Reformation Spain.

Before entering into a discussion that, of necessity, must deal with the power of the institution of preaching, let us recall that the sixteenth century was a period in which changing socioeconomic conditions presented radically new challenges to the power structure of Spanish society. People flocked to the cities from rural areas, they migrated from northern Spain to the South, and they abandoned the Peninsula bound for the New World. This geographic mobility, in turn, led to increased socio-economic mobility. Technical innovations, an increase in the supply of agricultural and manufactured goods for purchase, and the growth of money and credit as means of exchange resulted in a more diversified labor force and fomented the expansion of a "fourth estate" composed of merchants, bureaucrats, financiers, and professionals. These interrelated phenomena combined to produce a society that was future-oriented and actively pursuing new ways of seeing, thinking, and doing in the first half of the century. Soon, however, these forward-looking groups began to constitute a genuine challenge to the traditional sources of authority (the Church, the Monarchy, and the upper echelons of the hereditary nobility). These challenges, in turn, brought an air of uncertainty to the Peninsula, and as José Antonio Maravall explains, "the inconsistency of *status* engendered social instability" ("From the Renaissance" 21; emphasis in the original). Maravall argues that this growing perception of instability finally led the privileged elites of the monarchical-seigneurial order to begin to actively reconsolidate their eroded power base around 1600, a process that he refers to as the "refeudalization" of the Spanish society (see *Culture of the Baroque*).

While the reaction of the dominant groups in secular society would make itself felt around the turn of the century, the Church, in contrast, had already begun to take new steps to counteract the trend toward the decentralization of its authority as early as the Council of Trent (1545-1563). Although the Inquisition had been actively engaged in the repression and/or suppression of dangerous marginal groups (Gypsies, crypto-Jews, *alumbrados*, Protestants, witches), by midcentury the nonconformity that threatened the Church's power base was not limited to such easily identifiable "heretics." The possibility of direct access to God without the mediation of the Church or one of its authorized representatives was deemed to present opportunities to challenge openly the Church's discourse and established religious practices. Faced with such possibilities, the Church felt an urgent need to develop new means of manipulation of public opinion and behavioral control that would be effective in reversing such dangerous trends among the general population. To this end, the ecclesiastical hierarchy began to reconsider the potential of religious oratory for ideological control.

One of the major outcomes of the Council of Trent was the (re)institutionalization of preaching as a means of (i) psychological manipulation and control and (ii) dissemination of propaganda favorable to the continued survival of the traditional society of estates founded upon the pillars of Church, Monarchy, and nobility. Although preaching had traditionally been a part of the propagation of Christianity, by as early as the fifth century it had already begun to be overshadowed by the liturgy of the mass as the focal point of Catholic religious observance. In spite of the proliferation of medieval *artes praedicandi* and preachers' aids, preaching soon became an activity of particular religious orders (especially the Franciscans and Dominicans) rather than an essential duty of all secular and religious clergy. By the mid-1500s, Spain was plagued by a dearth of preachers despite the fact that there was no shortage of priests or members of religious orders. That situation was to change as Tridentine mandates concerning the regulation and standardization of clerical duties required that priests, for the first time ever, preach sermons every Sunday and feast day as well as daily during Advent and Lent. Thus began a period (which would last throughout the entire seventeenth century) of mobilizing and training the Spanish clergy to be transmitters of the Church's discourse of religious, moral, and socioeconomic orthodoxy.

The key to the power of preaching as ideological control lies in the creation, manipulation, and dissemination of images that would create an aura of moral, theological, socioeconomic, and political harmony and homogeneity capable of supplanting an increasingly unorthodox social order. The reconsolidation of the ecclesiastical and secular power structures thus would be a product of a representation that would reaffirm a past reality. The ability, however, to resuscitate a past social order through ideological manipulation depended on proper reception of the discourse of the Church and of the dominant groups. The success of the reconsolidation of the eroded power base of the

Church and other elites depended not just on the imposition of the will of the dominant groups, but on the acquiescence of the dominated. As Foucault has shown, power, rather than being a monolithic "possession" or "privilege" of a hierarchy, is the product of a complex network of mediating institutions and mechanisms. The effects of this vast network reach all sectors of society and may be transmitted and amplified by those who are themselves dominated (26-27 +). Thus, for religious oratory to be effective, it had to impress listeners to the point of inhibiting a genuinely critical reception of the message and coopt them into modifying their beliefs, values, and behavior in accordance with the ideas transmitted.

The notion of reception in the process of manipulation was inherent in the traditional three-part goal of religious oratory derived from classical rhetoric. Solid doctrinal and moral instruction (*enseñar*) had to be combined with aesthetic appeal (*deleitar*) in order to persuade and produce a response (*mover*). The optimal response would be action motivated by emotion—compassion, piety, guilt, astonishment, awe, terror—rather than reason, and would preclude a logical dissection of the content and implications of the message. This type of desired response dovetailed perfectly with the prevailing modes of production and reception of culture in the 1500s and 1600s. Luiz Costa Lima uses the term "auditive" culture to describe a situation, such as that of Counter-Reformation Spain, in which most verbal artifacts, even those that existed in written or printed form, were disseminated orally and received aurally. In such a "culture of seductive persuasion," the dynamic nature of the oral performance was combined with new types of linguistic and conceptual constructs facilitated by writing. The result was the production of texts—in this case, sermons—performed live. They were characterized by novelty (instead of the traditional formulaic structure of storytelling) and by a type of rhetorical artifice designed to persuade by astounding and overwhelming rather than through logical argumentation, as in a text composed for analysis by an individual reader (Godzich and Spadaccini 47). Such texts, received simultaneously by all members of an audience, could serve as effective instruments of manipulation because of their power to act upon listeners as an uncritical community rather than as isolated individuals reading for private consumption (see Rossi-Landi).

The power of preachers to control public opinion in Counter-Reformation Spain and, subsequently, to channel behavior into patterns that would perpetuate the traditional hierarchical society of estates, depended on their ability to manipulate images and rhetoric in such a way as to leave their listeners astonished and incapable of intellectually challenging the validity of a message. This type of emotional and psychological manipulation would result in a "mass reception" of a message by illiterate or semiliterate listeners (Godzich and Spadaccini 47-49).

As Counter-Reformation sermons were first and foremost live performances, their reception was determined not only by the verbal signs (the actual text of the sermon), but also by the staging signs of the performance (e.g., voice, gesture, dress, setting, properties) (see Eco). The interaction between verbal and staging signs produced the theatricality that could operate so effectively on audiences intellectually unprepared to distance themselves from the overwhelming persuasive power of the total performance (see Alter).

The creation of an aura of mystique around the figure of the preacher was the first of many steps in the process of astounding listeners so that their minds and wills would become pliable material to be remolded according to orthodox religious and socioeconomic doctrines. The manipulation of an image of the preacher as a consecrated figure would in itself generate awe. To begin with, a preacher's ability to leave his listeners dumbfounded during the live performance of a sermon was intimately linked to his distance from the general population, as succinctly stated by Diego Niseno, Abbot of the Order of San Basilio Magno in Madrid, in an Advent sermon entitled "If the Evangelical Orator is to be the terror and astonishment of his listeners, he must be rarely seen or dealt with by men" ("Que si el Orador Evangelico ha de ser terror y assombro de los oyentes, ha de ser muy raras veces visto y tratado de hombres") (see *Asuntos predicables*).[1] In essence, Niseno encouraged preachers to be always like the wind: felt, but never seen (fol. 38). By keeping out of the public eye, they would enhance the mystery of their person and the potential power of their words. The Augustinian Pedro de San José explained this phenomenon more explicitly:

> How can the roving, gadabout Preacher expect what he
> says in the pulpit to be believed, if he does not know
> how to withdraw awhile from the conversations of lay
> people? If he spends all day visiting, is it so strange that
> his doctrine and person are despised? . . . But if he
> hides, if they see him as if by miracle, they will value his
> doctrine, they will carry it out, because since he was not
> raised with them, nor did he deal with them, they will
> venerate him all the more. Withdraw, then, Preaching
> Fathers, from all publicity, do not let yourselves be
> pawed by laymen. ("Para la feria quinta después del
> primer domingo," *Discursos morales* 247)[2]

The aura of mystique and authority that could be generated by a preacher who avoided excessive contact with the public was enhanced by the staging signs of the actual performance. The settings for sermons themselves preconditioned audiences to be manipulated emotionally, sensorially, and psychologically. Sermons performed in churches or convents were often presented against a backdrop of highly dramatic polychromed baroque statuary. The glass tears, disheveled wigs of natural hair, crowns of thorns, wounds painted blood red, tragic facial expressions, and symbols of pain and persecution that adorned images of Christ, the Virgin Mary, and various saints and martyrs predisposed sermon-goers to be susceptible to a rhetoric of awe or terror. In addition, multiple painted hieroglyphics or emblems, whose mysterious hidden meanings could be deciphered only by the superior faculties of the preacher, adorned many places of worship. These graphic images, often on display before the sermons began, were also effective in stimulating emotional states in listeners that could later be exploited during the actual sermon.

As the seventeenth century progressed, many preachers became masters of theatricality and learned to heighten the dramatic appeal of their persons and the sermon settings through the use of properties. Terror was routinely produced through the timely display of crucifixes or actual skulls and bones. Astonishment was produced through creative special effects such as the release of live doves adorned with tinsel at a particularly climactic moment (Medrano 188). Some preachers even transformed their churches into ecclesiastic theaters. An example can be found in Francisco Caus's description of a colleague's sermon:

> Even though it [preaching] is so contrary to the theater, he behaved in this exercise as actors do. Actors, to attract audiences, and make a profit, commonly use scenic effects in the theater called *tramoyas*, that because of their novelty draw perhaps bigger crowds than Sermons do, and, in this way they increase their earnings. In a similar way our Evangelical Actor ordered the Altar to be covered with a black veil; he put a skull in the middle, as if to be the title of that spectacle, accompanied by only two Images: of the Christ Crucified and the Virgin of the Sorrows; and with the candles that burned with melancholy, he formed a Theater suited for death. Then our fervent Minister appeared [on stage], and acted out the sudden onset of death and what one will gain or lose at that hour with such vigor that his words seemed to either be like [fish]hooks that caught or [drag]hooks that carried souls to God. . . . There are two types of death: one real, and one acted out. The real kind finishes everything; but the kind that is acted out is preserved. (*Oracion funebre en la* [sic] *exequias que el convento de San Sebastian de la ciudad de Xativa, de la Orden de San Augustin, consagro al Venerable, y muy Reverendo Padre fray Augustin Antonio Pascual, de la misma orden en 12 de octubre de 1691* . . . [Valencia: Imprenta de Francisco Mestre, 1692], quoted in Ledda 104)[3]

Other preachers went even further, actually incorporating live tableaux designed to overwhelm unsuspecting audiences of their sermons.

The ability of sermons to engulf their listeners in a wave of emotion that would impede any type of critical reception of the verbal message was even greater when the sermons were part of ecclesiastical celebrations (e.g., dedications of new churches, beatifications, canonizations), *autos de fe*, *fiestas*, ceremonies commemorating municipal or royal events, or other massive public spectacles. The elaborate backdrops or stages, luxurious costumes, pomp and circumstance of processions, ostentatious display of royal or religious artifacts and regalia, presence and participation of figures of sacred or secular authority, and special effects (ranging from music to fireworks) created an atmosphere that acted to astound an audience and suppress its ability to reason even before it was time for the sermon. Within the context of such multimedia events, the preacher began with an audience whose malleability was virtually guaranteed from the start.

The preacher's projection of an image that was in itself capable of inspiring awe in listeners and his ability to exploit the setting, whether a church or a public spectacle, set the stage for the actual performance of the sermon. Despite an emphasis on the moral dimension of preaching and the need to condemn vice and promote virtue in thought and action, it was a preacher's ability to perform in such a way so as to highlight the ingeniousness and innovations of his rhetorical artifice that was valued most highly. In this way, the affective impact of a preacher's words, more than the logic of his discourse, would engulf his listeners in a wave of emotion that would render them incapable of receiving a message critically.

Beginning around 1576, when Fray Luis de Granada published his *Ecclesiasticae rhetoricae, sive De ratione concionandi libri sex (Los seis libros de la retórica eclesiástica, o de la manera de predicar; Six Books of Ecclesiastical Rhetoric, or the Way to Preach)* in Lisbon, theoreticians began to privilege a style of preaching that was more oriented toward performance than toward information. Granada's rhetoric of religious oratory outlined parameters that would be more fully developed by successors in the seventeenth century. Granada believed that the best way to effect change was to appeal to listeners' emotions (*el afecto*) rather than to preach doctrine because "men sin more because of vice and the depravity of their emotions than because of ignorance of the truth; and depraved emotions can only be forced out by opposite ones, for as the saying goes, 'one nail is removed by another' " ("mas pecan los hombres por vicio y depravacion de su afecto, que por ignorancia de las verdades; y los afectos depravados, como un clavo con otro, han de arrancarse con afectos opuestos" [520-521]). The surest path, then, to stir listeners' hearts was not that afforded by reason, but that of an appeal to the senses. Thus, Granada exhorted his colleagues to capture their audiences' attention and goodwill through the aesthetic pleasure generated by artistic use of language.

The cultivation of rhetorical artifice quickly became a priority among Granada's successors, who were determined to entice and tantalize their listeners with ingenious conceits and magnificent-sounding verbal constructions. Linguistic and rhetorical novelty, rather than substance, much to the disdain of many clerics and rhetoricians, would soon come to be the characteristic of Counter-Reformation religious oratory as preachers attempted to disguise the goal of reestablishing orthodox modes of thought and comportment in order to protect an endangered social order.

But exploiting the capacity of rhetorical artifice to render audiences open to embracing a message was in itself insufficient. Granada advocated combining verbal imagery with the elegance of a polished delivery:

> As in all things, form is valued more than the substance
> that receives the form, I would venture that many
> priests, spending as much time and energy in artifice as
> in substance, pay almost no heed to elocution and
> pronunciation, when without them, the ignorant
> common people despise the most excellent artifice. (40)[4]

If the *vulgo necio* could be enticed by rhetorical artifice highlighted by an effective performance within the context of a multimedia event, they could then be led on to a state of astonishment (*suspenso*). At this point, a captive audience could then be further manipulated by a preacher to feel anger, compassion, fear, terror, admiration, awe, or any number of emotions whose impact would be to render listeners open to the most insidious type of ideological manipulation.

The power of the preacher to manipulate could be enhanced further by his capacity to re-create a scenario in the minds of his listeners with such vividness that they would be able to visualize the images inherent in the verbal signs. Granada, for example, emphasizes the idea that "nothing moves the listeners more than painting something with words, so that it does not seem like it is being described as much as it is taking place before one's very eyes: being generally known that all the emotions are greatly stirred when something's greatness can be seen" ("nada los conmueve mas [a los oyentes] que el pintar una cosa con palabras, de manera, que no tanto parezca que se dice, cuanto que se hace y se pone delante de los ojos: siendo notorio que se mueven muchísimo todos los afectos, poniendo á la vista la grandeza de las cosas" [538]). A preacher's ability to paint pictures with words was akin to his transporting his audience to a theater (538). Just as a scene acted out on a sixteenth- or seventeenth-century stage could become confused with the real existence of semiliterate or illiterate theatergoers, the force of a narrative brought to life by an effective preacher could overwhelm sermon-goers so as to make them unable to disengage themselves from what they heard or saw, and so open them up once again to manipulation. In the same vein, Francisco de Ameyugo pointed to the overwhelming power of drama to leave ideas engraved upon the hearts and minds of sermon-goers when he stated that "the truth represented in a dead way moves no more than if it were fiction, and a fiction represented in a lively way, moves as if truth were unfolding before one's eyes" ("la verdad muertamente representada no mueve mas que si fuera una ficcion, y una ficcion vivamente representada, mueve del mismo modo, que si estuviera a los ojos la verdad" [72]).

Although there were, throughout the seventeenth century, constant appeals by rhetoricians to prudently temper the drama of performance with the naturalness and decorum required by the holiness of the office of the preacher, the parallels between the stage and the pulpit were recognized. Diego Niseno, for example, states that the preacher, like the actor, must excel in portraying different characters "on stage" to produce calculated responses in his listeners and take special care not to destroy the illusions he creates at the end of the performance.

> It is well known that the theater is the place where acting is done, where different roles are imagined and played, first of a King, then of a lover, a lady, a saint, a sinner, a courtier, a shepherd, and of many others that the action requires: in this the actor and Preacher do not fail to agree; because he [the preacher] in order to move the listeners' emotions, should play various roles and characters, first an angry God, to restrain the proud;

then a loving father, to inspire the weak; then a King,
who can easily punish; and a shepherd who wants to
defend lovingly, and many other characters and roles
that can occur to him. . . . After playing his role, he
should return to his dressing room, and not be seen by
the people, because it would be a great affront for he
who acts, to remain within sight of the people without
anything to do or say, exposed so that they could boo
him. In that the pulpit should be similar to the theater,
and the preacher like the actor, who upon finishing his
role or completing his sermon, should exit and hide until
it is necessary for him to preach again. (Fols. 39-39v)[5]

Despite a general recognition of the similarities between oratory and theater, the need to avoid excess rhetorical artifice and
theatricality was a constant throughout the 1600s. The manipulation of images through sermons as a vehicle for disseminating
ideas that would facilitate the reconsolidation of the eroding
power base of the Church, Monarchy, and nobility was ultimately tied to the preservation of the aura of authority, gran-
deur, and infallibility of these three institutions in order to halt
the increasing autonomy of the individual and/or of new social
groups. The preservation of this aura depended first on the careful structuring of the verbal message both to enhance what
could create powerful positive images for the future and to conceal the suspect realities of the present moment. The Portuguese
Jesuit António de Vieira, for example, in selected words from
"Pensamientos Predicables. Sacados de papeles del Author. Sobre el evangelio del dia de San Iosef. (Tratanse las calidades de
un animo real.)", speaks of the need to maintain an air of secrecy to sustain power:

There is no surer sign of the end of an Empire, and a
Monarchy, than the destruction of the curtain of their
mysteries and the veils of their secrets. Kingdoms and
Monarchies sustain themselves with mystery more than
truth, and if their mysteries are revealed, their truths
will be defended with difficulty. Opinion is the
sustenance of Empires, secrets are the soul of opinion.
(*Aprovechar deleytando* 149)[6]

While these thoughts focused primarily on the secular realm, they were equally applicable to the ecclesiastical domain. This process of creating a representation that projected a desire rather than portraying a reality, however, could be undermined if the performance of the verbal test were overly dramatic and provoked laughter in the audience. Fray Francisco Sobrecasas exhorted his colleagues to be mindful of maintaining the decorum essential for the reconsolidation of the power of the Church, saying:

> There is a difference between the Actor, and the [Evangelical] Orator in their actions: as the Actor's main goal is to artfully delight the mind and the senses, he should adjust his voice to his actions, in such a way that what is born from his lips is newly animated with actions so that eyes and ears are nourished by the liveliness of lips and hands. The Orator has three goals: to move, to teach, and to delight. . . . the Orator should not limit himself to delighting the Audiences to the extent that he wastes . . . his time in acting: his primary goal is to move and teach. (455)[7]

Excessive theatricality could break the magic of the spell cast over an unsuspecting and uncritical audience and provoke the one emotional response capable of producing disengagement from the process of manipulation: laughter. Testimonies from the period point to the fact that laughter was the outcome of some preaching and that some sermon-goers reacted to sermons as if they were comedies. For example, already in 1604, Bartolomé Ximénez Patón reported that many sermon-goers commented on their frequent attendance saying "there was no cheaper comedy than hearing that preacher, nor was there a buffoon [available] for a lower fee" ("no avia comedia mas barata que oyr aquel predicador, ni truhan velazquillo mas de valde . . ." [*Eloquencia española en arte*, Toledo, fol. 11v], quoted in Ledda 96). In the mid-1600s, Juan Antonio Xarque criticizes many sermon audiences as being "merry people whose goal in hearing sermons is none other than going where the ladies are, because at that time of day there is no other entertainment than waiting for the theaters to open" ("gente divertida, cuyo fin en oyr los sermones, no es otro que ir a donde van las damas, porque en aquella hora no hay otro entretenimiento, hazer tiempo para la comedia" [291]).

When these key elements—the mystique of the persona of the preacher as a source of truth and authority; the awe-inspiring backdrops against which sermons were performed; the acute manipulation of rhetorical artifice and the drama of live performance—were carefully combined and exploited, preachers could render their audiences incapable of evaluating the validity of the verbal text. Captivated by the power of the multimedia event they were taking part in, they were moved to embrace the conservative content of the message without recognizing their role as objects of an artful process of ideological manipulation.

The discourse of the Church and the monarchical-seigneurial order as disseminated by Counter-Reformation preachers was religiously, socioeconomically, and politically orthodox. Its tenets included the following: the superiority of the spiritual realm with regard to the material world; the primacy of the Catholic faith and of the Church as mediator between God and his earthly subjects; the necessity of unquestioning obedience to ecclesiastical and civil authorities, who have been chosen to be God's representatives on earth; the perfection of a social order comprised of three immobile estates as ordained by Divine Providence; and the meaning of human existence as linked ultimately to salvation with one's own estate.

An examination of two sermons, preserved in writing some fifty years apart, will highlight how some of the key concepts of this conservation ideology were transmitted to sermon-goers. It should be noted, however, that the concepts presented in this essay have been extracted from a plethora of conceits, rhetorical word plays, and at times somewhat rambling and tangential meditations loosely linked to the topic of the sermons. Here, they form a coherent discourse capable of being scrutinized by a solitary reader for logic, validity, and relevance. Yet, within the context of the live performance, these concepts would have easily been accepted by illiterate or semiliterate audiences captivated by the entire multimedia experience. The impact of any one sermon or any one preacher on individuals or groups was variable, yet the constant bombardment of the Spanish populace by preachers extolling these basic concepts over months, years, and decades would firmly instill these ideas in listeners' minds and wills.

The first example is the sermon "Oración primera de la Dominica 24 después de Penthecostes" by the Franciscan Fray Diego de Arce, preached in Alcalá de Henares sometime between 1578 and 1606. The crux of the message, a literal interpretation of St. John's apocalyptic prophecies within the context of the Counter-Reformation, is that the coming of the Antichrist and the destruction of the known social order of the universe are imminent. Evidence of the impending disaster can be found in the destruction of the unity of the Western world by the propagation of Lutheran "heresy." Before Luther, according to Arce, the world's peoples lived together under one Father (the Pope), one Mother (the Church), one sun that shone on all (Christ), and one atmosphere breathed by all (the Holy Scriptures). Luther, who had been a shining star as a preacher, soon became a fallen star because of his disobedience. He abandoned his religious vocation for a secular life-style, his vows of celibacy for marriage, his poverty for wealth, and his abstinence for gluttony. His fall from grace through rebellion against ecclesiastic authority and the established social order upset the delicate balance of this archetypal world of unity, light, and purity, debilitating the Church and all Christian republics alike. Indeed, in Arce's view, Luther became the author of all contemporary ills. In portraying the destructiveness of Luther's acts, Arce employs the metaphor of noxious smoke (Lutheranism) that obscured the light of the sun (Christ) and fouled the pure air (Scriptures), thus poisoning and suffocating the human soul. He continues by relating how this smoke engendered an army of giant locusts (*langostas*) that ravaged the world, provoking civil wars, perverting the balance between the sacred and secular realms, desecrating churches, and spreading vice where virtue once had reigned supreme.

Arce skillfully constructed the rest of the sermon around the notion that rebellion against established authority engenders monsters. Rather than logically explaining to his listeners in further detail the real-world consequences of a reordering of the social structure, he manipulates them psychologically with terrifying tales of disobedient human beings turned into monstrous locusts, thus carefully playing upon the prevalent fears of demons, apparitions, witches, and other supernatural beings. To ensure that his listeners, most likely all baptized Catholics, would identify with the metaphor of the locust and experience horror at the thought of being transformed into grotesque creatures, he links disobedience not only to heretical Lutherans, but to all who fail to act according to their estate or role in the social order, calling them "friends of Lutherans." Thus, "gluttons" who ignore the mandate to uphold obligatory fasts; the "sacrilegious" who refuse to confess; the "idle" who believe that salvation is a question of faith alone, separate from good works or from fulfilling the responsibilities of one's station in life; "incontinent" members of religious orders who violate their vows of celibacy; "apostates" (monks) who turn monasteries into palaces of sensual delight; and "avaricious and ambitious princes" who try to confiscate the wealth of the Church to satisfy their greed—representatives of all three estates (*labradores, oradores,* and *nobles*)—are all as vulnerable as practicing Lutherans and just as likely to be transformed into horrifying locusts.

Once Arce sets up a structure in which all listeners, tied to the particular sins of their estate, must heed his admonishments or lose their human form, he proceeds to a highly visual description of the beast, a composite of other monsters. Each part of the locust is a graphic portrayal of an act of disobedience or excess. The locust is weighed down by a huge belly (gluttony) which prevents it from walking or flying. Its carapace is a coat of impenetrable mail (stubbornness in not admitting error when wrong). Its face is that of a man (the deception of sweet, but devious, Lutheran preaching that encourages further disobedience) and its hair is that of a woman (sensuality and lust). It wears a crown of fake gold (arrogance and ostentation), and has lion's teeth (gossip and blasphemy) and a scorpion's tail (the poison of Lutheran heresy). It behaves as if it were a war horse, ears laid back, eyes glaring, nostrils flared, frothing at the mouth, mane erect as it snorts and paws the earth. Its master is the Devil. These horrifying creatures pursue humans mercilessly, Arce warns his listeners with vehemence. Even if they escape the fate of becoming locusts, they may not elude the monsters' poison. Once stung by the tail, the victims foam at the mouth, vomit, and cry thick tears. Their hair stands on end, and their bodies convulse in a cold sweat.

These terrifying images of sin transformed into material reality (enhanced by the drama of live performance) should have frightened Arce's listeners into emotional submission and made them open to embracing a life-style consistent with the orthodox discourse of the Church and the monarchical-seigneurial order. After stunning his audience with the tale of the locust, he reassures them by insinuating that Spain is relatively free from the wrath of the locust because of its fidelity to the true Faith and its privileging of the glories of the spiritual realm over the transitory rewards of the material world. He says, "As much as the soul exceeds the body; the spirit, the flesh; eternity, time; the spiritual realm, the temporal world; such is the joy of our Spain in enjoying the light of the Gospel amidst so many people who do not have it" ("Pues quanto excede el alma al cuerpo; el espiritu a la carne; la eternidad al tiempo; lo celestial a lo terreno; tanta es mayor la dicha de nuestra España en gozar la luz de el Evangelio en medio de tantas gentes que carecen de ella" [fol. 31v]). Yet, lest his audience become too lax in their obedience to the Church's doctrine and civil authority, Arce reminds them that Lutheran Germany was once Catholic like Spain. Thus, he emphasizes, human nature is not incorruptible and the threat to Spain is omnipresent. The sermon ends with a prayer of support for the Inquisition, the institution responsible for keeping the heresy that destroyed Germany out of Spain.

Arce's strategy is clear. He manipulates his audience psychologically by linking their probable real-life failings to the possibility of persecution by or transformation into a beast that is likely both too horrible to imagine and yet too real to ignore. Rather than providing logical reasons for remaining faithful and obedient to both ecclesiastical and secular authority, he plays on his audience's irrational fears. If they do continue or return to a life-style consistent with Church doctrines and the traditional social order, it will have been motivated by an appeal to the emotions fabricated through rhetorical and conceptual artifice rather than by the existence of a real danger to the audience's physical well-being. The inclusion of the prayer for support of the Inquisition is juxtaposed effectively. A sufficiently frightened audience might have readily welcomed the repression of the feared institution if it could guarantee their personal safety.

The Jesuit Padre Gerónimo Continente takes a different approach in the mid-seventeenth-century mission sermon, "On man's fate" ("Del fin del hombre"[26–47]). He constructs his discourse as a commentary on the relationship between the spiritual world and the human condition. Beginning with an orderly meditation on the purpose of human existence, he reviews different goals: the acquisition of material wealth, the fulfillment of one's desires, the exercise of moral virtue, the contemplation of divine creation. Yet, he subsequently discards all of these options in favor of the orthodox Catholic position: the goal of human existence is to attain salvation according to the designs preordained by Divine Providence. In order to remind his audience that all human beings have the right to enter the Kingdom of Heaven, he paints a visual picture of Ezekiel's chariot and deciphers its symbolism. Its eagle, lion, ox, and human motifs, he explains, illustrate the four estates of human society: the prophets,[8] the nobility, the clergy, and the common people (el vulgo). In a similar fashion, the chariot's four wheels represent the four continents (Asia, Africa, Europe, and America) as well as the four seasons of the year. According to Continente, the inclusion of all estates, all regions of the known world, and all seasons of the human life cycle provides indisputable proof of God's plan for the redemption of all humankind.

Having thus demonstrated the nature of God's Kingdom, Continente proceeds to condemn those who fail to enter because of their own failure to gain admittance. Like Pharaoh, who kept the ancient Israelites from entering the Promised Land by putting them to work in building projects, the Pharaohs of contemporary times similarly enslave themselves to their material existence and thus deny themselves access to eternal salvation. Confronting his audience, he launches an accusatory litany of questions:

> I ask you, Faithful, are there still Pharoahs in the world? Are there people who are lost and condemned? Are there people, who, tied to the straw and clay of worldly possessions, despise celestial ones? O what sorrow that Christians and members of God's chosen can be found

who imitate Moors and Gentiles in their deeds and customs! who do not care about their eternal salvation? who remember neither their souls nor God because they squander themselves in the straw and clay of earthly interests? (42)[9]

Before the momentum generated in this interrogation can subside, he exhorts his audience to direct its energies toward spiritual redemption rather than material benefits by highlighting the struggles of the *labrador*, the soldier, and the merchant, the three types of listeners most likely to be in his audience:

In order not to become fainthearted in this journey and conquest of the celestial Kingdom, watch for the abundant prize, wait for the reward and crown of glory. For if the farmer endures the cold of winter, the fire of summer, the frost of the night, and the heat of the day, to reap his harvest in August; reason enough for the Christian to be encouraged, with the hope of the harvest that is to sustain him eternally. The soldier loaded down with armor, at an enemy frontier, with a harquebus on his shoulder, a sword in his hand, exposes himself to great risk for a brief pillage and the honor of his King: for those celestial treasures, for the true honor that the supreme Emperor will give you, seated at His table, fight with valor and perseverance. The merchant goes about traipsing across the earth, plowing through the waves, taking trips, overcoming danger, defeating difficulties, to obtain four doubloons: who should delay, knowing that he should possess those immense riches that neither the thief can steal nor time consume? . . . All of these [people] labor for a crown, that soon withers away; and as we wait for the immortal crown, the possession of the ultimate good, the clear view of God, are we to be lazy and remiss? On the contrary, let us be fervent, subdued, and attentive to the wish that his Majesty has for our eternal health; let us avail ourselves of all means in all estates [conditions] and events of this life to attain our ultimate goal of doing penance for our sins. (44)[10]

The audience's acceptance of these sentiments was the key to the reconsolidation of the traditional society of estates threatened by the upward mobility of certain members of the third estate and the emergence of a fourth estate of professionals and bureaucrats. Yet, because Continente firmly supported the notion that "the fear of punishment moves more than rewards" ("mueve mas el espanto del castigo, que el premio" [see "Aprovación del P. Martin de la Naja," 16 April 1651, n. pag.]), he ends his message with a hair-raising tale designed to frighten his listeners into acquiescence before they had the opportunity to evaluate the message critically.

The story focuses on a young noblewoman, torn between following the ways of her virtuous Christian father (Heaven) and those of her ostentatious and idle mother (Hell). Bit by bit, she falls prey to the wicked influence of her mother, who was

> dressed in fiery flames; on her head she was wearing a venomous serpent that was boring into her head and, with unspeakable pain, eating her brains; toads were grazing on her eyes; rabid dogs were tearing her hands to shreds; and an infernal monster was opening her breast with its claws; she had her feet fettered in chains of fire. (46)[11]

At the point of being lost to her mother and to the pursuit of worldly pleasures, the young woman is saved by the intercession of the Virgin Mary. Thankful for a second chance, the young woman renounces her former life-style and enters a convent. This climactic ending leaves the audience overwhelmed and open to believing that an overemphasis on success and wealth in this life is not only fleeting, but life-threatening as well. Again, as in Arce's sermon, the emphasis is on persuasion through evocation of fear rather than through an appeal to logic through rational discourse. The danger posed by a potential fourth estate perceived by both the Church and the secular power structure could be most effectively counteracted by instilling terror of other-worldly punishments.

Although for most Spaniards living in the late 1500s and in the 1600s "sermon" was synonymous with oral performance, by the early 1600s, religious oratory was being disseminated in a variety of print forms. The interaction between these print manifestations and oral performance was multifaceted and complex.

In the first place, the publishing of collections of sermons (*sermonarios*), usually by individual preachers who selected from the best works of their entire careers, was an important step in institutionalizing the genre. As early as 1559, the Inquisition prohibited the circulation of all manuscript sermons with references to the Scriptures, the Holy Sacraments, or the Christian faith—in essence, all manuscript sermons—to prevent their misappropriation by heretics. Some twenty years later, in 1577, the Tribunal mandated the confiscation of all manuscript sermons in the possession of clerics other than their authors (see Smith 35-36). Clearly, the intent behind these edicts was to suppress the possible circulation of ideas not conforming to orthodox doctrine. By removing written sermons from the informal sphere of the exchange of (often anonymous) manuscripts and forcing them into the domain of the press, their content could be purged of any ideological impurities. Before publication, *sermonarios* had to be approved by representatives of the author's order and by an inquisitional censor in order to ensure that they contained nothing in conflict with the Catholic faith or morality (usually referred to as "good customs"). Their official *aprobaciones* were published at the beginning of each volume. Such volumes, officially endorsed by the Church hierarchy, served as popular reference books for preachers, who used them to prepare their own sermons. Although the rhetoric books and preachers' manuals of the day exhorted priests and friars to pursue their theological studies zealously in order to acquire the necessary erudition to be effective evangelical orators, the truth was that the average preacher cannibalized *sermonarios*, patching together bits and pieces of others' discourses and sometimes even preaching them as printed. This way of using approved sermons among ecclesiastics greatly facilitated the ideological homogenization of the Church's message and increased the efficacy of preaching as a mediating force in Spanish society.

The readership for *sermonarios* was primarily clerical, but there did exist a small lay audience, limited by illiteracy and lack of resources to purchase books. Juan Rodríguez de León, for example, speaks of "great ladies and ministers" who used *sermonarios* as books of devotion in their private chapels (138-139). Preachers who published their sermons were cognizant of their lay readers and of the ability of sermons to reach audiences more numerous than those present at any given oral sermon. In his "Sermon para el Domingo Tercero de Adviento," Diego Niseno speaks of the lasting quality of the printed sermon:

> The piety of he who writes is greater than that of he who preaches, because the Preacher's counsel perishes over time; the Writer's counsel lasts for eternity. The Preacher only teaches those who live in the present; but the Writer, those who will come in the future. The former's sermon, a one-time event, is over quickly; the latter's lesson, repeated a hundred thousand times, is never diminished. When the Preacher is no longer present, the succor of preaching ceases to exist; but the Writer, as he lives on in his pages, continues on well after death. (Fol. 47v)[12]

Despite the recognition of the fact that, in print, a sermon's message could multiply almost indefinitely, other preachers voiced concern that printed sermons could receive a different, less favorable reception than oral ones. In his 1613 *Santoral*, the Cistercian Fray Angel Manrique acknowledged the difference between the private act of reading and the emotional and sensorial effect of the live performance:

> You will hear a preacher's Sermon, and it seems so fine that you consider no word to have been wasted nor anything to be lacking in all his proofs. Fond of him and of his words, you ask for the paper and read it, and it does not seem half as good as when you heard it. Why is this so? The preacher gave life to what he said with his voice, with his actions, with his style of preaching, with his movement; but it is impossible to put any of this down on paper. (Quoted in Herrero García lvii)[13]

Isolated from the impact of the staging signs of the performance and from the sense of belonging to a community of listeners reacting simultaneously to shared experience, the solitary reader had the opportunity to subject the verbal test to close scrutiny.

Yet, other preachers, recognizing the difference between reading and listening, modified their sermons to take this shift in the mode of transmission into account. The Jesuit Tomás Sánchez, for instance, indicated to his readers that his published texts were expanded versions of his original sermons performed live and that they were edited especially to be read. Should readers find them to be too long and tedious to swallow, he suggested that they behave as if guests at banquet, partaking only until satisfied and then politely folding their napkin (n. pag.).

The frequency of the type of critical reception permitted by the solitary act of reading was in all probability quite low. Most readers of *sermonarios*, either clerics or members of the dominant groups in society, would have been in agreement with the messages disseminated. Thus, their prior mind-set would have preconditioned a favorable reception. Indeed, they may have been unaware of the manipulatory nature of a sermon's verbal text because of their previous ideological commitment. Moreover, the purpose of their reading within the context of private devotion or meditation would have most likely preconditioned a type of ritualistic conformity with the message. Furthermore, the type of genteel savoring of portions of a text advocated by preachers like Tomás Sánchez may have impeded the more coherent type of analysis that digesting the entire text in a single sitting would have facilitated. Finally, even when these privileged readers sensed the manipulation inherent in sermons, they most likely engaged in what Godzich and Spadaccini refer to as "elite reception" of a text in which they identified themselves culturally with the goals of the manipulators (48).

The more accessible type of print sermon was the chapbook sermon, published either as a self-contained text or as an addendum to a historical account (*relación*) of a contemporary event of importance. Sermons in *pliegos sueltos*, rather than being intended like the *sermonarios* for private meditation or study, functioned primarily to commemorate events deemed significant by those wealthy enough to finance their publication (once again, the Church, the Monarchy, and members of the upper echelons of the hereditary nobility). Because of their appeal as news items, their relative affordability, and the ease with which they could be shared through reading aloud (resulting again in a live performance), chapbook sermons were an effective means of recirculating ideas first spoken from the pulpit to nonreading audiences. A brief commentary on one example, Fray Francisco Riojano's "Triumph of Spain" ("Trivnfo de España"), will highlight the manipulatory power of this type of printed sermon. The chapbook version, published about two months after the actual event, commemorates the military victory of the forces of Philip IV over the armies of Louis XIII of France at Fuenterrabía in 1638. The timeliness and newsworthiness of the topic would have created an immediate audience for the *pliegos*, and we can imagine their being read aloud enthusiastically in plazas, marketplaces, or on street corners throughout Spain. The sermon content itself reinforces the conservative religious, political, and socioeconomic values of the power structure by portraying the victory of the smaller Spanish forces over the superior French ones as the triumph of invincible, true Spanish Catholicism over cowardly Calvinist-Lutheran-Huguenot heresy. Listeners would have become easily engulfed by the rhetoric of the discourse read aloud and open to the persuasive process of ideological manipulation.

The interaction of sermons as oral performance and in print form allowed for the emergence of a pervasive infrastructure for the dissemination of propaganda favorable to the realization of the goals of the Church and the secular monarchical-seigneurial order. An enormous cadre of vehement preachers, speaking regularly in churches and at public spectacles throughout Spain, produced a flow of conservation ideals that reached all sectors of society. The subsequent publication of some of these oral sermons in book form facilitated the efficiency of this type of ideological manipulation by providing preachers with ready-made, and, more important, ecclesiastically approved models. Against this backdrop of constant bombardment from the pulpit, certain messages were disseminated even further as sermons in chapbooks (*pliegos sueltos*) were read aloud to common people hungry for sensational news. In turn, this additional exposure to the works of certain preachers stirred up greater enthusiasm among the masses for attending oral sermons. Finally, the ideals held to be true by the elites were reinforced as they perused sermons during their private devotions. Thus, the constant recycling from the sphere of oral performance into the domain of consumption through print and back again into the realm of performance kept the Church's conservative system of thought circu-

lating continuously throughout Spain until well into the
eighteenth century.

Notes

1. All quotations from primary sources are printed with the original spell-
ing, accentuation, punctuation, and typographical conventions, with exceptions
in brackets. All translations are the author's.

2. ". . . como quiere el Predicador callejero, y andariego, se de credito a lo
que en el pulpito dize, sino sabe retirarse un rato de la conversacion de criaturas?
Si todo el dia lo passa en visitas, es mucho que se desprecie su doctrina, y su
persona? . . . Pero si se esconde, si le ven por milagro, estimaran su doctrina,
pondranla por execucion, que porque no se crio con ellos, ni los trato, por esso le
veneran mas. Retirense pues, Padres Predicadores, a toda publicidad, no se de-
jen manosear de criaturas . . ."

3. "Con ser tan contrario de las comedias, se portava en este exercicio como
los comediantes. Estos, para llamar gente, y tener ganancia, suelen disponer en
el Teatro algunas apariencias, que llaman Tramoyas, a cuya novedad se junta tal
vez mayor concurso que para un Sermon, y con esto aumentan su grangeria.
Assi nuestro Representante Evangelico, mandava cubrir con un velo negro el Altar; ponia una calavera en medio, como titular de aquel espectaculo, assistida
solo de dos Imagenes, de Christo Crucificado, y de la Virgen de los dolores; y
con las velas, que melancolicamente ardian, formava un Teatro proprio de la
muerte. Alli salia nuestra [sic] fervoroso Ministro, y con tanta viveza represen-
tava los sobresaltos del morir, y lo mucho que va en ganar, o perder aquella
hora, que parecian sus palabras, o ançuelos que prendian, o garfios que tiravan
almas para Dios. . . . Ay dos manera [sic] de muerte: una verdadera, y otra representada. La verdadera lo acaba todo: pero la representada lo conserva."

4. "Y como en todas las cosas se tenga en mas la forma, que la materia que
recibe la forma, me adivino que muchos predicadores, gastando tanto tiempo y
trabajo en la invencion que se ha como en la materia, no se cuiden casi nada de
la elocucion y pronunciacion, cuando sin estas formas, el vulgo necio comunmente menosprecia las invenciones mas excelentes."

5. "Bien se sabe que el teatro es el lugar donde se representa, dõde se ven
fingir y hazer varios papeles, ya de un Rey, ya de un amante, ya de una dama,
ya de un santo, ya de un pecador, ya de un galan, ya de un pastor, y de otros
muchos q[ue] la accion pide y requiere: en esso no dexan de cõformar el representante, y el Predicador; porque deve, para mover los animos de los oyentes,
representar varios papeles y figuras, ya la de un Dios enojado, para refrenar al
sobervio; ya la de un padre amoroso, para alentar al flaco; ya la de un Rey, que
facil puede castigar; ya la de un pastor q[ue] amoroso quiere sustentar, y otras
muchas figuras y representaciones que a cada Predicador se le pueden ofrecer.
. . . Que en haziendo su papel luego se entra en el vestuario, y no se dexa ver del
pueblo, porque fuera grã desayre para el que representa, quedarse a vista del
pueblo sin tener que hazer ni dezir, y se expusiera a que le silvaran. Pues en esso
ha de ser el pulpito parecido al teatro, y el Predicador como el representante,
q[ue] en haziendo su papel, en acabando su sermõ le han de entrar y esconder
hasta q[ue] sea necessario bolver a predicar otra vez."

6. "No hay mas propria señal de acabarse un Imperio, y una Monarquia, que romperse la cortina de sus misterios, y los velos de sus secretos. Los Reinos, y las Monarquias sustentāse mas de lo misterioso, que de lo verdadero, y si se manifiestan sus misterios, mal se defie[n]de[n] sus verdades. La opinion es la vida de los Imperios, el secreto es el alma de la opinion."

7. "Ay diferencia entre el Comediante, y el Orador en las acciones; que el Comediante como su fin principal es deleytar con el arte las potencias y sentidos, deve regular de tal forma las acciones á las voces, que aquello que de los labios nace, se ha de animar con las acciones nuevamente; para que oídos, y ojos tengan en la viveza de labios, y manos su alimento. El Orador tiene tres fines: mover, enseñar, y deleytar. . . . el Orador no deve ceñirse tanto al deleyte del Auditorio, que gaste en la . . . representacion el tiempo: su fin principal es mover, y enseñar."

8. The mention of an estate of prophets is a rhetorical device that allows the preacher to exploit fully the symbolism of the Biblical reference. There was no equivalent for this estate in contemporary sociopolitical thought.

9. "Pregunto, Fieles, ay al presente Faraones en el mu[n]do? Ay gente perdida y rematada? Ay personas, que aficionadas a las pajas, y barro de los terrenos bienes, desprecian los celestiales? O gran dolor! que se hallen Christianos, y gente del pueblo de Dios, que imiten en sus obras, costu[m]bres a los Moros, y Gentiles? Que no traten de su eterna salud? Ni se acuerden de su alma ni de Dios, por derramarse en las pajas, y barros de interesses terrenos?"

10. "Para no desmayar en esta jornada y conquista del Reyno celeste, mira al premio colmadissimo [sic], atiende al galardō, y corona de gloria. Que si el labrador passa el frio del invierno, el fuego del verano, la escarcha de la noche, y el calor del dia, por hazer su cosecha en el Agosto; razon es se aliente el Christiano, con la esperanza de la cosecha, que le ha de sustentar eternamente. El soldado cargado de hierro, en frontera de enemigos, el arcabuz al ombro, la espada en la mano, se pone a grandes riesgos por un corto pillaje, y honra de su Rey: por aquellos tesoros celestiales, por la honra verdadera, que te hará el supremo Emperador, sentandote a la mesa, pelea con valor, y perseverācia. El mercader anda midiendo la tierra, sulcando la mar, haziendo viages, venciendo peligros, rompie[n]do dificultades, por adquirir quatro doblas: quien ha de emperezar, sabiendo que ha de posseer aquellas riquezas inmensas, que ni el ladrō las roba ni el tiempo las consume? . . . Todos estos afanan por una corona, que presto se marchita; y esperando nosotros la corona inmortal, la possesion del sumo bien, la vista clara de Dios hemos de ser perezosos, y remissos? en ninguna manera, sino que seamos fervorosos, mortificados, y atentos al deseo que tiene su Magestad, de nuestra eterna salud; a valernos de tantos medios en todos los estados, y sucessos desta vida, para alcanzar nuestro ultimo fin haziendo penite[n]cia de nuestros pecados."

11. "envestida de llamas de fuego; en la cabeça traìa una venenosa sierpe, que se la taladrava, y con dolor indezible le comia los sessos; escuerzos, y sapos se apacentavan en sus ojos: perros rabiosos la despedazavan sus manos: y un monstruo infernal le abria el pecho con sus uñas: los pies tenia travados con cadenas de fuego."

12. "Mayor es la piedad del que escrive, que la del que predica, porque los avisos del Predicador fenecen con el tiempo; los del Escritor, eternidades duran.

El Predicador solo enseña a los presentes; pero el Escritor a los venideros. El sermon de aquel una vez se acaba presto; pero la licion deste, repetida cien mil vezes, nunca se disminuye. Quando falta el Predicador, cessa el socorro de la predicacion; pero el Escritor como vive en sus papeles, passa mucho mas allà de la muerte."

13. "Oiréis un Sermón à un predicador, y paréceos tan bien que no juzgáis palabra por perdida ni hay cosa que dejar en todas sus razones. Aficionado de él y de ellas, pedís el papel y leéis, y no os parece la mitad de bien que cuando le oisteis. ¿En qué está eso? En que el predicador daba vida a lo que decía con la voz, con las acciones, con el modillo de decir, con los meneos; pero en el papel es imposible escribirse nada de esto."

Works Cited

Alter, Jean. "From Text to Performance: Semiotics of Theatricality." *Poetics Today* 2.3 (1981):113-139.

Ameyugo, Francisco de, O. S. A. *Rhetorica Sagrada y evangélica ilustrada con la práctica de diversos artificios retóricos para proponer la palabra divina*. Zaragoza: Ivan de Ybar, 1667.

Arce, Fr. Diego de. *Miscelánea Primera de Oraciones Ecclesiásticas, desde el Domingo veynte y quatro después de Penthecostes, hasta la Vigilia de Natividad*. Murcia: Diego de la Torre, 1606.

Continente, Pedro Gerónimo, S. J. *Predicación fructuosa, sermones al espíritu sobre los motivos, que hay más poderosos para reducir los hombres al servicio de su Criador. Van comprimidos con raras historias*. Zaragoza: Diego Dormer, 1652.

Eco, Umberto. "Semiotics of Theatrical Performance." *The Drama Review* 21.1 (1977):107-117.

Foucault, Michel. *Discipline and Punish: The Birth of the Prison*. Trans. Alan Sheridan. New York: Vintage, 1979.

Godzich, Wlad, and Nicholas Spadaccini. "Popular Culture and Spanish Literary Theory." *Literature among Discourses: The Spanish Golden Age*. Ed. Wlad Godzich and Nicholas Spadaccini. Minneapolis: Univ. of Minnesota Press, 1986. 41-61.

Granada, Fr. Luis de. *Los seis libros de la retórica eclesiástica, o de la manera de predicar*. 1576. *Obras de Fray Luis de Granada*, Vol. 3. Ed. Buenaventura Carlos Aribau. Madrid: Biblioteca de Autores Españoles, 1945. 488-642.

Herrero García, Miguel. *Sermonario clásico*. Madrid: Escelicer, 1947.

Ledda, Giuseppina. "Forme e modi di teatralità nell'oratoria sacra del seicento." *Studi ispanici* 1982:87-107.

Maravall, José Antonio. *La cultura del Barroco*. Barcelona: Ariel, 1980. [Eng. trans. Terry Cochran. *The Culture of the Baroque*. Minneapolis: Univ. of Minnesota Press, 1986.]

_____. "From the Renaissance to the Baroque: The Diphasic Schema of a Social Crisis." *Literature among Discourses: The Spanish Golden Age*. Ed. Wlad Godzich and Nicholas Spadaccini. Minneapolis: Univ. of Minnesota Press, 1986. 3-40.

Medrano, Sebastián Francisco de. *Relación de la fiesta, que se hizo a la dedicacion de la Iglesia Parroquial de S. Miguel de los Octoes, fundada en esta villa de Madrid*. N.p.:n.p., n.d. [1623.] Rpt. in *Relaciones breves de actos públicos celebrados en*

Madrid de 1541 a 1650. Ed. José Simón Díaz. Madrid: Instituto de Estudios Madrileños, 1982. 184-189.

Niseno, Diego. *Asuntos predicables, para todos los Domingos, del Primero de Adviento al último de Pascua de Resurección*. Madrid: Francisco Martínez, 1627.

Riojano, Fr. Francisco. *Trivnfo de España, y hazimiento de gracias, por la gran vitoria, que con divinos socorros consiguio el Exercito de nuestro gran Catolico Monarca é inuicto Rey Don Felipe, Quarto el Grande, del de Luis Treze, Christianissimo Rey de Francia, en Fuente-Rabía. Sermon que predico . . . en . . . S. Pablo de Valladolid, a la Real Chancillería y Civdad . . . Domingo diez y nueue de Setiembre del mil y seiscientos y treinta y ocho años. Estando en publico el soberano Dios de los Exercitos, Christo Sacramentado, que Galan de su santissima Madre, quiso assistir de fiesta á la celebridad de sus glorias*. Burgos: Pedro de Huidobro, 1638.

Rodríguez de León, Juan. *El predicador de Las Gentes San Pablo. Sciencia, preceptos, avisos y obligaciones de los predicadores Evangelicos con doctrina del Apostol*. Madrid: Mª de Quiñones, 1638.

Rossi-Landi, Ferruccio. *Semiotica e ideologia*. Milan: Bompiani, 1972.

San José, Pedro de. *Discursos morales para las ferias menores de Quaresma*. Alcalá: Mª Fernández, Impressora de la Universidad, 1652.

Sánchez, P. Tomás. *Las seis alas del Serafin, en seis Sermones de los seis iueues de Quaresma. Predicados en el Real Convento de la Encarnación de Madrid*. Madrid: Antonio Francisco de Zafra, 1679.

Smith, Hilar Dansey. *Preaching in the Spanish Golden Age: A Study of Some Preachers of the Reign of Philip III*. Oxford: Oxford Univ. Press, 1978.

Sobrecasas, Fr. Francisco. *Ideas varias de Orar Evangelicamente con reglas, para la forma: y eleccion de libro para la materia*. Zaragoza: Pedro Lanaja y Lamarca, 1681.

Vieira [Vieyra], António de. *Aprovechar deleytando. Nueva idea de pulpito christiano-politica; delineada en cinco Sermones varios, otros discursos: predicados por el Reverendissimo. . . .* Valencia: Bernardo Nogués, 1660.

Xarque, Juan Antonio, S. J. *El orador Christiano sobre el Miserere, sacras invectivas contra los vicios, singularmente dirigidas a fomentar el santo zelo con que los Religiosos de la Compañia de IESUS se exercitan en el Ministerio Apostolico de las Misiones*. Zaragoza: Miguel de Luna, 1657.

◆ Chapter 4

The *Moriscos* and Circumcision

Bernard Vincent

(translated by Susan Isabel Stein)

In her study on the *moriscos* from Sigüenza and the Cuenca region, Mercedes García Arenal, on the subject of circumcision, records the declaration of a *morisco* from Belmonte who appeared before the Inquisition in 1630. According to him, "all the *moriscos* of the kingdom of Valencia, about half from Aragón, and none from Andalucía and Castile were circumcised" (149). To what extent can we believe such isolated and late testimony given twenty years after the expulsion? Is this merely a gratuitous statement or does it express a widespread belief among the *moriscos*? In this essay, I would like to offer an overview of our current knowledge of the practice of circumcision, along with the initial results of a study I have recently undertaken.

Little attention has actually been focused on the theme of circumcision among the *moriscos*. Pedro Longas dedicates only two pages to this topic in his excellent *Vida religiosa de los moriscos* (262-264), while Mercedes García Arenal has noted the scarcity of references in the Cuenca Inquisition. The only two references she has found concern an Aragonese *morisco* and a group of *moriscos* from the Valencia region (59). Cardaillac notes that Bernardo Pérez de Chinchón's *Antialcorán* includes two sermons comparing baptism with circumcision (384), and reminds us that, according to Aznar Cardona (314) and Jaime Bleda (Halperin Donghi 99+), the *moriscos* circumcised their sons following the *aid Kabir*. Tulio Halperin Donghi cites Chinchón, the ardent Dominican and fierce enemy of the *moriscos*, and also presents a series of proofs of the generalized practice of circumcision among the Valencian *moriscos*. Thus, almost all the *moriscos* prosecuted by the Inquisition confess to being circumcised.

We have only a few references that, on the surface, would seem to confirm the words of the Belmonte *morisco*. We need to delve further, since we must take into account both the relative silence of the texts and the scant interest of the investigators. Circumcision is not mentioned in the Koran, nor does it occupy an important place in the texts on Islamic law. Ancient poetry and the *hadith*, however, testify to its firm roots in the culture, and Muslim settlements worldwide were soon to acknowledge its significance. It is interesting to note that one of the Spanish terms for circumcision is *retajar*, from one of several Arab verbs employed for this practice. In effect, the Arabic language employs the word *Kh.t.n.*, which means: (1) to circumcise; (2) to give a banquet in celebration of a circumcision; (3) to truncate, to shorten; and (4) to become someone's ally through marriage. Just as frequently, Arabic uses the word *T'.h'.r*, meaning (1) to separate, to take away; (2) to be pure or clean; and (3) a euphemism for circumcision. Only Ibn Manzur's *Lisan al-'Arab* records this third definition for *T'.h'.r*:

> . . . to follow the tradition of circumcision; the Muslims called it *t'at'hir* (purification) as opposed to the Christians who replaced the tradition of circumcision with the immersion of their newly born. . . . Circumcision is true purification, not the practice established by the Nazarenes.[1]

As we can see, this definition reflects the concerns of the *morisco* minority perfectly. It is sufficiently polemical to continue the debate—here we need only to think of Bernardo Pérez de Chinchón's aforementioned sermons—between *moriscos* and Christians.

The fact that the Arabic word *retajar* entered into Spanish, and that circumcision itself remained a controversial issue among Christians and *moriscos*, proves that this practice was firmly ensconced in the Hispanic Muslim community. Again, we must search for concrete signs. I can add nothing new to the Aragonese trial except for one ambiguous document. In an *auto de fe* that took place in Zaragoza in 1582, we encounter a *morisco* circumcised in order to please his future father-in-law, who would permit the marriage only on this condition. Thus, the discovery of this specific individual confirms that an adult, or at the earliest an adolescent, had not been circumcised (AHN, Bk. 989).

Granada offers us more opportunities for research, as we can select data from various sources. First, we know that instructional literature did not ignore the issue. Among the recommendations of the assembly of the Royal Chapel of Granada (November 1526), we find the following:

> We also command that from now on no surgeon or doctor or any other person may give permission to the newly converted of this kingdom, with or without information, to cut off the foreskin of the penis, without express permission from the prelate or the chief magistrate (*corregidor*), nor should he personally remove it, under penalty of loss of property and permanent exile from the kingdom for whoever does so without permission. (Gallego Burín and Gámir Sandoval 203)[2]

Forty years later the situation had not changed much, since the 1565 provincial council of Granada reiterated the same terms. At any rate, enforcement did not become a firm objective. Bishop Martín de Ayala, promoter of the 1554 Guadix synod, knew this from experience, and he therefore preferred to have the *moriscos* consult an Old Christian midwife or matron at the time of birth and seek a priest shortly afterward to verify if the newborn child had been circumcised (Gallego Burín and Gámir Sandoval 34).

These precautions by secular and religious authorities demonstrate their awareness that circumcision had hardly been eradicated. The chronicler Mármol Carvajal echoes public sentiment when he describes the baptism of the infant *moriscos: "*After they baptized some of the infants, they secretly washed them with hot water to rinse off the chrism and holy oil, and performed their circumcision ceremonies, and gave them Muslim names" (167).[3] Indeed, all the cases we have studied attest to this belief. One striking case is that of an Old Christian, Alonso Vázquez, son of a juror from Granada, who in 1545 was circumcised in the presence of a notary. The operation, required because of Vázquez's precarious health, was performed by a surgeon: "Antonio Martínez cut the aforementioned Alonso Vázquez de Acuña's prepuce from his penis with a razor and stopped the flow of blood with a cauterization by fire *in the presence of myself, the aforementioned notary, and the witnesses*" (Domínguez Ortiz and Vincent 267).[4] Why was such an official act needed, save for the fear that his being circumcised might sooner or later identify him as a *morisco*? This act reveals, better than any statement, that circumcision was a generalized practice among the *morisco* minority.

The odyssey endured by a Frenchman in the 1560s is equally eloquent. Accused of theft when living in Andalucía, he is condemned to the galleys. After being set free, he begins his return journey, and on his way through Granada converts to Islam. He escapes, but is finally captured by the Inquisition in San Clemente, La Mancha. "They inspect him, disrobe him, he is *circumcised*" (Cardaillac 77; emphasis in the original). His circumcision is an unequivocal sign of having embraced Islam, no less for those who arrest him than for the Grenadines who converted him. Similarly, upon discovering the horribly mutilated body of Farax Aben Farax, leader of the December 1568 rebellion, the *moriscos* from the town of Guéjar strip the body in order to determine the side to which he belonged (Mármol Carvajal 209).

Finally, it is surprising that we do not find any more references to circumcision in the *relaciones de causas* of the Inquisition besides those that appear in the confessions of Christians converted to Islam during a stay in the Magreb (García Fuentes). We cannot arrive at any conclusion about this lack of information, since in other documents on inquisitorial visits, we find some *moriscos* condemned for having circumcised their sons (AHN, Inq. Leg. 1953-1972). Isabel Pérez de Colosia has found similar cases in Martín de Coscojales's visit to the bishopric of Málaga in

1560, and quite a few others in the visits during the 1580s (181-198). As circumcision was not considered a serious offense by the inquisitors—I will return to this point later—there was insufficient justification for imprisonment. In the kingdom of Granada, this type of case was always judged on the spot.

Documentation, while dispersed, seems sufficiently coherent to confirm that, contrary to the initial testimony of the Belmonte *morisco*, the vast majority of *moriscos* from Granada practiced circumcision. Conversely, with the detailed documentation available about the Valencians on this subject, there is no doubt about the prevalence of this practice in that region. Nonetheless, I would like to make known the results of a study that may greatly contribute to our knowledge of the subject, especially since it is the first to incorporate quantifiable data. The study is based on the confessions of all the adult *moriscos* from three towns in the Valencia region (Carlet, Benimodo, and Benimuslem) obtained by the inquisitors through the promulgation of an edict of grace in 1574 (AHN, Leg. 544).[5] (See Table 1.) The final question asked of the New Christians concerned circumcision.

Table 1.

	Carlet	Benimodo	Benimuslem	Total
No mention	24	3	–	27
Uncircumcised	35	4	12	51
Circumcised	206	90	16	312
Unclear cases	1	–	–	1
Total	266	97	28	391

Of the 391 recorded cases representative of half the males from the three towns, we must eliminate twenty-seven for omitting, either intentionally or unintentionally, any reference to circumcision; in most of these cases, we can assume that the notary forgot to record the answer. The older males would not have been asked, because they would have been circumcised prior to the 1525-1526 period of obligatory conversion. For this reason, we must consider the number of circumcised males as representing the minimum rather than the maximum percentage. The only doubtful case is that of a boy who, according to his mother, was five years old and circumcised, and according to his father, two years old and uncircumcised. Of the 363 men and boys who answered intelligibly, 312 were circumcised, that is, a minimum average of 86%. This average obscures the individual differences: while 85.5% of the men from Carlet are circumcised, the index rises to 95.6% in Benimodo and drops to 57.8% in Benimuslem.

We cannot overlook the possibility of false testimony. After all, it is possible that the Benimuslem *moriscos* collectively adopted defensive measures against the inquisitors not taken in Carlet or Benimodo. In any case, I am convinced that the figures come close to the truth and that we are facing three very different situations. Judging from several sources, Benimuslem's small community of one hundred inhabitants was considerably acculturated. Not only do nineteen of the forty-six inhabitants appearing before the inquisitor affirm that they have always been faithful Christians, but there are many others, unlike the *moriscos* from Benimodo and Carlet, who seem to have abandoned their Muslim name. On the other hand, the community of Benimodo, with almost three hundred inhabitants, appears to present a united front. The four uncircumcised are boys under two years of age who will more than likely be circumcised when circumstances permit. It would probably be safe to say that at least until 1574, all the boys in Benimodo were circumcised.

Although not identical, the situation in Carlet resembles that of Benimodo. The *moriscos* preserved their identity in a more general manner, but there are undeniable signs of weakening, no doubt slight and perhaps quite recent, but increasing nonetheless. We must remember that the town of Carlet, with approximately one thousand inhabitants, is located in the southern part of the Valencian farmland that extends from Játiva to the kingdom's capital, and which is home to an Old Christian minority. Table 2 shows the ages of the uncircumcised in all three towns and reveals their differences. While the majority of uncircumcised in Carlet is comprised of boys up to five years of age, there are five cases of probable uncircumcised from eight to thirty-five years of age. This is certainly insignificant in view of the total number of circumcised individuals, but why the large number of uncircumcised boys ranging from two to four years of age? In Benimodo, a more isolated and well-preserved town, the

numbers are quite different. Little needs to be said about Benimuslem, as the data confirm this community's greater fragility.

Table 2. Age of the Uncircumcised

Age	Carlet	Benimodo	Benimuslem
Less than 1 year	7	2	1
1 year	4	2	–
2 years	7	–	–
3 years	8	–	–
4 years	2	–	3
5 years	1	–	1
6 years	–	–	1
7 years	–	–	–
8 years	2	–	3
9 years	1	–	–
10 years	–	–	1
14 years	–	–	1
15 years	1	–	–
35 years	1	–	1
Total	34	4	12

The inquisitorial inquest also clarifies under what circumstances
the males were circumcised, and at what specific age.

Only one testimony addresses the subject directly. A *morisca*
from Carlet declared that she did not know who had circumcised her son, Zaad-Jaime Sabba, twenty years of age, and
added: "Elel Arquich came here and said, 'I need your son' and
took him and then later returned him, crying and circumcised,
and this occurred when the boy was only six months old." Lacking more information, I will assume this declaration to be correct
and collate it with the data in Table 3. From the outset, we can
see that there is no single model. The boys of Benimodo are circumcised at an early age, before they turn two. In Carlet, the
range of ages is much wider, from two to six years, the dominant age of circumcision being between three and four years.

The following hypothesis may explain the differences we
have observed. Tradition demanded that circumcision be performed very early, during the first year of life, and this custom
was upheld until the 1560s. Tulio Halperin Donghi notes that a
barber from Concentaina and a resident of Aspe went from
town to town circumcising two- to three-month-old babies (100).
After this date, and once the *moriscos* became the object of per-

Table 3. Circumcised and Uncircumcised Boys

Age	Carlet		Benimodo	
	circumcised	uncircumcised	circumcised	uncircumcised
Less than 1 year	–	7	–	2
1 year	–	4	–	2
2 years	2	7	1	–
3 years	3	8	1	–
4 years	6	2	4	–
5 years	7	1	1	–
6 years	7	–	4	–
7 years	6	–	1	–
8 years	8	2	1	–
9 years	6	1	–	–

secution, circumcision was delayed. In places where the *moriscos* defended their culture without difficulty, such as Benimodo, the delay was relatively brief. In other places, to elude the painstaking controls of the priests as well as the eventual vigilance of the Old Christians, the ceremony occurred much later. It is possible that this delay was extended even further, and that the chroniclers of the seventeenth century were correct in stating that circumcision did not take place until the age of seven (Bleda, fols. 33-34) or eight (Aznar Cardona II: fol. 50). Such a pattern would simultaneously reveal both temporal and geographical differences.

Who performed the circumcisions? Reading between the lines in the answers of the interrogated, we discern various profiles. Certainly, the need to keep circumcision a secret obliged the *moriscos* to make it a family affair. Luis Azmet Ferrer affirmed that his seven-year-old son was circumcised by his father-in-law. Zaad Digues, a twenty-year-old, had always heard that his maternal grandfather performed the ceremony. Violante Mandet did not hesitate to confess to the inquisitor that her sons were circumcised and that "they were circumcised by her father because as they are afraid of the Holy Office, all secretly circumcised their sons, or had them circumcised" (Halperin Donghi 100).[6]

Yet Abraham Mandet, whose profession, unfortunately, we do not know, not only circumcised his sons and grandsons, but also provided his services to at least two other families in Carlet. He was a resident of Benimodo—this detail is important because there does not appear to be an official circumciser in Carlet or Benimuslem. Mandet's name was easily given by the interrogated, since he had died after reaching Argel. The *moriscos* of these three towns frequently resorted to "foreigners," as they were systematically and tersely labeled, as their answer regarding who performed circumcisions. The names of some who were out of danger or had already been judged were at times given, as in the case of a man named Celim from the Buñol region. Another was the man known as the *Virrey de Chiva*, who circumcised nineteen boys from Carlet and Benimodo in the years preceding the investigation of 1574 and who was probably the "foreigner" whom the majority prudently pretended not to know. It is tempting to establish a parallel between this person who, according to many witnesses, would have been condemned to the galleys by the Inquisition, and the tailor from Chiva mentioned by Halperin Donghi (García Ballester, *Los moriscos* 189-192).[7]

Thus, we find several circumcisers in the heart of the *morisco* community, frequently hiding behind a trade whose skills and tools are also of service in the ceremony: in Chiva, a tailor and his scissors; in Concentaina, a barber and his razor. It is true that the barber often functioned as a surgeon. Yet apart from these specialists, anyone, man or woman, could act as circumciser. It was therefore possible to circumcise sons clandestinely without calling attention to oneself. The necessity of acting with the utmost secrecy does not explain the lack of professional circumcisers, however. One could not make a living primarily as a circumciser, since the tariffs were very low. The barber from Concentaina charged one *real* (thirty-four *maravedís*) per operation. In Carlet and Benimodo, the tailor from Chiva charged three *sueldos*, that is, one and one half *reales*; Rafael Carrasco cites three cases in which the fee for the service was raised to five *sueldos*, or a little less than three *reales* (205). The salary of a day laborer at this time fluctuated between two and three *reales*. The circumciser enjoyed little of the social position and esteem held by the *alfaquí*.

It is important to note the circumciser's limited professionalism, a characteristic emphasized by Tulio Halperin Donghi; this contributed greatly to the survival of this practice among the *mo-*

riscos. Halperin Donghi states that circumcision was relatively tolerated by the Inquisition because it was not at the nucleus of an organized religious resistance. This statement needs to be qualified. The Christian authorities considered the circumciser to be an essential agent of Moslem proselytism. Did not the renowned Grenadine Francisco Núñez Muley, in his famous memorial to Philip II, emphasize the fact that the circumciser was one of the three individuals excluded from the Pope's general pardon of the *moriscos* in 1526 (Foulche-Delbosc 214)?[8] Or was being circumcised not considered a fundamental sign of one's adherence to Islam? The accusations convicting the barber of Concentaina, Martín Zaad Baroni, are quite clear:

> He performed this (circumcision) so that Christian children would become Moors because until they are circumcised, they are not taken for Moors. . . . The aforementioned, desiring that the damned and condemned sect of Mohammed be extended and increased, has taught various people the Muslim ceremony of circumcision. . . . One of the persons to whom the aforementioned taught the skill and ceremony has performed circumcision . . . and we must believe that many others whom he has taught have done the same . . . since this ceremony is considered their baptism. (García Ballester, *El ejercicio médico* 17)[9]

If the Christians' concern with the practice of circumcision was constant, and they attempted to eradicate it accordingly, the means of doing so varied considerably. From 1520 until 1560, their course of action was essentially preventive, until it resulted in a full-fledged repression. In summary, there was an initial effort to neutralize potential circumcisers by means of allegedly valid legislation. I have already mentioned the dispositions adopted from 1526 on by the assembly that gathered at the Royal Chapel; the papal pardons that Francisco Núñez Muley alluded to in his memorial; and the dispositions of the Guadix synod of 1554. Other texts also have the same intent. The instructions sent from Charles V to the archbishop of Granada Pedro de Alba in December 1526, as well as the recommendations of the Valencian synod of 1561, include a section concerning the necessity of strict vigilance of *morisco* midwives, since it was believed that they were the ones who circumcised newborn infants (Gallego Burín and Gámir Sandoval 207). Instead, the presence of an Old Christian doctor or surgeon was recommended.

It was long believed that the measures controlling only professional circumcisers were sufficient. But here, as in other areas dealing with the politics of *morisco* conversion, the Spanish sovereigns had deceived themselves. They had not counted upon the crypto-Muslims' admirable capacity to adapt to new circumstances; by delaying the age of circumcision, the *moriscos* rendered the legislation practically invalid. Nor had the sovereigns counted upon the *moriscos*' indomitable spirit of resistance. The practice of circumcision became more and more of a challenge. Thus, the Valencian inquisitor Pedro de Zárate warns Francisco Alguerri, a native of Puzol who defends his true Christian faith:

> Being a Christian, he did not have any reason for
> coming here or any need for the public pardon, but the
> fact that he is the son of *moriscos*, that he has a Muslim
> name, that he lives among them, and that he is
> circumcised, leads us to assume therefore that he is a
> Muslim and that it remains to be seen how he fulfills the
> aforementioned pardon. (n. pag.)[10]

The search for circumcisers became more systematic. Many were captured in the inquisitorial net: the previously mentioned Virrey, the tailor from Chiva, and Martín Zaad Baroni, the barber from Concentaina, as well as Angela Ganina in 1573, Pedro Ganin, a relative of hers, and Francisco Hilel in 1594 (AHN, Inq. Leg. 551/20, Leg. 552/6).[11] A circumciser from Salem, a town near the valley of Gallinera, was condemned to be burned at the stake in 1587. By that time, the entire Muslim population was threatened. We have already seen that prior to 1570, punishment was limited to imposing fines during inquisitorial district visits, and even these were infrequent and meager. After 1570, both the numbers and quantities of the fines increased. The Inquisition expanded its activities, and more assistants in the circumcision ceremonies began to appear in the *autos de fe*, as in Valencia in 1587 (AHN, Inq. Bk. 937, fol. 22). The fact that circumcision is addressed by a separate question in the confessions extracted from the *moriscos* of the Valencian farmland is not a simple coincidence. Finally, the terms cannot be made any more explicit than they are in another Inquisition text, dated 1581:

> Because experience has shown so far that all the *moriscos* of this kingdom are circumcised and that they circumcise their infant sons, it has seemed fitting to become stricter with the parents and to condemn them all to be whipped if a son is discovered to be circumcised. (AHN, Inq. Bk. 936, fol. 300)[12]

In the face of increasing dangers, the *moriscos* prove themselves to be very agile at dismantling the traps patiently set for them by the Inquisition. The eldest know they are free from danger, in which case they take pleasure in declaring, like Miguel Ali Bambala, that "he is circumcised because he comes from the era of the Moors." Younger males accuse those responsible for their circumcision, such as Miguel-Ali Mintri, a twenty-five-year-old native of Benimuslem, who affirms that his parents circumcised him. Yet, since the implicated parties were deceased, the confession had no effect. The majority of people not only feigned ignorance of the circumcised's identity, but they tried to shed responsibility as well; the act always took place in their absence.[13] If someone within the family does claim responsibility for the crime, it is usually the wife who does so, as if the *moriscos* expected the Inquisition to be more lenient with women. Some even go so far as to appear suspiciously contrite: Nicolás Coayar Ferrer's mother, from Carlet, confessed that "her mother forced her to circumcise an unknown person, and this fact grieves her exceedingly."

I perceive this intelligent and efficient defense as the main reason that the practice of circumcision was preserved among the *moriscos* of Valencia and Granada. Lack of sufficient evidence forces me to be more cautious with respect to the Aragonese *moriscos*. Neither can we overlook the fact that the large regional groups are never completely uniform. The difference among groups is the main lesson to be learned from this brief study. Until we have carried out more research, we run the risk of formulating rash hypotheses.

Ultimately, what is the meaning of the battle surrounding the issue of circumcision? Naturally, we can point out that the

Christian authorities prosecuted any show of adherence to Islam, but this explanation is not enough. I suggest two others that, to me, seem more comprehensive. The first refers to the Inquisition's methods in attempting to confuse the accused: it extracts from the victim whatever proof it requires. Circumcision was a *crime* whose materiality the *moriscos* could not deny. Once this was made evident, it became much easier to obtain a general confession. My second hypothesis derives from the simplistic view both sides held of Islam. Limiting Islam, as did the inquisitor Pedro de Zárate, to Muslim ascendance, a Muslim name, and circumcision, is tantamount to defining the religion through its most external manifestations. This view was also shared by the *moriscos* themselves, who, almost always stripped of theological support, clung to the most superficial indications of identity. Being circumcised in Spain in the decade of the 1570s was a declaration of Muslim faith.

Notes

1. This same terminology can be found in the *Qámús al-Muhlt de firúzabádi de Ibn durayd* and the *Lisan al-'Arab.*, furnished to me by Abdel Waheb Meddeb.

2. "Asi mismo mandamos que de aquí en adelante ningún cirujano ni médico ni otra persona alguna de licencia a los nuevamente convertidos de este reino, con información o sin ella, para cortar parte del principio de su miembro, sin expresa licencia del prelado o del corregidor, ni lo corte él, so pena de perdimento de bienes y de ser desterrado del reino perpetuamente el que lo hiciere sin licencia."

3. "Cuando habían baptizado algunas criaturas, las lavaban secretamente con agua caliente para quitarles la crisma y el olio santo, y hacían sus ceremonias de retajarlas, y les ponían nombres de moros."

4. "Antonio Martínez cirujano cortó al dicho Alonso Vázquez de Acuña el dicho capullo de su miembro con una navaja y restañó la sangre con un cauterio de fuego *en presencia de mí el dicho escrivano e de los testigos.*"

5. See AHN, Leg. 544; there is another volume that belongs to a private collection.

6. "Los retajó su padre de esta porque como tienen miedo del santo oficio cada uno procuró secretamente de retajar o hacer retajar sus hijos."

7. In this work, which the author has recently published with the help of R. Blasco, we find excerpts from the trial of barber-surgeon Jerónimo Tang, a circumciser in the Grenadine region who was condemned by the Inquisition in 1601 (García Ballester, *Los moriscos* 189-192).

8. "In which pardon it was expressly declared that three persons were excluded: the *alfaquí* who revealed the sect or part of it, the surgeon who had performed circumcisions, and I do not remember the third . . . "

9. "Lo hazía (retajar) para que los niños cristianos fuesen moros porque hasta que son retajados no son tenidos por moros . . . quel suso dicho queriendo que la dicha maldita y reprobada secta de Mahoma se extendiese y acrecentase ha enseñado a diversas personas la dicha ceremonia de Mahoma de retajar. . . . Una de las dichas personas que el suso dicho enseñó el dicho oficio y ceremonia por su enseñamiento ha retajado . . . y se ha de creer que lo mismo habían hecho muchos de los otros a quien así mismo lo ha enseñado . . . que esa ceremonia es su bautismo."

10. "Siendo cristiano no tenía para qué venir aquí ni tiene necesidad del perdón que está publicado pero que de ser el hijo de *moriscos* y tener nombre de moro y vivir entre ellos y estar retajado se presume que es moro por tanto que él vea lo que le cumple acerca de la gracia que se trató."

11. Rafael Carrasco has provided me with these references. I propose a detailed examination of this trial in order to study, if possible, the ceremony of circumcision. Refer to note 2 as well.

12. "Por la experiencia que se tiene que todos los *moriscos* de este reino están retajados y van retajando a sus hijos de pequeños ha parecido comenzar a tener un poco de rigor con los padres y condenarles a todos en pena de azotes por solo hallarse el hijo retajado."

13. Two examples, among others, of this system of defense: Leonor Crispi of Benimodo, a mother with three sons "whose own mother had them circumcised when she was absent and she does not know by whom" ("que su madre della los hizo retajar estando ella ausente y no sabra a quien"). Her relative, Angela Crispi, also with three sons, does not hesitate to give details: "Her father had them circumcised; she does not know who else was present. Being away, upon returning she found her sons crying and she asked who had done it and her father was upset because she had asked" ("Su padre della hizo retajar no sabe a quien mas que estando fuera y volviendo los halló a los hijos llorando y preguntó quien los había hecho y la reño su padre porque lo preguntaba"). Naturally, the intermediary parties mentioned in these declarations had passed away.

Works Cited

Archivo Histórico Nacional (AHN). Various documents.

Aznar Cardona, P. *Expulsión justificada de los moriscos españoles y suma de las excelencias de nuestro rey don Felipe el Católico Tercero deste nombre.* Huesca, 1612.

Bleda, J. *Defensio fidei in causa nophytorum, sive Morischorum regni Valentiae totiusque Hispanae.* Valencia, 1610.

Cardaillac, L. *Morisques et Chrétiens. Un affrontement polémique (1492-1640).* Paris: Klincksieck, 1977.

Carrasco, Rafael. "Le refus d'assimilation des Morisques, aspects politiques et culturels d'après les sources inquisitoriales." *Les Morisques et leur temps.* Paris: Table Ronde Internationale, 1983. 169-216.

Domínguez Ortiz, Antonio, and Bernard Vincent. *Historia de los moriscos: Vida y tragedia de una minoría.* Madrid: Revista de Occidente, 1978.

Foulche-Delbosc, R. "Memorial de Francisco Núñez Muley." *Revue Hispanique* (1899): 205-239.

Gallego Burín, A., and Alfonso Gámir Sandoval. *Los moriscos del Reino de Granada según el sínodo de Guadix de 1554*. Granada: Univ. de Granada, 1968.

García Arenal, Mercedes. *Inquisición y moriscos: Los procesos del tribunal de Cuenca*. Madrid: Siglo Veintiuno, 1978.

García Ballester, Luis. *El ejercicio médico morisco y la sociedad cristiana*. Granada: Univ. de Granada, 1975.

―――. *Los moriscos y la medicina*. Barcelona: Editorial Labor, 1984.

García Fuentes, José María. *La Inquisición en Granada en el siglo XVI*. Granada: Departamento de Historia de la Univ. de Granada, 1981.

Halperin Donghi, Tulio. *Un conflicto nacional: moriscos y cristianos viejos en Valencia*. Valencia: Institución Alfonso el Magnánimo, 1980.

Ibn Manzur, Muhammad ibn Mukarram. *Lisan al-'Arab*. Cairo, n.d.

Longas, Pedro. *Vida religiosa de los moriscos*. Madrid: E. Maestre, 1915.

Mármol Carvajal, L., ed. *Historia de la rebelión y castigo de los moriscos de Granada*. Vol. 21. Madrid: Biblioteca de Autores Españoles, 1946.

Pérez de Colosia, Isabel. "La religiosidad en los moriscos malagueños." *Religion, Identité et Sources Documentaires sur les Morisques Andalous*. Vol. 1. Túnez, 1984.

Chapter 5

Aldermen and Judaizers
Cryptojudaism, Counter-Reformation,
and Local Power

Jaime Contreras

(translated by Susan Isabel Stein)

The year 1560 was a time both of loud public loyalties barely disguising clearly political motives and of forced silence. Those closest to the King openly asserted that in the new governmental program of Philip II, religious heterodoxy was to be viewed as social and political dissidence. They insisted that, for this reason, the Tribunal of the Faith, whose charge it was to protect orthodoxy, must be converted into a political institution of maximum importance.

This, in short, was the premise of the Counter-Reformation program begun in that year. Obviously, the program was not disinterested; on the contrary, it intended to win majority support. In effect, what was being proposed was the establishment of a new social paradigm that would bring together both the nobility and the religious values of Counter-Reformation dogma. The embodiment of the model was to be the Old Christian nobility, since it conflated, to the point of stereotype, noble lineage determined by blood and religious faith without any stain of heresy. While not excluding them altogether, such a focused sociocultural "program" of acculturation indeed marginalized minority groups that represented less monolithic values. In any case, the dominant ideological discourse formulated at the beginning of 1560 by powerful Church sectors, and solidly backed by the Crown, emphasized social class over religious difference. The original and universal Christian faith was to find its most appropriate stronghold in the heirs to ancient family lines. The Old Christian who also belonged to the nobility thus became the archetypal Christian.

This "fact" was propagated from the pulpit, repeated patiently in the confessional, and selectively imposed by the Tribunal of the Faith. Yet this dominant discourse could not completely silence the few critical voices of a now distant Erasmism that argued against the convergence of lineage and faith. Although their arguments were unheeded during this period, several respected men rejected the concept of purity of blood, reasoning that the dogma of faith concerned moral issues and was hardly dependent upon heredity. "Virtue does not follow honor and glory, but rather they must come after virtue," the *converso* Antonio de Torquemada wrote in 1552; other "antistatute" contemporaries propounded the same argument (Maravall 45). Apprehensively witnessing the growing specter of "pure blood," these dissidents stated that virtue was not hereditary because sin did not reside in the blood, nor did evil develop according to race, nor was infamy born along with lineage. On the contrary, all people, born of God's will, shared the same origin and had been redeemed by the universality of Christ's sacrifice (Sicroff 134-169).

Yet one does not need to examine closely the insubstantial rhetoric of racial and religious arguments to discover that they eluded far more serious issues. Underlying the controversy over purity of blood is a strong social conflict manifested in a variety of ways; Henry Kamen has suggested that the tensions over the statutes of "pure blood" resulted from their benefiting an elite that wished to protect its power and influence (326). The dominant social discourses of the sixteenth century addressing New Christians merely repeated earlier stereotypes against the Jews. Perhaps because of the repressive religious atmosphere, *conversos* were viewed in the same light as the former dwellers of the Jewish ghettos. The underlying cultural desire to segregate socially was always present for Christians of Jewish origins, although it was not always manifestly hostile. In an effort to alleviate the chronic weakness of the Royal Treasury, the King readily agreed to the sale of offices and noble titles. This, in turn, satisfied the social aspirations of the newly rich. Indeed, what better customers were there than these recently enriched *conversos* in need of social rehabilitation? As we shall see, however, their attempts to improve their social standing created tensions among the various social groups.

Only religious reasons were sufficiently convincing to prevent what money made possible and what could not be legally forbidden: the social mobility of certain newly rich commoners, who could then occupy positions in municipal government, achieve honors within the Church, and finally, receive appointments to the highest levels of the royal administration, such as the councils, magistrates, and high courts. These posts offered an easy entry into the privileged estate of the nobility.

Such mobility, relatively frequent during the early sixteenth century, intensified unexpectedly during the 1540s and 1550s as the Monarchy continued to sell offices, sinecures, and titles. These years witnessed considerable upward mobility, allowing a "social ventilation" that rendered social classes permeable. The process occasioned angry responses, mostly from the groups of commoners adversely affected by this social change, as well as from those noble groups (*hidalgos* and *caballeros de sangre*) who, because of these sales of titles of nobility, risked losing the distinguishing marks of their identities. Caught in the cross fire, those who either had scaled the social ladder or were aspiring to do so were much more fearful of the angry populist demagoguery that immediately labeled them as upstarts, than of the nobility's grudging acceptance.

It was only too easy for the lower classes to oppose social mobility through wealth by voicing moral and religious arguments laden with racist undertones. A strong tradition of anti-Semitism provided an entire arsenal of simplistic and stereotyped arguments whose inflammatory rhetoric goaded mass prejudice and justified social exclusion. Américo Castro spoke, in this sense, of the pressure applied by the "peasant culture" (*cultura villana*), and even if this were not the only or the most important force, it confirms their "participation"—what Castro termed the "hates" of the *menudos*—in the racial exclusivity of the statutes (149-150).

Not coincidentally, the principal propagandists behind the legalization and acceptance of "purity" belonged to the third estate, nourished by the pride and exclusivist mysticism characteristic of all individualist meritocracies. Juan Martínez Silíceo, Archbishop of Toledo and the belligerent defender of purity of blood, was arguably its most significant representative, from what little we know of his life (Domínguez Ortiz, *Los Judeoconversos* 37). He was born in Villagarcía, a distant village in Extremadura, to humble laborers, and his character, forged through immense struggle and sacrifice, proved unyielding—too much so, perhaps, to those whose courtly habits were formed under the tolerance of Erasmian universalism and pacifism. Silíceo proved the real possibility of the triumph of the lower classes. His own case demonstrated that, through a combination of wealth, effort, and chance, social ascent was indeed possible. As the sole dispenser of "graces and mercies," the King could, if he wished, cut through class lines by proffering noble status to those with wealth. Wealth in itself was not a guarantee of nobility, however, especially if there was strong competition from other sectors. Rich laborers often found themselves displaced by the commercially competitive and financially astute New Christians, who were equally wealthy and supported by strong family and clan ties. Wealth alone, therefore, could not be the deciding factor. Lineage, a concept developed in the fifteenth century, was revived along with concurrent legal and religious stipulations, all notoriously segregationist, and soon became the means of dividing New Christians from rich peasants of Old Christian lineage. Silíceo was simply evoking the anti-Semitic tenets that had justified the medieval pogroms, the "Sentence-Statute" of 1449, and the enclosure of the Jews in ghettos prior to their expulsion. If, as several fifteenth-century chroniclers asserted, the Jew came from a dishonored race, so too, then, did the New Christian (Sicroff 31).

Thus, the "lineage of the laborers" became institutionalized as a social class parallel in importance to that of the nobility. Lorenzo Galíndez de Carvajal's famed report comments on the social status of Charles V's Royal Council, calling the Emperor's attention to the fact that many of his famous councillors are "Old Christians from peasant families" (Castro 180-181). Its tenor is considered representative of the atmosphere surrounding the court, and seems to suggest that the nobility now shared its highest values with the venerable and pure lineage of the wealthy peasants.

This unique state of affairs, though well known to all, cannot be fully understood without taking into account the socioeconomic factors that fueled an exceptionally productive peasant economy during almost the entire century from 1450 to 1550. The family was the basic unit of agricultural production, and its surplus capital created an extremely powerful urban market whose interaction with the countryside stimulated a functional and intense commercial circuit.[1] This economic bonanza inspired the hope of social reform, and, although unsuccessful, "democratizing" impulses were felt all over Castile.

Economic growth continued for a time, but soon there were signs of exhaustion. By 1540, it was no longer so easy to join the nobility; ascendant social ventilation became a more complicated endeavor and began to shut down. When Silíceo published his statutes for the Cathedral of Toledo, he specified in no uncertain terms that the process of social mobility should be more selective. The statutes outlined what the criteria should be in the future, thus restricting conditions for social change. These criteria were based on two main precepts: nobility, ensuring the hierarchy of privilege, and purity of blood, guaranteeing social worth. Silíceo, born to peasants of pure blood, thus ensured his own success. Men like Silíceo encouraged social outrage over "impure blood." Rather than forget their origins, these wealthy men, educated and ambitious, in the highest positions of power, dignified them instead. "In Spain," wrote the unknown author of a seventeenth-century manuscript, "there are two kinds of nobility: the greater, which is the *hidalguía*, and the lesser, which is the purity of the Old Christians. Although the former is more honorable, it is an affront to lack the latter, for in Spain we esteem a commoner with pure blood far more than a nobleman without it" (Domínguez Ortiz, *Los Judeoconversos* 183).

Nobility and purity: two paradigms that, as far as the lower classes were concerned, should have been of equal significance, but were not. The efforts of the more numerous Old Christians to assume cultural leadership in society ultimately failed against the controlling group: the nobility (Maravall 95). In spite of the efforts of men like Silíceo, the nobility triumphed in the end. Furthermore, while the problem of purity unleashed heated, and at times tragic, discussions, wealth was still the most effective means of ensuring social ascent. Many New Christians, relying upon an effective tradition of family and clan solidarity, were able to rise to positions of social and political prominence with relative ease.

Nonetheless, things were not always simple; as with any sociocultural concern, questions of purity were decided by the exigencies of the historical moment. The years following the promulgation of the Statutes were particularly quarrelsome, and those on the side of purity of blood represented a real threat to those whose social aspirations were the least bit suspicious. There were two main reasons for the advocacy of pure blood during the mid-sixteenth century. The first, social in nature, was based on the nobility's efforts to maintain its control of municipal councils, especially in the unappropriated urban centers. The second reason was the wave of religious mysticism that engulfed Castile during these years.

Little is known about the efforts to retain nobles in municipal offices, other than the information stemming from parliamentary discussions (Domínguez Ortiz, Las clases 121-145; Clavero 103-116). From 1538 on, there were constant discussions regarding the nobility's interests in occupying municipal offices. The members of parliament repeatedly insisted that the urban offices of aldermen should be occupied by noblemen of pure blood rather than by merchants or manual laborers with purchased titles of nobility (Domínguez Ortiz, Las clases 123).[2] This insistence demonstrates the extreme resistance encountered from the lower classes, as the aristocratization of municipal service meant that the powerful taxpaying peasants would be marginalized at a time when many cities still remembered the violence they had experienced not long ago (Yun Casalilla 224-225, 370-371).

The peasants' resistance was weakened in the mid-sixteenth century when, with the King's consent, the municipal offices, particularly those that could be inherited, fell inexorably into the hands of the nobility. In Toledo in 1566, despite strong government opposition, Philip II chose nobility above wealth or peasant origins as the most important criterion for municipal employees. Yet even this practically irrevocable decision provoked near-violent conflicts among the local aristocratic families and clans. It was not uncommon for them to hurl accusations of impure blood and heresy at each other as well as at their political enemies. Such unfounded and pitiless attacks fostered community tensions, especially when dangerous institutions such as the Holy Office intervened. This, I believe, is what occurred in the cases that follow.

The second reason that helps to explain the "collective furor" over purity of blood was the spirituality that characterized the middle years of the century. The religious tensions form part of the broader social conflict; indeed, the conflict cannot be understood without taking them into account. The process of aristocratization effectively proscribed the social mobility of some wealthy individuals, whose frustration was then focused on other goals. Martin Luther, the Reformation, and the "heresy" of the "impure" New Christians were thus converted into the central enemies of the reigning cultural-ideological system.

The campaign of exclusion begun at this time was manifestly xenophobic and wished to transform the heretics—Protestants and crypto-Jews—into scapegoats for the Monarchy's evils.[3] These minorities had to suffer the wrath of the majority whenever they disagreed with the dominant ideology. Luther and the Protestants were heretics and foreigners, and toleration of them presented a social threat; while the crypto-Jews obviously were not "foreigners," it was believed that they had inherited an innate tendency toward heresy. Like their predecessors the Jews, their exclusion was justified by their presumed inability to assimilate Christian values. The Inquisition—then heavily politicized—determined that heterodoxy and foreignness were dangerous and scandalously dysfunctional elements in society. The defenders of purity of blood believed that Protestants, crypto-Jews, and New Christians constituted a heretical opposition as well as a front for political dissidence, and by stereotyping them as such, they imposed this view as much as possible.

In Yuste, Charles V meditated upon his failures: Germany divided, Flanders in revolt, the faded dream of the "Universitas Christiana" . . . all was ruined. Only one cause remained: heresy, and for this, the flames burned everywhere. The frightful brilliance of the fires, however, has too often blinded the historiographic perspective. The court's presence in the famous *autos* of Valladolid, the renown of the alleged Lutherans there and in Seville, and the shock of the Archbishop of Toledo's imprisonment have taken center stage in history (Tellechea). Yet the flames that consumed Spanish Protestantism should not make us forget the fires burning elsewhere; fires less publicized but no less tragic burned the Judaizers far away from the court, in smaller towns such as Llerena and Murcia (Contreras, "Criptojudaismo" 77-100). There, the Tribunal of the Faith did not hesitate to call heretical what was essentially a conflict of the urban elite.

Those who expired in the flames had attempted to maintain their social status and municipal positions through their commercial success and the vague connections to their Jewish origins. Accusing them of following the "Law of Moses," the Tribunal reacted accordingly. Those who opposed the concept of purity of blood, whether they had gained noble rank through wealth or were attempting to do so, were accused of an even more serious crime: heresy. The Inquisition then took sides. The Crown, impassive, fell into a demoralizing silence that gave free rein to unscrupulous and vengeful bands. Nonetheless, in some towns, there were those who protested.

Francisco de Valibrera was born in Murcia and was heir, along with his brothers, to the fortune of his uncle, the renowned alderman Juan de Valibrera, and his wife Catalina de Arroniz, also from a wealthy Murcian family. Indignant but somewhat fearful, Francisco wrote once again to his Majesty reminding him that he had sought justice from Don Fernando de Valdés, the Archbishop of Seville and then Inquisitor General, but, he wrote,

> Your Majesty is aware that the Archbishop has been
> remiss in both means and result . . . (therefore) it is Your
> Majesty's duty, as King and Superior above all others to

find out as soon as possible why these incidents have
occurred, since they have never before happened in
Spain, nor, by God's mercy, may they occur anywhere
else. In this case, decorum should not be kept, but the
events be made known so that the entire kingdom see
and understand how this justice has been carried out.
The holy and just Office [of the Inquisition] is
administered by men, and as such they are liable to err.
(AHN, Inq. Leg. 2779, Expd. 21)

The Council responded with silence to Valibrera's desperate
petitions. He wanted the King to review personally the incidents that had taken place in Lorca and Murcia. He had many
reasons to be aggravated. He did not believe that members of his
family were dogmatist heretics in charge of the Jewish synagogue supposedly discovered by the city's inquisitors. His entire family had been accused and three brothers burned at the
stake along with his aunt and uncle, Juan de Valibrera and Catalina de Arroniz. His relatives, the Lara family, had also been
decimated: Alvaro, another alderman; his brother Diego, the
King's chaplain; and their cousin Lope de Chinchilla, jurisdic-
tional official of Ontur and Albatana . . . all were burned at the
stake. Francisco de Valibrera was convinced that the Tribunal
had acted unjustly. Only the King could repair the terrible damage.

Francisco's appeal to royal justice, "as Superior above all others," and thus bypassing the Tribunal's jurisdiction, reflects the
popular belief that inquisitorial justice could be restrained by the
King's authority. Others like Francisco had also pleaded for assistance. Francisco Dávalos de Chinchilla, Lope de Chinchilla's
eldest son, had requested not only that the reports of the Murcia
inquisitors be sent to the King—which the Inquisition then conveniently withheld—but that the King also hear "those who are
detained in the Holy Office's prisons in Murcia" (AHN, Inq.
Leg. 2023, n. 29, fol. 3r, Dávalos letter June 15, 1560). Many
people did not believe that the Tribunal acted impartially,
guided by strict proof of heterodoxy. A muffled rumor of collective frustration and repressed hatred grew in Lorca and Murcia
against the inquisitors and their supporters.

The many letters and appeals sent to the King created much distrust and disillusionment at court. The Crown's silence was untenable; moreover, it was known that members of the Ayllón family, a family with a long tradition in municipal government, had gone to Rome, and through influential *converso* connections, had managed to send two petitions to Cardinal Alciato harshly criticizing inquisitorial action. Juan and Francisco Ayllón denounced to the Holy See the "arbitrary" *relajación* of their father Pablo Ayllón and their brothers Luis and Agustín, the former jurors on the Murcia council, and the latter a lawyer of the district. News that his Holiness had been shocked soon reached the King, who, it was thought, would name the Archbishop of Granada to head an investigation (AHN, Inq. Leg. 2022, Expd. 84; Blázquez Miguel 135). All of this bothered the King's councillors, who thought that an internal problem was being turned into a conflict with the Holy See. The court therefore decided to pay attention to all the reports received up to that time.

The first report was signed by a clergyman and New Christian from Lorca named Francisco Ruiz de Murcia, who in the early 1560s had drawn up an unusual criminal complaint against Doctor Cristóbal de Salazar, "Inquisitor of the Bishopric of Cartagena." The complaint was signed by the "sons and heirs of Pedro de Murcia and Francisco Castellanos, deceased residents of Lorca" (AHN, Inq. Leg. 2022, Expd. 77, fols. 1r-19v). According to the document, the deceased men's heirs went before the King to "prosecute Doctor Salazar" for his frequent and notorious offenses "made against my father Pedro de Murcia, in prison." They also asked that his Majesty take up the defense of other friends and relatives, all of them tried before Doctor Salazar as Judaizing heretics and faithful believers in the "sect of Moses."

Francisco Ruiz de Murcia's complaint intended to disprove the accusations as well as point out the Inquisition's arbitrary procedures. He demanded the restoration of his family's social and personal honor and asked that the inquisitor and two of his closest officials be disqualified and exiled from Lorca and Murcia. The complaint was made at a difficult political moment, when many social groups and some renowned theoreticians were engaging in the polemic on the possible relationship between purity of blood and heresy. For these groups, the repressive actions taken against the inquisitor proved their point: Catholic dogma was not compatible with the descendants of the Jews, even if they had converted. Such "incompatibility" led to the crime of heresy and consequently had to be eliminated with the full weight of the law. The events in Lorca and Murcia corroborated the belief that "blood" was thicker than water: indeed, a synagogue had been discovered in both towns.

Alleging that his honor and reputation had been tainted, Francisco Ruiz de Murcia represented the opposite side of the controversy. He insisted that justice was on his side because neither the laws of the land nor those of the Church stated that his Christian faith and the Jewish blood that possibly coursed through his veins were mutually exclusive. All the members of his family had long been decent Christians, and for this reason he did not believe himself or his family to be suspect.

Salazar and his assistants had committed serious procedural irregularities; far from arriving at the truth, they had caused irreparable damage to Francisco Ruiz de Murcia's family and spread panic throughout the town of Lorca. Ignoring the trial procedures that he was obligated to follow and obey, the inquisitor had allowed evidence to be falsified, and he twisted confessions until he had obtained accusations against more than one hundred people (AHN, Inq. Leg. 2022, Expd. 77, fols. 1r-v).[4] According to Ruiz, Salazar planted spies in jail who instilled fear in the prisoners and influenced the form and content of their testimonies. Salazar also disregarded prison secrecies, encouraging the prisoners to talk fearfully among themselves so as to guarantee the standardized testimony preferred by the judge. Salazar spread panic throughout the jail, overcoming even the strongest resistance with torture and fear: "they terrorized the witnesses with threats of death and other intimidations so that they would admit the falseness and perjury of what they had previously testified" (AHN, Inq. Leg. 2022, Expd. 77, fols. 1r-v). In his letter to Philip II, Ruiz stressed that many of the accused, acting on a blind impulse of survival, said exactly what the judge wanted to hear: "Desiring only to survive, aware of the great amount of evidence against them, they swore as truth what never was or could ever be true" (AHN, Inq. Leg. 2022, Expd. 7, fol. 16r).

The testimonies and trials affected the entire town. Ruiz did not give up, as his complaint was intended to bring the inquisitor to trial. His success would depend on the institution's own admission of its unjustifiable zeal; it would also explain why the Inquisition had so grievously disrupted the town's peaceful coexistence.

The inquisitor's injurious actions brought to the fore those feelings latent beneath the apparent social normalcy: the Old Christian-New Christian dualism triggered deeply seated tensions and contradictions. In effect, a careful reading of Ruiz's document uncovers factions within the Lorca community that the Holy Office obviously exploited for its own purposes. The Tribunal was thus transformed into an agent provocateur (Jaguaribe).

What really happened? We must study the clergyman's document to understand what occurred; even then, the whole truth will never be known. Its language is difficult and complex, detailing the many names and families that intertwine within a collective history. Often the report goes from Lorca to Murcia and doubles back on itself in a whirlwind of men and women entangled in a set of inextricable relationships.

As we have seen, at the mid-sixteenth century, the town of Lorca, close to Murcia, was inhabited by judges and inquisitors of the faith, who disturbed the town's tranquility on all levels. In 1561, Lorca had only 1,989 residents counting those of Huercal and the Casas de los Alumbres (Molinié Bertrand 298). The town was so small that everyone knew one another, friends met often, and enemies could not avoid each other. Wielding authority for ten long, difficult years, the Inquisition attempted to destroy what it considered a strong nucleus of New Christians who practiced the "Law of Moses."

How many were tried? Figures are uncertain, but over one hundred cases are documented. The inquisitors believed that such drastic surgery "would eradicate the evil" and the city would thus regain its civic health. Yet the tragedy would be remembered for decades. Moreover, the events in Lorca merely foreshadowed what happened in Murcia the following decade, when Judaizers were completely exterminated and upheaval reached all social levels. We know far more about Murcia than we do about Lorca. We know names and families, and we can thus more precisely reconstruct the sequence of events that led the victims to the stake, into exile, or into total social and economic ruin unobliterated even by death. First, however, we need to return to Lorca.

The events seem to have begun around 1550, when the Licentiate Quevedo, as mayor of Lorca representing both the King and the *corregidor* of Murcia, spoke out rather brashly one day in Lorca's town square. Publicly brandishing his power, he aimed threats at a woman named Magdalena López, an elderly widow of "one Monzón." Quevedo loudly proclaimed that "he swore by God and by the sign of the Cross that he personally would see to it that the inquisitors burn such a bitch as Magdalena López" (AHN, Inq. Leg. 2022, Expd. 77, fol. 8r). These harsh words barely hid their accusation of heresy. But was Magdalena López a heretic?

Behind the mayor's accusations and threats was an issue of personal honor. Everyone in the city had known for some time that Quevedo was a declared enemy of Magdalena López. Everyone knew the cause of the hatred: Quevedo was having an affair with Magdalena's daughter-in-law "Ribellas." Feeling insulted in "her own honor and that of her son," Magdalena sought redress. Juan de Monzón, her other son and Ribellas's brother-in-law, attempted to restore the family's honor: one day he followed the lovers and surprised them as they were leaving the mayor's house. Publicly denouncing his sister-in-law, Juan stabbed the mayor. Another time, Magdalena saw Ribellas leaving her lover's house. There were shouts, insults, and denunciations against her daughter-in-law, whom Magdalena "treated very badly, pulling her hair and scratching her face and saying many ugly words to both of them" (AHN, Inq. Leg. 2022, Expd. 77, fol. 8r). The mayor took this as an affront to his authority. For this reason, perhaps, he conceived the most terrible revenge: the public accusation of Magdalena López as a heretic.

What did Quevedo really know about heresy in Lorca? It was public knowledge that Magdalena had *converso* blood. Although she often squabbled with them, she was related to the Murcias and the Castellanos, two wealthy families of merchants and tailors considered by all to have Jewish blood. She was also related to the married couple Lorenzo García and Catalina Sánchez, both tailors, against whom the Tribunal had been particularly harsh (AHN, Inq. Leg. 2797, n. 13; *Auto de fe* September 8, 1560). She also knew many other New Christians in Lorca and maintained a close relationship with the alderman Juan Gutiérrez de Padilla, one of the town's richest men (AHN, Inq. Leg. 2022, Expd. 1; Domingo de Lázaro, *Auto de fe* March 15, 1562). Yet, even though Magdalena's status as a New Christian might provoke petty jealousies from a neighbor, it was neither a public dishonor nor a crime. Lorca's large population of New Christians had never caused problems. Either Quevedo must have known something we will never know, or his thirst for revenge made him act irrationally.

Whatever his motives, at the heart of the argument was Quevedo's relationship with Inquisitor Salazar in Murcia. Given their positions, they often litigated against each other, but behind these institutional confrontations were two officials of the royal administration with parallel careers. Courtesy was obligatory between them and could become friendship if the collaboration between them so dictated. Their visits became more frequent; there was an exchange of gifts and a show of goodwill on both sides—nothing extraordinary between two authorities. Yet Francisco Ruiz de Murcia saw them as planning a strategy for vengeance: "and in order to carry out his intent," the complainant wrote, Quevedo "formed a solid friendship with Salazar and visited him frequently in Murcia, sending him many gifts of pigs, pheasants, rabbits, and other things" (AHN, Inq. Leg. 2022, Expd. 1, notes 36-39).

According to Ruiz, Quevedo wished to bring Magdalena López before the inquisitional Tribunal to accuse her of Judaizing. To achieve this end, he acted shrewdly. Having gained Salazar's friendship and defined his objective, all he needed now were witnesses who would testify against Magdalena. Quevedo knew how to exploit his enemy's family squabbles: thus he obtained witnesses from the woman's own family. Her two daughters-in-law testified against her—Ribellas and Salvadora Pérez Cañamares, married to Juan Monzón, the son who had publicly denounced his sister-in-law and the mayor. Two other female relatives testified against her—Catalina López and Teresa de

Morata, members of the Murcia family with whom Magdalena was at odds. The final family witness was the accused woman's slave, who had intimate knowledge of her mistress's habits. To these five family witnesses Quevedo added some of his own faithful friends—Juan Vélez, his servant who also acted as bailiff; "La Carriona," his housekeeper; and Rodrigo de Mérida, a prisoner who knew Magdalena. These witnesses reveal Quevedo's extraordinary ability for scheming as well as his readiness to exploit his own personal power.

The witnesses were "brought" before the Tribunal notary; prejudging the accuracy of its contents, Salazar pocketed the summary. He immediately ordered Magdalena to prison. No one questioned the validity of the testimonies or the legality of the procedures, but this was not too important in these circumstances, because the judge and the inquisitor determined the validity of the witness and the testimony. When the trials resulted in executions, however, people asked themselves how the trials could have been held in such a way. Although people found out that there had been pressures and threats of torture aimed at whoever doubted or wished to retract their testimony, nothing could be done. What was certain was Salazar's power over the group of witnesses testifying against Magdalena.

The accusations were flatly stated: that she was a Judaizer; that she performed Jewish ceremonies like those mentioned in the Edict of Faith read by parish priests at church; that she went to the meat market and took the meat home to shred; that on Friday afternoons she laid clean clothes on the bed, cleaned the oil lamps, and gave her husband and children clean shirts; that she did not work on Saturdays; that she went to meetings with other New Christians where books in Hebrew were read.

These stereotypical accusations were literally taken from the Edict of Faith, and could hardly correspond to any real facts. The miserable witnesses, pressured and terrorized into defending themselves from something they did not understand, confused fiction and reality. They accused Magdalena of doing precisely what the inquisitors asserted Judaizers did in secrecy. For Salazar, that was enough, because the Edict of Faith was the literal truth.[5]

Little else can be said. Possibly to some New Christians, these accusations sounded like vague, almost forgotten echoes of the past. Possibly for others, the heresies mentioned in the Edict formed nothing more than a collection of inherited customs; possibly, also, what was meant to repress and extirpate these customs ironically became a source of knowledge that rediscovered and stimulated the original ethnic culture (Revah 54). Although aware of their own ethnic identity, very few of the Lorcan New Christians had achieved a feeling of belonging to the Jewish community and adherence to Mosaic law. There were, however, family-like groups throughout the years who considered themselves separate minority entities, even if they had risen substantially on the social scale. In general, the relatively numerous local New Christians maintained a separate, albeit diffused cultural identity. This became quite obvious as the statutes of pure blood began to obsess certain people and to mobilize certain wealth. Buying purity could achieve a certain social tranquility, but whoever stirred up the past risked detection. Social mobility was also risky; in this case, the laws of exclusivity of those who had already made the journey hit the newcomers hard.

The opposition between Old and New Christians had never created social strife in the past, but as soon as a few individuals began to extol their purity, the wound was opened. Magdalena's imprisonment in 1550, the witnesses who accused her, and above all the form in which inquisitorial justice sought a solution for the trivial problem of illicit love were of great concern to some influential people who were surprised to discover their own origins.

As usual, the judge's strategy was to disrupt the internal solidarity of the group he wished to destroy. Through the inquisitor's manipulation and astute awareness of their family problems, the two daughters-in-law seriously compromised their relative. This provoked even more family tension, and created the desired atmosphere of revenge. The inquisitor awaited the results.

Soon after Magdalena's imprisonment, her daughter-in-law Salvadora Pérez, Juan Monzón's wife, went to the scribe's house to assuage her guilt. She stated that "she went to him to relieve her conscience and retract what she had falsely said about Magdalena." The scribe had clear instructions, however, and "seeing that she wanted to contradict herself, he told her that if she did so, she would have her back torn open by lashings and other dire punishments; he frightened her so much that she did not dare to say the truth" (AHN, Inq. Leg. 2022, Expd. 77, fol. 4r).

But Salvadora could not remain silent. Emotionally upset, she sought relief among her own friends. Yet it was not in Lorca, but rather in Murcia that she confessed to a priest at the monastery of San Francisco. Aware of the seriousness of her confession, the priest refused to absolve her, and with her permission, he consulted the convent's preacher, Friar Luis de Valdecañas (AHN, Inq. Leg. 2022, Expd. 1, *Auto de fe* March 15, 1562). This friar was none other than the great rabbi of the conventicles of the Lorca and Murcia Judaizers. Aldermen, jurors, merchants, and lawyers of both towns congregated with him to praise the Lord of Israel. This is yet another of the many histories deserving separate treatment that complete this case. It thus turned out that Salvadora knew the identity of some of the Franciscan friars; suddenly Inquisitor Salazar could understand the true meaning of the many double entendres and ironic comments that usually went unnoticed in daily conversation. Without realizing it, Salvadora gave Salazar a lead; from that day on, he began to construct, piece by piece, the "great crypto-Jewish conspiracy."

In the convent, Father Luis de Valdecañas listened to the confessor, Father Pedro de las Nieves, as well as to Salvadora, and discussed the issue with other priests, colleagues in the "secrecy of the sect." All agreed that, "so the truth be known," the best thing was to speak directly with the inquisitor. The scene was tense and harsh, a preview of the tragic events to follow. Francisco Ruiz narrates the events: "the abovementioned inquisitor treated Friar Valdecañas and the other friars who went with the abovementioned woman [Salvadora] very poorly with many ugly words and ordered Salvadora Pérez arrested" (AHN, Inq. Leg. 2022, Expd. 77, fol. 6).

It was unthinkable then, but those who were now speaking as Christians would one day confront one another at the Tribunal: the inquisitor as the judge, and the friars as victims led to the stake. They discussed Salvadora, and the friars could not stop the inquisitor from sending her to the secret prison. No one, however, spoke of heresy, and the prisoner was condemned for having violated the secrecy of the Tribunal. Salazar also reprimanded the friars—he said—for overlooking the serious obligation they incurred in paying attention to witnesses who violated the sacred Tribunal's secrecy. He made no other accusation.

Salazar preferred to wait. He had jailed two people, and Juan de Monzón, the son and husband of the two prisoners, would be the third victim. Not surprisingly, Juan tried to stop this persecution of his family, but he was hardly the one to do so. The Holy Office knew of his aggressive behavior against Quevedo and his insults aimed at Ribellas. This was enough to condemn him. Salazar thought that by lightly "pressuring" the two women, they would implicate Juan and testify against new people. Magdalena and her daughter-in-law were tortured; the former resisted for some time, but the latter soon gave in. She confessed that her husband had induced her to retract her testimony when she had fearfully gone to the Tribunal's scribe.

This was sufficient. Juan was imprisoned and accused of obstructing the Holy Tribunal's justice. He was also accused of attending meetings "of the ceremonies of Moses." He denied it, but he could not escape from the inquisitor's vengeance. The Inquisition document is concise, but explicit: "Juan de Monzón was so seriously tortured that he was driven insane" (AHN, Inq. Leg. 2022, Expd. 77, fol. 4r). New names appeared and the web of those implicated continued to spread. Some years later, Juan was burned at the stake.

By then, Magdalena had been tortured many times and finally could resist no more. She testified to everything the inquisitor wished to hear. The shock waves that hit Lorca were due to her declarations. Those accused insisted that they were blatant lies, that the scandalous and tragic sequence of events was an outrage. Francisco Ruiz de Murcia, defending his family against Magdalena's accusations, charged that it was all a cruel farce brought about by hatred. He demanded that the iniquity be brought to light "for if there is the smallest error as regards the principle of any cause, there will be grave errors in the means and in the ends" (AHN, Inq. Leg. 2022, Expd. 77, fol. 17r).

The "errors" mattered little to the inquisitor; what really mattered were Magdalena López's many accusations. Despised and humiliated, she accused both rich and poor, nobles and commoners of performing the rites of the law of Moses. Most important, she accused her relatives, the Murcia and the Castellanos families, of Judaizing. The entire town was consumed by this insanity. More than two hundred people filled the Tribunal jails; more than one hundred were subjected to a harsh trial.

Salazar had achieved his goal, disrupting the town's harmony in the process. Preeminent families who barely remembered their Jewish origins saw themselves suddenly exposed to public scorn and even to trial by the inquisitors. Town councillors such as Leyba Ponce, Mateo Castillo, or Gutiérrez de Padilla, such jurors as the Torrecilla brothers, Doctor Valverde, and other members of the local elite suffered the infamy of suspicion and the social scorn of other groups who refused to acknowledge their status. The Lorcan councillors and aldermen accused by Magdalena, Salvadora, and Juan quickly realized that certain hostile families, backed by the Inquisition, had instituted a systematic vendetta against them. Quevedo, Salazar, and Alonso Sánchez were the front rank of the Old Christian clans—and some New Christian families—favored by the *anticonverso* psychodrama initiated by the Lorca mayor's illicit love affair.

There could be no doubt in Lorca: the Tribunal of Faith, arguing from the lofty principles of orthodoxy, transformed itself into an instrument for the "ennoblement" of municipal power. This resulted in an open political struggle among various sectors of the urban elite, with the inquisitors taking sides.

The losers in the struggle lost their positions, while the winners, in the majority Old Christians, quickly took over the vacant seats. In 1555, for example, when several municipal scribes had died at the stake and many others were prisoners of the Tribunal, the victors prepared to divide the spoils. The aldermen (the most important public office) had been able to "perpetuate themselves"—that is, they could now hold the office for life and even will it to their heirs. Since the mid-1540s the office of juror, the second-ranking post, received the most applications (Owens 289). On April 20, 1555, the new mayor of Lorca, the lawyer Baltazar de Gama, decided to send a memorandum to the King proposing that the jurors of the city should be, like the aldermen, lifelong appointees rather than elected officials.

With the Tribunal's attack on New Christians, it was logical to suppose that there would be few buyers of Jewish blood for the juror positions now available. If, when the King had increased the number of aldermen in the 1540s, the New Christians had augmented their municipal presence, now, with the Tribunal's help, it was time for the wealthy commoners who bragged about their lineage to "perpetuate" the newly acquired positions and thus enter the nobility.

Nothing, they said, could be achieved without pure blood; social ascent, political power, and juridical power were all denied. If the nobility could acquire some of the municipal posts through their privileges, the wealthy commoners, basing themselves on their ancient lineage, would not accept competition from the rich descendants of Jews (AGS, CJH, Leg. 85, n. 1). Indeed, this competition had to be eliminated, and the concepts of purity and orthodoxy were thus incorporated into the official propaganda.

Lorca, with its small population of two thousand, could not carry out the process of elimination. All there knew their neighbors' origin. It was much more difficult to carry out the process of assimilation of New Christians in Lorca than in the rest of Castile; there had been no expulsion, since the Jewish community had not opted for exile, but rather for the conversion of all its members, a collective decision that left no individual option (García Servet 97). Since everyone knew everyone else's background, anti-Semitism, culturally repressed, soon found an object to rally against.

Social conflict erupted when the frenzy over purity of blood conflated with the growing financial problems of the crown from the 1540s to the 1560s. By selling titles of nobility, the King allowed for indiscriminate social mobility. A royal letter patent of 1557 declared that "because of the great needs that his Majesty faces, he has agreed to provide one hundred fifty noble titles to anyone of any estate or lineage, no matter what his profession or origin" (AGS, CJH, Leg. 36, n. 200). Such a liberal offer created much rancor; taking sides, the Tribunal of Faith then tried as heretics those it considered to be disloyal competitors. Although the numbers of victims are not exactly known, many families were permanently marked with the stigma. One witness, Mateo Ruiz, who saw his father die in prison, spoke fearfully of "more than sixty deaths and other innumerable damages" (AHN, Inq. Leg. 2022, Expd. 77, fol. 16r).

In Murcia, the Tribunal did not offer a very edifying spectacle. Chaos was apparent everywhere: this microcosm was a reflection of the factional structure of the entire town. At war with each other were families, clans, and kinships whose network of patronages comprised public life in both Lorca and Murcia (Geller; Kettering). The urban elite's main objective was to keep municipal power, prestige, influence, and enrichment for themselves.

It was difficult to prevent political and administrative institutions from being affected by these preexistent social organizations; the cathedral chapter, the bishopric, the ministers, and officials of the magistrate were all influenced and shaped by the same councils. Entire families, clans, and "bands" vied for the office of alderman, juror, or some other important municipal post. To the extent that there existed a process of "right of patrimony"—that is, the possibility of transferring an office to a third party, even by testament—municipal power became the center of all political disputes (Tomás y Valiente; Owens 34-35). The power elite's struggle thus remained a battlefield between lineages and kinship alliances, a permanent rivalry increasingly bloody and violent as endogamous boundaries became more limiting. These urban groups also felt the polarization of Old and New Christian. Religious, aldermen, jurors, lawyers, and merchants were all traumatized by the division. The virulence increased as the differentiation between pure and impure became a symbol of difference among families. What had been solely a political struggle assumed a totalizing exclusivity that threatened the very existence of the nobility.

The crisis came to a head when the Tribunal started receiving accusations claiming the existence of groups, meetings, and conventicles. The accusations, made by commoners, incriminated people of high rank. Thus, names were forwarded of aldermen, mayors, merchants, priests, and friars. The Tribunal already knew and suspected some of these people; in fact, some of the ministers had special ties with them. On closer observation, these people relied on a public system of patronage with the Inquisition, particularly with some of its officials and ministers. With very few exceptions, the issues of purity of blood had been of little consequence to the Murcian Tribunal officials. They only began to feel concerned when so many of the accused went to the secret prisons; otherwise, they continued to participate in the same structures of town factions and bands.

The Tribunal did not isolate itself from local conflicts. On the contrary, it seems that the inquisitors became quite active in promoting the conflicts until—abandoning their own roles—they succeeded in disrupting the social status quo. It is interesting to note that the Tribunal was an essential cause of the town's internecine struggles, as its councillors readily admitted. They were intrigued by the urban power structure's potential for conflict and, quite likely, they were seduced themselves by its power and influence.

From these facts, we can arrive at some conclusions. The inquisitor Sánchez Cabrera, for example, educated, courteous, and polished, "did not awaken much sympathy" among some officials, who found him to be grave and reserved, "not very friendly and acts seriously." In general, people found him to "act justly" and apparently this reputation for seriousness had won him the magistrate's sympathy, for they became friends. Their friendship was criticized by the magistrate's powerful enemies, the Riquelme family and the Bishop of Cartagena, who had long been allied against him. Inquisitor Sánchez Cabrera soon found himself involved in the conflict. The first of the enemy band's supporters to criticize was Gonzalo de Avilés; then, the bishop's prosecutor, Dr. Obregón; finally, Luis Excasa, litigant for the bishopric (AHN, Inq. Leg. 2023, Expd. 18, Tribunal Letter to Council, April 22, 1551). They intended to remove Sánchez Cabrera from office; to this end, proper procedure was that the Suprema send an inspector to gather information. He arrived to hear slander, lies, and half-truths. The Riquelme family and the bishop accused Sánchez Cabrera of surrounding himself with *converso* friends, close friends of the Laras (who were also aldermen), and relatives of the Sotos (AHN, Inq. Leg. 2023, Expd. 19). While this was true, it was also true that, until now, it had never been a crime to befriend the old alderman Diego de Lara and his wife, Beatriz de Soto. It was a serious accusation, proof of the widening gap in that society, and it tarnished the reputation of both the Laras and the Sotos. By the beginning of the 1560s, Sánchez Cabrera was exiled from Murcia and therefore did not witness the *auto de fe* that would burn twelve members of these families at the stake.

What provoked these problems? In Murcia the social factions created a conflict parallel to the clientele structure. Nothing but exclusion and marginality existed outside the tight bonds of patronage. Sánchez Cabrera had seemingly done nothing inordinate to incur the Riquelmes'—and, by extension—the bishop's ire. When serving as ecclesiastical judge in Granada, however, he had imposed ecclesiastical over secular jurisdiction in the investigation of the murder of Francisco Riquelme, a clergyman of lesser orders killed in a brawl. Riquelme's family had pushed to have the case heard by the mayors and judges of the chancellery, but Sánchez Cabrera had been able to impose the Church's jurisdiction (AHN, Inq. Leg. 2023, Expd. 18, Tribunal Letter to the Council, April 17, 1551).

This was the reason for the hatred between the inquisitor and the Riquelmes. Sánchez Cabrera arrived at Murcia with the stigma of exclusion upon him. Since nothing could be done about this, he acted according to its implied code of conduct. Family loyalties did not allow for personal autonomy; marginalization by partisanship placed one in the opposing group. Thus, the enmity of the Riquelmes assumed the friendship of the Sotos.

Naturally, very soon insidious rumors were heard in Murcia which were then transformed into formal accusations. The bishop criticized Sánchez, and the powerful Riquelme family observed how the inquisitor asked the rich *conversos* for money, while dealing very harshly with Old Christians. The accusation, finally, was serious: "That you had close friendships with certain converted Jews and factions and that you shut yourself up with them both day and night" (AHN, Inq. Leg. 2023, Expd. 17, Tribunal Letter to the Council, April 16, 1551).

What was the inspector insinuating? Had social coexistence splintered into factional groups using racial origins as the reason for their conflicts? So it seems. Yet the tension stemmed more from social reasons and the specific values of Spanish theocratic society. Thus, the opposition between Old and New Christians did not really create any line of social division; its ethnic implications, however, lent moral arguments to justify the struggle for power.

To speak of inquisitors and Tribunal officials as *conversos* or as having Jewish blood may seem paradoxical, but it is not surprising. This strong-willed realm of endless ambitions and scrutinized consciences also included groups, bands, and factions that made up its collective life. Loyalty to superiors and ambition for power were the most permanent variables. Some were against and others were in favor of the Tribunal of Faith; it too was thus divided into hostile groups. Salazar, the inquisitor who disrupted the status quo and geared the Tribunal against *conversos* and crypto-Jews, blamed the evils of the Murcia Inquisition on the fact that "neither the Inquisition nor its ministers were pure, and so everything was tainted" (AHN, Inq. Leg. 2023, Expd. 3).

Salazar was indeed obsessed with the lack of purity in the Judaizing community of Lorca, especially in the case of the *converso* officials. He had no scruples in accusing them by name: secretaries Rodrigo de Saravia, Diego de Herrera, and Lope de Ungo; Commissioner Diego de Alarcón; and his own colleague, the Inquisitor Licentiate Gasco. Salazar investigated his ministers' family skeletons; he obtained precious data that he used to devise lineages. He remembered having heard that in the village of Corral de Almaguer in the province of Ciudad Real "the inhabitants were surprised that Licentiate Gasco [a native of the village] had been appointed inquisitor, since he was a *converso* on his mother's side, herself a native from Mondéjar in the province of Guadalajara" (AHN, Inq. Leg. 2023, Expd. 25, Accusations 51 and 57, fols. 12r-14v). Through Salazar's intentionally caustic comment, the Supreme Council was made to understand that Gasco's "friendship" with notorious Murcia *conversos*— Diego Hernández, the city's tax-gatherer, or Pedro de Montiel, custom-house official—could be explained by his blood.

Yet Licentiate Gasco was not the most closely linked to the area's *converso* families; others had much tighter bonds, like the *converso* secretaries Rodrigo de Saravia and Diego de Herrera. Saravia's situation was especially uncomfortable, as he was from Lorca and knew all of Salazar's victims. There were desperate allegations made by accused individuals that Secretary Saravia "was a relative of theirs." Saravia suffered grievously the stigma of his origins and his ties to kinship and town. Seated in the secret chamber, he experienced in his own person the trials of his friends. Saravia was relieved of his duties and denied entry into the secret chamber "because in these dealings in Lorca he showed an excess of passion" (AHN, Inq. Leg. 2023, n. fol., Salazar's testimony, June 23, 1558). This was a severe blow for an old man who for more than fifty years had sought the protection of inquisitorial bureaucracy to escape from marginalization.

Rodrigo de Alarcón, the Tribunal's commissioner, was familiar with his colleague's history, and recounted some significant details. Saravia was, at the present time in 1552, more than seventy years old. He had been born around 1480, at the height of the persecutions against Judaizers, when anti-Semitism permeated all levels of society. Perhaps there still existed for the Jews of Lorca a vague memory of that period, when, after having converted in 1492, they left the Castillo ghetto in an effort to begin a new era of tolerance and integration. Perhaps Saravia's family had been among those who so moved. In any case, Saravia was a witness—one of the few remaining—of those tragic events. A survivor, he had sought the means to obscure his origins. He must have been very young when he became a Tribunal official in Murcia. This provided him more camouflage than other locations, but his *converso* background was known, and while it was tolerated most of the time, it always caused him problems.

In 1517, when the young Charles V arrived in Spain, Saravia was in Valladolid, where he had to account to the Supreme Council for his behavior at the trial of Fernando Narváez, a scribe who had been relaxed due to his adherence to the religion of Moses. During the trial, it was said, Saravia had obstructed justice and counselled Narváez on how to deceive the judges. Now in Valladolid he had to explain not only his own origins, but also the strange and dark ties between him—an Inquisition official—and a Judaizer in the Murcia Tribunal prison.

Valladolid, where the young monarch had come to attend parliament, was then a hotbed of conflicts. Tribunals, high courts, municipal councils, and even the advisory boards all reflected the violence and tensions of the times. Thus, Saravia's case, which usually would have required a detailed investigation, was dismissed in 1518 with hardly any notice. He returned to Murcia a free man.

He was soon accused again, however. In 1520, Rodrigo Arroniz, a member of an important Lorca family, was imprisoned by the Tribunal. Many witnesses accused him of Judaizing, and it was discovered that Arroniz was "a close relative to Saravia on his mother's side." The Arroniz family was known as New Christian and very prone to Judaizing: the accused's father, Lope Alonso de Lorca, had been "a Judaizing New Christian, condemned, and relaxed [turned over to the secular authorities] as a heretic by the Holy Office"; a cousin, the Licentiate Santiesteban was also a famous heretic relaxed around 1515, and another relative, Francisco Vicente, an apothecary, who had raised Saravia as his own son, met a similar fate.

With so many antecedents, no one in the Tribunal doubted the origins of Secretary Saravia. He was an example of a *converso* who could never forget that he was one. He sought a position that would protect him from suspicion and guarantee his reputation and social worth, but his conduct in the Tribunal had betrayed him repeatedly. Saravia always upheld the values defining his background: the value of patronage, the obligations to his town, and the ethnic ties he had felt from childhood all superseded the "social and political" exigencies of his recently adopted Christian creed. He would always be a convert, even though he was a member of the Tribunal. Thus, at the age of seventy, after fifty years of service to the Holy Office, where he had known other colleagues of his race, he still feared that his family would be marginalized after his death. Suffering from memory loss and almost senile he asked the Supreme Council that "his son Cristobal Saravia be granted his position." This would finally prove his integration into society. It was not to be: the Council received negative reports on young Saravia's impure blood and his tendency toward delinquency (AHN, Inq. Leg. 2023, Expd. 3, Tribunal Letter to Council, November 20,

1552). Unfortunately for the elder Saravia, the paranoia regarding purity of blood had recently reached new heights, and he was familiar with the slanderous remarks of those colleagues who exploited the difficulties of the times for their own benefit.

The activities of the *converso* Diego de Herrera, Saravia's colleague and close friend, was perhaps the most vivid example of the tensions characterizing life in Murcia at the beginning of the Counter-Reformation. Like Saravia, Herrera had also come under attack from some of his Old Christian colleagues. The Licentiate Molina, a Tribunal prosecutor in Murcia and faithful supporter of the Counter-Reformation, demanded that his subordinates renounce their social ties; according to him, society should not dictate to the Inquisition. Thus, the new strategy demanded that the Tribunal dissociate itself as much as possible from onerous social obligations. Molina wanted the Inquisition run on two principles: efficiency and independence. The Murcia Inquisition, like other districts, had long suffered the "pressures from outside friends." Who were these "friends"? Secretary Herrera's friends were "townspeople and obvious Jews." For officials like Molina, inquisitorial authority was diminished when powerful locals, including *conversos*, influenced Inquisition officials.

Herrera always sought to diminish penal rigor meted out against his ethnic brothers. According to the prosecutor in Diego Miñano's case, Herrera's comportment was intolerable and disproportionate. Miñano, a *converso*, had been imprisoned three times previously, "and made a prisoner a fourth time"; the judges finally voted in favor of the confiscation of property in a public *auto de fe*. This was the usual sentence in such cases, but Herrera implored that the sentence be reduced and that "[Miñano] not be physically present in a public *auto de fe*." Herrera protected his friend: Miñano, owner of the most important game house in the city, did not have to suffer the public humiliation of an *auto de fe*.

This was not the only case in which Herrera used his political power to aid members of the *converso* community. For Francisco de Llerena, whose grandparents were burned at the stake in the final bloody years of the fifteenth century, Herrera hid evidence, prevented the decree of a prison *auto*, tried to suspend the Tribunal hearings, and finally arranged for the settlement to be brief and private in the Tribunal court. Francisco de Llerena's *converso* origins were never publicly denounced (AHN, Inq. Leg. 2796, Expd. 14).

These two brief examples from Herrera's career reveal significant aspects of the *converso* world's cultural sociology: the extreme zeal in avoiding any public decree about ethnic origins, as well as the enormous pressure placed on the Tribunal. These two aspects were inseparable, since "tainted" origins revealed publicly represented a serious threat to survival. Diego Herrera could be seen as an efficient "agent" within the Tribunal of Faith for the most important *converso* clans of the city. Their prosecutor Molina knew who these clans were: almost all of them belonged to the ancient kinship of the Sotos and the Laras. The alderman Alvaro de Lara; his brother, Diego de Lara; their cousin, Lope de Chinchilla; and Juan de Valibrera, another alderman and close relative, were members of the city's patrician class whose power and influence had lasted for almost fifty years. Closely interrelated, these families shared servants, friends, and relatives, and were placed in the municipal institutions of Lorca and Murcia as aldermen, judges, *provisores*, officials, priests, and scribes who had acquired honors and fortune. The prosecutor Molina identified them as notorious *conversos* and spread an old and popular rumor. These *conversos* were prone to Judaizing, and it was even said that some of them went to meetings and sacrilegious conventicles.

What began as a rumor soon became suspicion, and the insistent precaution of the great Murcia "patrons" to avoid public exposure of their *converso* origins led eventually to the accusation of heresy. Interestingly, this collective neurosis did not originate in the Tribunal, but was conveniently triggered by the resentment and old hatreds among other leaders and rival patrons. Inquisitor Cristóbal de Salazar, a recent arrival to Murcia from Granada, who thought very much like Molina, capitalized on the Tribunal's punitive force. Arguing in favor of independence and efficiency, he believed in the Holy Office's fight against heresy, without realizing that the Tribunal was a tool in the struggle among local factions. He assumed that all the racist arguments defending the Statutes of Purity were solid, and thought that the crusade against New Christians should be organized like the one against the Protestants.

In effect, the obsession with purity based on moral arguments that barely justified social interests arrived at extreme measures in zones with marked internal conflicts among the urban elite. Many internal demons were thus let loose. It was said that the sin was in the blood, that there could be no trust in the best intentions of a vitiated character. In such circumstances, it was easy to see how a *marrano* could potentially be a Jew (Revah 55),[6] just as a New Christian could easily be discovered to be a *marrano* (Yerushalmi 35).[7] Only in these circumstances, in the midst of such violent conflict, could the discourse on purity of blood condition faith. The manifestations of one's faith originated in one's blood: impure blood could only produce religious aberrations. Could there be a better justification for segregation? Supporting these arguments, the Murcian inquisitor Salazar therefore did not doubt the rumors that his friend from Lorca, the Licentiate Quevedo, had threatened Magdalena López—a New Christian from way back—to burn at the stake. What the inquisitor did not know was that this fanatical zeal hid social forces that attempted to aristocratize and feudalize the urban structures of power and that contributed so significantly to the history of Spanish absolutism. The Counter-Reformation not only propagated a religious ideology—it also imposed a social model and affirmed a political structure.

Notes

1. The bibliography on the subject is extensive. See Gentil da Silva, Carande, Salomon, García Sanz, and Clavero.

2. "Las Cortes de 1538 pidieron que los nobles fueran admitidos a los municipios que no tenían acceso. Las de 1566 solicitaron que los mercaderes y oficiales mecánicos no pudieran tener cargos concejiles" (Domínguez Ortiz, *Las clases* 123).

3. On the xenophobic character of the anti-Lutheran campaign, see Jiménez Monteserín, Dedieu, and Contreras, "The Impact."

4. "Y el dicho Salazar hizo agravar las conciencias de más de cuarenta personas que han dicho y testificado contra el susodicho Pedro de Murcia e los demás difuntos mis partes, e contra más de otras cien personas haciéndoles decir y testificar falsamente contra ellas" (AHN, Inq. Leg. 2022, Expd. 77, fols. 1r-v).

5. On the insufficiency of inquisitorial sources regarding the Jewishness of *marranismo*, see Rivkin, Cohen, and Netanyahu.

6. "The 'judaism' of the *marranos* was essentially a potential one, most often transformed into real Judaism by entry into a Jewish community" ("Le 'judaisme' des marranes était essentiellement un judaisme potentiel que l'entrée dans une communautée juive transformait le plus souvent en jadaisme réel").

7. "Paraphrasing Professor Revah's statement, I would say that it is perhaps more important to realize that, even before he began to 'Judaize,' every New Christian was a potential *marrano* whom any number of circumstances could transform into an active one" ("Paraphraseant le propos du professeur Revah, je dirais qu'il peut être encore plus essentiel de reconnaître que, avant même qu'il commençait a 'judaiser,' tout nouveau chrétien était marrane potentiel qu'un certain nombre de circonstances diverses pouvait transformer en un marrane actif").

Works Cited

Archivo General de Simancas (AGS), Consejo y Juntas de Hacienda (CJH). Various documents.

Archivo Histórico Nacional (AHN), Sección Inquisición. Various documents.

Blázquez Miguel, J. *El Tribunal de la Inquisición en Murcia.* Murcia: Comunidad Autónoma de la Región de Murcia, 1986.

Carande, Ramón. *Carlos V y sus banqueros: La vida económica en Castilla 1516-1556.* Madrid: Sociedad de Estudios y Publicaciones, 1965.

Castro, Américo. *De la edad conflictiva.* 4th ed. Madrid: Taurus, 1976.

Clavero, Bartolomé. *Mayorazgo: Propiedad feudal en Castilla, 1369-1836.* Madrid: Siglo XX, 1974.

Cohen, M. "Toward a New Comprehension of the *marranos.*" *Hispania Judaica* 1 (1961): 23-25.

Contreras, Jaime. "The Impact of Protestantism in Spain. 1520-1600." *Inquisition and Society in Early Modern Europe.* Ed. Stephen Haliczer. London: Croom Helm, 1987. 47-63.

_____. "Criptojudaismo en la España Moderna: Clientelismo y Linaje." *Revista Areas* 9 (1988): 77-100.

Dedieu, Jean Pierre. "El modelo religioso: Las disciplinas del lenguaje y de la acción." *Inquisición española: Poder político y control social.* Ed. Bartolomé Bennassar. Barcelona: Edición Crítica, 1971. 208-228.

Domínguez Ortiz, Antonio. *Los Judeoconversos en España y América.* Madrid: Istmo, 1971.

_____. *Las clases privilegiadas en el Antiguo Régimen.* Madrid: Istmo, 1973.

García Sanz, Angel. *Desarrollo y crisis del Antiguo Régimen en Castilla la Vieja. Economía y sociedad en tierras de Segovia, 1500-1814.* Madrid: Akal, 1977.

García Servet, Gerónimo. *El humanista Cascales y la Inquisición murciana.* Madrid: José Porrúa Turanza, 1978.

Geller, E. *Patronos y clientes.* Madrid: Júcar, 1985.

Gentil da Silva, José. *Desarrollo económico, subsistencia y decadencia en España.* Barcelona: Ciencia Nueva, 1967.

Jaguaribe, Helio. *Political Development: A General Theory and Latin American Case Study.* New York: Harper & Row, 1973.

Jiménez Monteserín, M. "Los luteranos ante el Tribunal de la Inquisición de Cuenca, 1525-1600." *La Inquisición Española: Nueva visión, nuevos horizontes.* Ed. Joaquín Pérez Villanueva. Madrid: Siglo XX, 1980. 689-737.

Kamen, Henry. "Una crisis de conciencia en la Edad de Oro en España: Inquisición contra limpieza de sangre." *Bulletin Hispanique* 88 (1986): 321-356.

Kettering, Sharon. *Patrons, Brokers, and Clients in Seventeenth Century France.* Oxford: Oxford Univ. Press, 1986.

Maravall, José Antonio. *Poder, honor y élites en el siglo XVII.* Madrid: Siglo XXI, 1979.

Molinié Bertrand, Annie. *Au siècle d'Or. L'Espagne et ses hommes (la population du Royaume de Castille au XVIe. siècle).* Paris: Económica, 1985.

Netanyahu, Benzion. *The Marranos of Spain from the Late XIVth to the Early XVIth Century According to Contemporary Hebrew Sources.* New York: American Academy for Jewish Research, 1966.

Owens, John B. *Rebelión, monarquía y oligarquía murciana en la época de Carlos V.* Murcia: Univ. de Murcia, 1980.

Revah, I. S. "Les Marranes." *Revue des Etudes Juives* 118 (1959-60): 3-77.

Rivkin, E. "How Jewish Were the New Christians?" *Hispania Judaica* 1 (1961): 105-115.

Salomon, Noël. *La vida rural castellana en tiempos de Felipe II.* Barcelona: Planeta, 1973.

Sicroff, Albert A. *Los estatutos de limpieza de sangre: Controversias entre los siglos XV y XVII.* Madrid: Taurus, 1985.

Tellechea, José Ignacio. *Fray Bartolomé de Carranza y su tiempo.* 2 vols. Madrid: Univ. Pontificia, 1968.

Tomás y Valiente, F. "Las ventas de oficios de regidores y la formación de oligarquías urbanas en Castilla." *Historia, Instituciones y Documentos* 2 (1975): 115-137.

Yerushalmi, Yosef Hayim. *De la Cour d'Espagne au ghetto italien.* Paris: Fayard, 1987.

Yun Casalilla, Bartolomé. *Sobre la transición al capitalismo en Castilla y Salamanca.* Ediciones de la Comunidad de Castilla-León, 1987.

◆ Chapter 6

Magdalens and Jezebels in Counter-Reformation Spain

Mary Elizabeth Perry

Guard your daughters "as dragons," Juan de la Cerda exhorted parents in a book published in 1599, and teach them the obedience and modesty essential to female purity (242r). Few parents may have actually read the Franciscan as an expert in raising daughters, but his advice nonetheless reflected a widespread belief in Counter-Reformation Spain that chastity was to be valued above all other virtues for women and that it was the most vulnerable female quality. In the peculiar mathematics of Counter-Reformation moralists, the female who lost her chastity acquired in exchange a frightening license to break every other taboo. The unchaste woman, in this view, posed not only a threat to the social order, but a real danger to the salvation of men's souls. Fray Juan's injunction took on an urgency unusual in the books of the period that prescribed ideal behavior for women. Far more than empty rhetoric or formulaic misogyny, his demand that parents act as dragons implies a deep concern about the real presence of unchaste women in his society. Parents and clerics could police women and girls as much as possible to protect their chastity, but effectiveness in keeping them under control depended upon the extent to which females inter-

nalized these beliefs. The very fact that all women did not remain chaste in Counter-Reformation Spain shows very clearly
that strategies for moral control did not succeed. They failed, in
particular, for those women who lacked a dowry for either marriage or convent.

The Spain of Fray Juan could not preserve chastity in all females, but it attempted to lessen the threat of unchaste women
through the use of three institutions: the brothel, the Magdalen
house, and the prison. An examination of each of these institutions shows that they played central roles in Counter-Reformation attempts to provide a homogeneous moral order believed
necessary to political stability in this period. It also reveals an
ambivalent attitude toward unchaste women. On the one hand,
they could be seen as victims of circumstances such as poverty
and seduction, Magdalens who could be saved from their sinful
ways; on the other hand, they could be viewed as agents of evil,
as Jezebels who seduced young boys and infected others with
disease and debauchery. Officials in Counter-Reformation Spain
might disagree on possibilities for redeeming unchaste women,
but they agreed that they should be enclosed, whether in the
brothel, the Magdalen house, or the prison.

Prior to the sixteenth century, the brothel had been tolerated
in many towns and cities as a "necessary evil" that was believed
to function as a cesspool in a castle.[1] Ordinances dating from the
fourteenth century in Seville decreed the public brothel as the
proper place for women "who do not want to be good and
chaste and want to sell their bodies" (*Ordenanzas* 63). Such
women could be more closely supervised in a public brothel, the
ordinance declared, than in the "monasteries of evil women,
who use their bodies for evil in the sin of lust, and who have a
director, in the manner of an abbess" and "carry out their lusts
and evils, more covertly than the public brothels" (63r-64).

Paradoxically, the same ideology that valued female chastity
also supported prostitution, for the chastity of some women
could be ensured by the fact that men would have access to
other women who would sell their sexual services. In this society of arranged marriages and preoccupation with purity of
blood (*limpieza de sangre*), males usually married later than females and sought wives whose chastity had been protected.

Prostitutes who provided sexual services for young unmarried men acted as deviant insiders essential to the moral order (Perry, "Deviant Insiders" 138-158; Perry, *Gender and Disorder* 42-62, 171-191). Clearly they strayed from the moral restrictions on female sexual activity, but they were believed to divert males from more serious sins of homosexuality, incest, adultery, rape, and propositioning honest women. Before the sixteenth century, most towns and cities attempted to control prostitution by restricting it to certain zones and requiring prostitutes to wear a visible insignia that would distinguish them from respectable women. Seville, for example, required prostitutes to wear a yellow head-covering and to carry out their trade in the public brothel. The ordinances for this city, which became a model for regulations in other towns in southern Spain, also allowed for fines for prostitutes who failed to observe these two restrictions (Galán Sánchez and López Beltrán 163). Rather than a single structure, the public brothel in Seville and in towns such as Valencia and Málaga included several small houses located together in one neighborhood (Caffarena 21-22; Carboneres 14).

The brothel could be accepted in the towns and cities of early modern Spain because regulations required legal prostitutes to observe certain rules that integrated them into a socioreligious order. Since the late fifteenth century, laws had prohibited prostitutes from working on Sundays and feast days. These regulations imposed some discipline on the lives of prostitutes, but even more important, they also imposed some control on the activities of men. A desire to keep prostitution within a socioreligious order may have motivated these regulations as much as a wish to protect the souls of prostitutes and provide them some days of rest. Whether motivated by fear or compassion, the requirements implied that prostitutes would not decide independently to attend mass or to refrain from work on Sundays.

Administration of the public brothel became an income-producing monopoly often granted to certain favored individuals, called *hostalers* in Valencia and *padres* in Seville. *Hostalers* could be male or female, but by the sixteenth century, brothel *padres* were always male (Carboneres 14-17; Perry, *Gender and Disorder* 57). Alonso Yáñez Fajardo received exclusive power over the brothel of Málaga from the Catholic Kings in gratitude for his heroism in the battle for Ronda (Caffarena 19-20). Since this monopoly would have no value if prostitutes were tolerated outside the brothel, the royal government called on local officials to enforce laws against free-lance prostitution. At the same time, officials in Málaga responded to complaints about the brothel administration by requiring Yáñez to reform the brothel regulations (Caffarena 21-22).

Effective supervision of prostitutes required local officials to enforce laws against pimps and procuresses, but it should be noted that antipimping laws also protected the interests of brothel administrators. In 1469, the Cortes that met in Ocaña complained that prostitutes, "through giving money to their ruffians or to other persons, become impoverished and owe some debts to the said *padre* or *madre*" (quoted in Galán Sánchez and López Beltrán 167). To solve this problem, the assembly required the prostitute to pay fees to the brothel administrator before she paid anyone else. In this same year, Enrique IV of Castile decreed one hundred lashes for any prostitute who had a pimp.[2]

The laws of the kingdom that prohibited anyone from living off the earnings of a prostitute implied that women who sold their sexual services did so because they were made to work, usually by a man. Defining five categories of pimps, the law first prohibited "bad rascals" who kept women in the public brothel. A second group acted as brokers in selling the sexual services of women in their homes, and a third group sold those of slaves or servant women in their homes. The fourth type of pimping occurred when a man was "so vile that he pimps his own wife," and the fifth type was to receive some payment for allowing a married woman to commit fornication in one's home.[3] Proponents of legalized prostitution argued that the brothel would help to prevent such evil exploitation of women.

The paternalistic assumption that the brothel system could protect prostitutes served several social functions. It reinforced the power position of officials and clerics who could play the role of authority in rituals that portrayed their power as acceptable because it was compassionate. In addition, passing regulations to protect legal prostitutes neutralized their danger. If they were portrayed as weak and vulnerable, their deviance seemed less threatening. Their vulnerability also helped to provide an explanation for why these women would become prostitutes. Finally, protective rules for prostitutes established boundaries for the deviance that could be tolerated in this city. Women could sell themselves to men, but men could not sell them into the brothel; prostitutes could violate sexual codes for respectable women, but they must attend church. Although such attitudes seem contradictory, they clearly illustrate how society set limits on deviance.[4]

During the period of the Counter-Reformation, brothels became subject to closer public supervision. The Crown, in particular, urged local secular officials to play a greater role in enforcing prostitution laws. Moreover, regulations passed in the sixteenth century reduced the powers of brothel administrators and held them accountable for enforcing prostitution laws. Local officials in Valencia decided in 1562 to limit the amount of rent that *hostalers* could charge prostitutes; they also prohibited the *hostaler* from loaning money to prostitutes and thus getting them so deeply into debt that they could never leave the brothel (Carboneres 103-107). From private fiefdoms administered for their own enrichment, the position of brothel administrators then became similar to that of petty bureaucrats (Puig and Tuset 71-82).

Sixteenth-century regulations assumed that brothel administrators would exploit prostitutes who were weak and vulnerable victims, and therefore they enforced formal protective measures. The ordinances of 1570 in Seville prohibited the brothel *padres* from accepting women who had been "pawned" into the brothel for a sum of money.[5] Pedro de León, a Jesuit who worked with people in the city's brothel, wrote of "ruffians" who pawned their women for ten or twenty ducats or more (Part 1, Chap. 4-6). Regulations forbade brothel administrators from accepting a pawned woman even if she agreed to the arrangement, and they forbade *padres* from keeping a woman in the brothel against her will even if she owed money. These rules clearly assumed that women were so commonly exploited economically and so easily duped into exploitative situations that the city government had to protect them from themselves and their men.

Protection and punishment, in fact, mingled in some confusion in pronouncements about unenclosed women. Prostitutes who observed regulations would be protected, but those who did not forfeited all social protection. In a similar fashion, women unrestrained by enclosure in the home, the brothel, or the convent deserved not only what violence they received at the hands of men, but also special punitive measures. "Neither wandering woman nor broken sword," warned a proverb of the period, emphasizing the link between unenclosed women and subverted authority (Juan de Espinosa 258).

As syphilis spread from port to port, local regulations emphasized mandatory medical examinations for prostitutes. The city of Valencia, for example, appointed a surgeon as medical inspector for the brothel in 1548 and some forty years later not only required all prostitutes to pass medical inspection, but also prohibited from prostitution any woman who had been treated in a hospital for *sement*, a term for venereal disease (Carboneres 95, 112-113). After an epidemic of syphilis hit Seville in 1568, this city adopted ordinances that required medical examinations of prostitutes every eight days and held brothel administrators responsible for enforcing this law. The surgeon hired to register and inspect women in the city brothel in 1572 warned that discharging infected prostitutes from the brothel was only exacerbating the problem because they simply continued their trade in the streets and taverns of Seville, causing "much damage" to public health. He urged that ill prostitutes should be transported from enclosure in the brothel to enclosure in a hospital.[6]

Counter-Reformation moralists began to question more loudly the pragmatic argument that legalized prostitution was a necessary evil and the best protection against disease. By the end of the sixteenth century, a controversy emerged between those who wanted to retain legalized prostitution and those who believed that it must be abolished as an offense to God. The longtime alliance of pragmatists and moralists crumbled as each side presented its position with increasing passion. Clerics such as Juan de Mariana had already begun to argue that prostitution was a serious social evil that multiplied in growing cities. Far more destructive than merely corrupting women, Mariana declared that prostitution had produced a generation of worthless men. "Many youths we have seen who, coming from places where there are no prostitutes, were very modest and sober," he wrote, "and later in the larger cities they found a liberty to sin, [and] suddenly changed into shameless and dishonest [men] losing estate, youth, health, and counsel, and ending up completely without any value" (446). Moreover, the brothel did not serve as a remedy for lust, he argued, but actually encouraged it. Women, who are much weaker than men, he observed, did not have brothels; and if prostitution were really necessary, then women would have to have "houses of boys" (447).

In the record of his ministry in Seville at the turn of the seventeenth century, Pedro de León described men and boys who frequented the legal brothel, damaging property and harassing priests who came to preach to the prostitutes.[7] He urged these men and boys, as well as the prostitutes, to leave their lives of sin. Some of the boys were as young as fourteen and already infected with venereal disease. The priest identified these males as "petty officials, workers, and apprentices of the field." In contrast to the belief from an earlier period that the brothel was a service for transient men, now it was apparent that the clientele of the brothel included many city residents, including young boys who could be corrupted by the prostitutes.

Opponents of the legal brothel mixed morality and hygiene in their appeals to abolish this institution. Syphilis seemed an especially terrifying threat because no one had yet found an effective cure. Cures used by prostitutes and surgeons merely treated the symptoms of the disease and could not prevent its return after a period of latency (Granjel 140). Some hospitals specialized in treating patients with syphilis, usually with a cure of *agua del palo*, a water solution of bark from a tree found in the Indies. Although a sixteenth-century writer praised this cure in the Hospital de San Cosme y San Damián in Seville, asserting that it was effective in thirty days, reports from the seventeenth century implied that patients could require repeated thirty-day treatments that were given each spring and fall.[8] Mercury treatments appeared to be more immediately effective, but they were also blamed for causing deaths. As one physician of the period stated, the mercury cures were more "damaging" than the disease (Rico-Avello 85-86; Garrison 589-634).

Many people in this period regarded syphilis not simply as a very virulent disease, but as a "divine illness" imposed by God as punishment for excess lust (Farfan, *Regimiento* 278). Applying contemporary medical wisdom to beliefs about sin, Francisco Farfan wrote that syphilis originated not in the New World, as others had declared, but as God's punishment on the army of Charles VIII of France, which had so brutally destroyed Naples in 1494 (279-279r). He warned that this "pestilence of Venus, and Heaven's lash" was extremely contagious because its humor was very penetrating. The "carnal act" alters and warms the parts of the body that become penetrated, opening the pores to its venom so that it can damage the liver, which "is the source and root of this evil" (280r). This disease did not spread simply through the sexual act, however, for Farfan declared that people became infected by eating or drinking from utensils used by those already infected or by wearing the clothing or using the same cloth that an infected person had used. Describing remedies such as diet, *agua del palo*, sarsaparilla, purges, potions, and sweatings, he said these were rarely effective. Even worse, he wrote, was the "vulgar practice" of trying to cure oneself of syphilis by expelling the venom when having sexual relations with a healthy person (289r).

Whether people of this period viewed the brothel as a breeding ground for disease or as a defense against it, they agreed that prostitutes who left the brothel had to be placed in another form of enclosure. Marriage would be preferable, and Jesuits in particular established shelters not as convents for converting prostitutes, but as places to reeducate them for "regular positions in the world," as Ignatius Loyola wrote, "above all for a proper marriage" (Rahner 17-18). Recognizing that many prostitutes were unhappily married, the Jesuit founder saw that a shelter for reforming prostitutes should help them regain self-respect and gradually bring them back to their husbands. In the statutes for the House of St. Martha that he founded in Rome for converting prostitutes, Ignatius wrote of these women: "Whenever the husband gives an assurance that he will resume married life with her, she is bound to return to him in peace, love, and conjugal loyalty" (Rahner 17-18).

Many supported charitable dowries for unmarried women who wanted to leave prostitution and marry, and in seventeenth-century Madrid, several men chose wives from the centers for reforming prostitutes (Pérez Baltasar 66). The Jesuit Pedro de León wrote of his success in getting a wealthy woman of Seville to give dowries of forty ducats to each woman he was able to convert from prostitution (Part 1, Chap. 4, fols. 10-14; Chap. 5, fols. 14-15). Even with a dowry, it must have been difficult for former prostitutes to find husbands, particularly in the seventeenth century when contemporaries noted that young men lacked the means to support themselves and marry, leaving single women to "perish in corners from hunger."[9] Moreover, clerics who wrote to the families of women who wanted to leave prostitution did not always find husbands or parents eager for their return home.

Magdalen houses could provide an alternative to marriage for converting prostitutes. As early as 1345, a "virtuous and good woman" who was a Franciscan tertiary proposed a house in Valencia to receive, shelter, and keep isolated all women who wanted to leave prostitution (Carboneres 22-24). The city government voted to contribute 500 *sueldos* to build the house, and nearly twenty years later city council members agreed to give 7,000 *sueldos* for an even larger house. As they became patrons of this house, now called the House of Penitents, they must have realized that converting prostitutes did not account for all of its growing number of inmates, for in 1396 the city council decided that this house would no longer receive wives placed there for "correction" by their husbands (Carboneres 41).

Counter-Reformation zeal to reform sinners increased the number of clerics who delivered special sermons to prostitutes on the feast day of Mary Magdalen. City officials frequently accompanied the cleric to the brothel on this feast day in Seville, where brothel administrators gathered the prostitutes to listen. They then marched the women who agreed to reform to the cathedral or another parish church where they would be publicly received as converts.[10] Although the numbers of prostitutes thus converted remains unknown, one historical account describes Fray Luis de Rebolledo, who preached so successfully to prostitutes on one Magdalen feast day that he converted twenty-seven of them (Pacheco n. pag.).

Many more Magdalen houses had to be founded during the Counter-Reformation to receive these women. In Málaga, Zaragoza, and Valencia "houses of penitents" appeared before the end of the sixteenth century, providing shelter for women who entered voluntarily to change their lives from prostitution. One historian has suggested that other women, such as widows and poor women, also found within these houses asylum and protection for varying periods of time (Muriel, quoted in Pérez Baltasar 28).

Some of these houses began as convents in which former prostitutes might enter a religious order. Augustinians established the Convent of the Sweet Name of Jesus in Seville in 1540 as a place to gather repentant women and up to six "honest" women (Llorden 7; Morgado 465-466). By 1551 this group had moved to a larger house, thanks to a generous grant from private donors, and it became a genuine convent following the rule of Saint Augustine. The abbess and nuns reported more than one hundred women in this convent by 1581.[11] Evidently, former prostitutes became segregated in assigned lay quarters, as the convent attracted gifts and daughters from pious families. By 1641 a papal brief decried this separation and reminded the convent administrators that the original purpose of the convent had been to provide a place where professed nuns could supervise and teach converting prostitutes. The brief stated that the lay quarters should not be separated from the rest of the nuns or the convent, nor should the convent be diverted from its original purpose of converting prostitutes. In particular, the brief declared, the lay quarters should no longer be required to shelter others such as women fleeing from their husbands or lovers (Llorden 12).

Discipline could be very severe in Magdalen houses, and former prostitutes were usually expected to follow a regimen of work and prayer that would correct their former sinfulness (Pérez Baltasar 26-28). In the house of penitents in Málaga, for example, women had to learn Christian doctrine, receive certification by a priest that they had changed their conduct, observe strict cloistering, pass a rigorous novitiate, and profess as Discalced Carmelites once they received the bishop's approval (Caffarena 26). Fortunately, they did not have to provide the usual dowry in order to become nuns.

In Valencia the house of penitents became the enclosure not only for converting prostitutes, but also for working prostitutes when city officials closed the brothel on Sundays and feast days. Quarrels broke out between the two groups of women, however, so that in 1605 working prostitutes were also sent to the Brotherhood of Santa Lucía, which had been accustomed to keeping them during Holy Week (Carboneres 120-128). By the middle of the seventeenth century, the number of days in which working prostitutes were locked up had increased so much that they were kept enclosed and away from the brothel during the entire forty days of Lent.

Some churchmen and officials in the seventeenth century recognized that the severe discipline of a convent could deter many women who would otherwise leave prostitution. At the Jesuits' Casa Pía in Seville, which functioned as a transition home for women leaving prostitution, one cleric in particular became noted for his compassionate treatment of these women and his attempts to make the Magdalen house less forbidding. Before he began work there, the Casa Pía contained only one or two converted women, but he soon had forty or more converted women in the shelter (Pedro de León, Part 1, Chap. 5, 14-15). Pedro de León wrote that these women usually stayed in the shelter only two or three days, until they could be released to their families or husbands, or had received a dowry or new position.

Sympathetic treatment successfully convinced many prostitutes to assume the kneeling, penitent position of Mary Magdalen. They received new importance and social approval as they willingly confessed to past sins and fervently declared their wish to change. Their confessions reversed their former degradation in Counter-Reformation society, converting their significance from profane to sacred (Hepworth and Turner 21). It could be argued, however, that conversion simply redefined degradation for these women, for they became reintegrated into society only by accepting another degraded status, that of the penitent who begged forgiveness.

Magdalen houses could function effectively for former prostitutes who voluntarily entered them, but they could do nothing about the problem of women who refused to stay in either the legal brothel or a convent for converted women. Traditional regulations required these Jezebels to be punished through public humiliation, whippings, having their nostrils slit, and exile. Forms of punishment changed, however, as the numbers of unenclosed prostitutes increased. During the sixteenth century, officials sent "incorrigible women" to prisons, which gradually adopted programs of work and correction (Pérez Baltasar 26-28). Noting that many "lost" and vagabond women wandered about Seville, the royal council directed local officials in 1596 to gather these women together in a house where they could be confined under supervision to support themselves from the work of their hands.[12]

Madre Magdalena de San Gerónimo had worked many years in a convent for converted prostitutes in Valladolid when Philip II called her to direct the Galera de Santa Isabel, a prison for women in Madrid. In 1608 she sent to the King a formal proposal for a special prison for recalcitrant women (Magdalena de San Gerónimo 304-316).[13] Long before the penitentiaries that developed in the modern period, Madre Magdalena's proposal influenced penal policies and promoted a gender-specific transition from corporal public punishments into private reformatory incarceration.[14]

Prescribing severe discipline for women who would not become penitent Magdalens, Madre Magdalena's proposal won the support of many officials. This nun did not sympathize with prostitutes who refused conversion, nor did she identify them as belonging to her own sex. Accepting the dichotomization of good and evil women, she proposed a harsh discipline of work, silence, and shaven heads for those Jezebels who refused to be good. She noted with pride that her plan had won considerable attention for its severity, "particularly being invented by a woman against women" (307). She carefully stated, however, that her treatise was not intended to impute the honor of virtuous women, only "the lost and evil ones, who insult the honesty and virtue of the good ones with their corruption and evil" (308).

Madre Magdalena drew upon her twenty years of working with such evil women in Valladolid, concluding that they were not simply a nuisance, but a true threat to the kingdom. At night, she wrote, they emerge as "wild beasts who leave their caves to look for prey," spreading disease among men, "family dishonor, and scandal among all the people" (309). Moreover, their evil example infected many respectable women "who fall into similar evil" (309). She indicted women younger than sixteen who solicited customers in the streets, as well as older women who literally sold girls of ten years and less and pretended to place other young girls in positions as domestic servants. "I know them well," she added, "the demon has taken possession of them and is so angry . . . that he will induce them to many evil things" (313).

To reinstill the fear of God in such women, Madre Magdalena proposed a prison "strong and well enclosed," with the royal arms and an unsheathed sword of justice over the door. The prison should include a dormitory, work room, and also a "secret prison where in particular the rebellious incorrigible ones will be punished" (310). The inmates would have their heads shaven and wear only burlap or rough clothing; they would be forbidden to speak together or to have visitors from outside. The five people in charge of the inmates were to guard them vigilantly with courage and "a hundred eyes" (311). Inmates who talked would be gagged, and those who tried to run away were to be chained or pilloried. To ensure that this discipline would bring about their conversion to better ways, she recommended that they be held for one or two years and that they be branded when they left the prison so that they could be identified as deserving punishment even more severe if they should be returned to prison. "This prison will be a warning," wrote the nun, "for many lost women to collect themselves and live well, through the fear and horror of this punishment and pain" (314).

The threat of disease justified such a prison, the nun declared, for disease threatened not merely prostitutes and their clients who were single. It threatened the entire society because prostitutes infected married men with "a thousand disgusting and contagious diseases," which these men then passed to their wives (309). Although congenital syphilis had not yet been identified, she and other moral reformers called for stringent measures to "remedy such great evil, devastation, and corruption of the republic" (315). She defended the severity of her proposal, pointing out that in times of epidemics, infected people were walled up within their houses to keep them away from others whom they might infect.

At the same time that Madre Magdalena sent her proposal to Philip III, Cristóbal Pérez de Herrera, the medical inspector for the King's galleys, wrote a similar treatise (319-324). His proposal for a workhouse for delinquent women lacked the severity of the nun's. In contrast to Madre Magdalena, he noted that even though they were bad women, "they will be treated in everything as women, who are of a more delicate nature" (322). They must work, he believed, not only as punishment or to earn their keep in the workhouse, but to learn a livelihood to support themselves after their release. This kind of punishment was better than public humiliation, which only served to confirm them as bad women. In fact, he said, women in Madrid had been given as many as 1,500 lashes without any effect in changing their lives, except that they might die from the whippings.

Women's prisons remained under local jurisdiction in seventeenth-century Spain and varied in their responses to the proposals of Madre Magdalena and Cristóbal Pérez. Regardless of their severity, these prisons did not solve the problem of unenclosed unchaste women. Declining fortunes in this period combined with repeated epidemics to increase concern with the state of public morals, particularly the moral frailty of girls and women. Pedro de León wrote of women who went to the orphanage in Seville, pretending to want to serve God by indoctrinating the young girls there in Christian virtue, but actually intending to teach them to be prostitutes. Seeing one "infernal stepmother" selling a young girl in the street, he intervened and rescued the girl (Part 2, Chap. 25, 191-192). He attributed the sinfulness of these women to their poverty and inability to marry. Prostitutes, too, could be perceived as victims of circumstances, their vulnerability to sin increasing with poverty. Clerics now more often portrayed them as sinners to redeem and correct, rather than as necessary evils.

Growing concern about the sin of prostitution led to a zealous movement in Seville during the early seventeenth century to convert all prostitutes and close the legal brothel. Preachers went to the brothel on Sundays and feast days, presenting prayers and sermons in rituals that attempted to convince prostitutes to convert, even as "scandalous men" made catcalls and faked conversions.[15] Conversion sermons also reached men, such as the brothel *padre* who asked if salvation was possible for him in his "evil profession." A Jesuit, perhaps caught offguard, did not urge him to leave his office, but assured him that he could, indeed, be saved if he guarded "the just and holy ordinances" of the brothel (Pedro de León, Part 1, Chap. 6).

By the end of 1620, preachers and pious laymen had effectively closed the brothel in Seville. One of the *padres* complained to the city council that the brothel had been closed for ten months because the preachers had driven the prostitutes away, and he noted that this was injurious to the city.[16] Closing the brothels did not prevent prostitution; it simply meant that prostitutes now spread disease and disorder throughout the city. Moreover, the chapels, hospitals, churches, and other religious foundations that had been given the rents from the brothel property were losing income on which they depended. He urged the city government to approve new prostitution ordinances that had arrived from Madrid and to forbid further "meddling" by preachers trying to convert prostitutes. The administrator of the girls' orphanage joined the *padre*'s protest, complaining that preachers who converted prostitutes on Mary Magdalen's day then placed these women in his orphanage, where there was neither room nor clothing nor sufficient discipline for them, and where they provided a bad example for his young girls.[17]

Finally in 1621 the city government decided to support the brothel *padres* against the reforming preachers, and it approved new regulations. While placing the usual restrictions on the brothel *padres*, the 1621 ordinances protected their privilege by reducing their number to two and doubling to two *reales* per day the amount they could charge each prostitute.[18] Moreover, the ordinances repeated the prohibition on any other person profiting from prostitution and explicitly prohibited servants of authorities from pimping "since for the most part those who have the said women in the said house of the brothel are servants of authorities, and it is not possible that their masters know of this" (Article 11).

These regulations again required regular medical inspections and added that the doctor should give each prostitute a certificate that she had been examined and found free from disease, but the great emphasis in these ordinances was on enclosing prostitutes in the brothel as a means to enforce order. Article 17 described "scandal," "turbulence," and "great inconveniences that result from the many women who pursue their evil profession night and day." Figuratively placing an unsheathed sword above the brothel door, as Madre Magdalena proposed for her prison, the new ordinances of 1621 made it clear that *padres* who enclosed wandering women preserved their own honor, and that of all men, by ensuring social order.

The debate over legalized prostitution in Seville revealed some basic gender assumptions of this period. On the one hand, pragmatists argued that prostitutes were an essential part of the moral order because men were so lusty that they would commit worse sins without brothels. On the other, moralists argued that women should not be made to serve the sinful desires of men in this way. Both agreed that unenclosed women posed a very real danger; but pragmatists believed that the brothel provided an acceptable form of enclosure, while the moralists did not. Significantly, brothels continued to have male administrators in Spain, although women supervised legal houses of prostitution in other parts of Europe at this time.[19] Moralists as well as pragmatists appeared to believe that social order in Counter-Reformation Spain required women enclosed under male supervision.

Social order, however, requires more than merely passing new ordinances. In fact, repeated legislation to regulate prostitution demonstrates that laws in themselves were not sufficient to establish social order, and neither were punishments. In 1623 Philip IV formally prohibited brothels throughout his kingdom.[20] Prostitutes did not disappear, of course, and neither did concern about unenclosed women. In fact, the distinction between wandering women and those of virtue continued to defy definition despite repeated attempts to do so by means of legislation. In 1639, for example, the city council of Seville approved for the fourth time regulations prohibiting women from going about with their faces covered.[21] In language similar to a proverb that warns against masked women, the 1639 law noted the danger of anonymous females and required all women, regardless of class or status, to allow their faces to be seen and recognized, under penalty of a fine of 10,000 *maravedís* for a first offense and 20,000 *maravedís* plus exile for a second offense. The law also warned that no one could use the privilege or status of her husband to circumvent its requirements. All women, not simply those required to identify themselves as prostitutes, were thus seen as dangerous and potential Jezebels.

Women kept slipping through these regulations, however, and countless complaints about their wandering reached the city council. A decade after passing the 1621 prostitution ordinances, city officials in Seville wrote to the King of their concern about the multiplication of prostitutes outside the brothel, a "bad example," they wrote, for "the daughters of the city."[22] Seven years later the administrator of the girls' orphanage complained that "many women of bad life who are called prostitutes" were using young girls, whom they called their daughters or nieces, to run after people for "their evil business."[23] Finally, in 1675, a royal official for Seville wrote to the Crown about the city's need for a prison for "lost and scandalous women."[24] The Queen Regent agreed with his plan to use for the prison the royal mint that had fallen into disuse. Symbolically, perhaps, incorrigible women could be stamped into conformity here where lumps of metal had formerly been stamped into coins of the kingdom.

Clearly the 1623 royal prohibition on prostitution had neither rid Counter-Reformation Spain of prostitutes, nor dismantled the brothel, the Magdalen house, or the prison for women. In Madrid the infamous Galera de Santa Isabel continued, as did Las Recogidas, a Magdalen house that had grown out of a Franciscan convent. Habitual female criminals went to the former, while women who offended the moral order went to the latter. Las Recogidas, in fact, received not only former prostitutes, but also women accused of adultery, public sins, and family rebellion, sometimes placed in the institution for "correction" by husbands, fathers, or other family members (Pérez Baltasar 51-52). The regulations adopted in 1692 for Las Recogidas seemed identical to those for other convents, except that a chapter on discipline called for prison terms to correct those residents of the institution found guilty of "dishonesty," scandal, aggression, false testimony, and theft (Pérez Baltasar 57-66). The Prelate (*Prelada*) would visit these women in prison to help them "correct themselves." She would also welcome them back to their Magdalen house when they demonstrated true penitence.

Whether they became inmates of brothels, Magdalen houses, or prisons, it seems very likely that the women selling their sexual services in Counter-Reformation Spain chose to do so not out of female perversity, but out of necessity. The economic decline that struck the kingdom in the seventeenth century affected most directly abandoned wives, daughters, and single mothers. Not all of these women became prostitutes, of course, for charitable donors tried to provide for those females who lacked husband or father to protect their chastity. Once they lost their chaste status, however, they became Magdalens and Jezebels.

Notes

1. For a sixteenth-century paraphrase of this traditional view of St. Augustine, see Francisco Farfan, *Tres libros* 730.

2. *Novísima Recopilación* Ley I, Título XXVII, Libro XII, quoted in Pérez Baltasar 14.

3. Ioannis Gutiérrez, *Praxis criminalis civilis et canonica in librum octanum nouae Recopilationis Regiae* (LVGDVNI: Sumptibus Lavrentii Anisson, 1660) 336-338; also see *Las Siete Partidas*, Partida 7, Título XXII, Leyes I and II, quoted in Pérez Baltasar 13.

4. Mary Douglas discusses the danger of anomalous people and the necessity of giving them definable boundaries in *Purity and Danger: An Analysis of Concepts of Pollution and Taboo*; see especially 95-102. Also see Erving Goffman, *Interaction Ritual: Essays on Face-to-Face Behavior* 47-49.

5. The ordinances regulating prostitution in Seville in 1570 are in *Tractatus varii, et collectanea*, in the British Museum, Egerton, 1873, fols. 155-156. These are also included in Juan de Mariana, "Tratado contra los juegos públicos," Vol. 30, 447-449.

6. Archivo Municipal de Sevilla (hereafter AMS), Sección 3, Escribanías de Cabildo, Tomo 11, Número 62.

7. Pedro de León, Part 1, Chap. 4, fols. 10-14, and Chap. 6, fol. 16; see also AMS, Siglo XVI, Sección 3, Escribanías de Cabildo, Tomo 11, Número 63, and Tomo 12, Número 44; and AMS, Sección Especial, Papeles del Sr. Conde de Aguila, Tomo 7 en folio, Número 20.

8. Morgado 365; AMS, Sección Especial, Papeles del Sr. Conde de Aguila, Tomo 32 en folio, Número 1.

9. Martínez de Mata 129. See also AMS, Papeles Importantes, Siglo XVI, Tomo 9, Número 1.

10. Pacheco n. pag. See Goffman 21-22, for a broader discussion of rituals of penance.

11. AMS, Sección 3, Escribanías de Cabildo, Tomo 14, Número 7.

12. AMS, Papeles Importantes, Siglo XVI, Tomo 9, Número 1.

13. See also Pérez Baltasar, who places Madre Magdalena's proposals in a larger context of correctional institutions for women.

14. See Michel Foucault, but note that several scholars have criticized his argument that public bodily punishments changed so quickly into private, discipline-imposing incarcerations. For an example, see Pieter Spierenburg, ed., *The Emergence of Carceral Institutions: Prisons, Galleys and Lunatic Asylums, 1550-1900*. Inquisition punishments during the Counter-Reformation, which included both public chastisement and private imprisonment, may also be seen as bridging the gap that Foucault considered a leap into modernism.

15. AMS, Sección Especial, Papeles del Sr. Conde de Aguila, Tomo 7 en folio, Número 20.

16. AMS, Sección 4, Escribanías de Cabildo, Tomo 22, Números 9-11. For evidence that religious groups benefited from the income of the brothels, see Archivo de la Diputación de la Provincia de Sevilla, Libros de Protocolos del Amor de Dios, Leg. 49, Expd. 2; also see the discussion in Perry, "Deviant Insiders" 145.

17. AMS, Sección 4, Escribanías de Cabildo, Tomo 22, Número 12.

18. The 1621 ordinances for Seville are in AMS, Sección 4, Escribanías de Cabildo, Tomo 22, Número 14.

19. For an example in southern France, see Rossiaud 289-325.

20. Pérez Baltasar 14; AMS, Nueva Recopilación, Ley 7, Título 26, Libro 12.

21. AMS, Sección 4, Escribanías de Cabildo, Tomo 29, Número 18.

22. AMS, Papeles Importantes, Siglo XVII, Tomo 5, Número 21.

23. AMS, Sección 4, Escribanías de Cabildo, Tomo 24, Número 26. For concerns in Valencia about procuresses who recruited girls and women into prostitution, see Graullera 109-119.

24. Archivo Histórico Nacional, Consejos, Leg. 7185.

Works Cited

Archivo de la Diputación de la Provincia de Sevilla, Libros de Protocolos del Amor de Dios, Leg. 49, Expd. 2.

Archivo Histórico Nacional (AHN). Consejos, Legajo 7185. *Documentos para la historia de Sevilla*. Ed. Antonio Domínguez Ortiz. Biblioteca Nacional 5-38856.

Archivo Municipal de Sevilla. Sección Especial, Nueva Recopilación.

———. Sección Especial, Papeles del Sr. Conde de Aguila. Tomo 7 en folio, Número 20; Tomo 32 en folio, Número 1.

_____. Papeles Importantes. Siglo XVI, Tomo 9, Número 1.

_____. Siglo XVI. Sección 3. Escribanías de Cabildo. Tomo 11, Números 62, 63; Tomo 12, Número 44; Tomo 14, Número 7.

_____. Papeles Importantes. Siglo XVII, Tomo 5, Número 21.

_____. Siglo XVII. Sección 4. Escribanías de Cabildo. Tomo 22, Números 9-14; Tomo 24, Número 26; Tomo 29, Número 18.

Caffarena, Angel. *Apuntes para la historia de las mancebías de Málaga.* Málaga: Juan Such, 1968.

Carboneres, Manuel. *Picaronas y alcahuetes, ó la mancebía de Valencia.* Valencia: El Mercantil, 1876.

Cerda, Juan de la. *Vida política de todos los estados de mugeres: en el qual se dan muy provechosos y christianos documentos y avisos, para criarse y conservarse devidamente las mugeres en sus estados.* Alcalá de Henares: Juan Gracián, 1599.

Douglas, Mary. *Purity and Danger: An Analysis of Concepts of Pollution and Taboo.* New York and Washington: Frederick A. Praeger, 1966.

Espinosa, Juan de. *Diálogo en laude de las mujeres.* 1580. Ed. Angela González Simón. Madrid: Consejo Superior de Investigaciones Científicas, 1946.

Farfan, Francisco. *Tres libros contra el peccado de la simple fornicacion; donde se averigua, que la torpeza entre solteros es peccado mortal, segun ley divina, natural, y humana; y se responde a los engaños de los que dizen que no es peccado.* Salamanca: n. p., 1585.

_____. *Regimiento de castos: Y remedio de torpes. Donde se ponen XVIII remedios contra el pecado de la torpeza: Y por otras tantas vías se exhorta el cristiano al amor de la castidad.* Salamanca: Cornelio Bonardo, 1590.

Foucault, Michel. *Discipline and Punish: The Birth of the Prison.* Trans. Alan Sheridan. New York: Pantheon, 1977.

Galán Sánchez, Angel, and María Teresa López Beltrán. "El 'status' teórico de las prostitutas del reino de Granada en la primera mitad del siglo XVI (las ordenanzas de 1538)." *Las mujeres en las ciudades medievales.* Ed. Cristina Segura. Madrid: Univ. Autónoma de Madrid, 1984.

Garrison, Fielding R. "An Epitome of the History of Spanish Medicine." *Bulletin of the New York Academy of Medicine* 7.8 (1928): 589-634.

Goffman, Erving. *Interaction Ritual: Essays on Face-to-Face Behavior.* Garden City, NY: Doubleday, 1967.

Granjel, Luis S. *La medicina española renacentista.* Salamanca: Ediciones Univ. de Salamanca, 1980.

Graullera, Vicente. "Mujer, amor y moralidad en la Valencia de los siglos XVI y XVII." *Amours légitimes, amours illégitimes en Espagne (XVI-XVII siècles).* Ed. Augustin Redondo. Paris: Publications de la Sorbonne, 1985. 109-119.

Gutiérrez, Ioannis. *Praxis criminalis civilis et canonica in librum octanum nouae Recopilationis Regiae.* LVGDVNI: Sumptibus Lavrentii Anisson, 1660.

Hepworth, Mike, and Bryan S. Turner. *Confession: Studies in Deviance and Religion.* London: Routledge & Kegan Paul, 1982.

León, Pedro de. *Compendio de algunas experiencias en los ministerios de que vsa la Compa de IESVS con q practicamente se muestra con algunos acaecimientos y documentos el buen acierto en ellos.* Granada: n. p., 1619.

Llorden, P. Andrés. *Apuntes históricos de los conventos sevillanos de religiosas agustinas.* El Escorial: Imprenta del Monasterio, 1944.

Magdalena de San Gerónimo, Madre. *Razón, y forma de la galera y casa Real, que el Rey nuestro señor manda hazer en estos Reynos, para castigo de las mugeres vagrantes, ladronas, alcahuetas y otras semejantes.* Valladolid: Francisco Fernández de Córdova, 1608. Rpt. in *Apuntes para una biblioteca de escritoras españolas desde el año 1401 al 1833.* Ed. Manuel Serrano y Sanz. Madrid: Sucesores de Rivadeneyra, 1903-1905. 304-316.

Mariana, Juan de. "Tratado contra los juegos públicos." *Biblioteca de Autores Españoles.* Vol. 30. Madrid: M. Rivadeneyra, 1855.

Martínez de Mata, Francisco. *Memoriales y discursos de Francisco Martínez de Mata.* Ed. Gonzalo Anes Alvarez. Madrid: Moneda y Crédito, 1971.

Morgado, Alonso. *Historia de Sevilla.* Sevilla: Andrea Pescioni y Juan de León, 1587.

Muriel, Josefina. *Los recogimientos de mujeres.* México: UNAM Instituto de Investigaciones Históricas, 1974.

Ordenanzas de Sevilla. Sevilla: Diego Hurtado de Mendoza, 1631.

Pacheco, Francisco. *Libro de descripción de verdaderos retratos de ilustres y memorables varones.* Seville: Ayuntamiento, 1599.

Pérez Baltasar, María Dolores. *Mujeres marginadas: Las casas de recogidas en Madrid.* Madrid: Gráficas Lormo, 1984.

Pérez de Herrera, Cristóbal. *Discurso de la reclusión y castigo de las mugeres vagabundas y delinquentes destos reynos.* Madrid: Luis Sánchez, 1608. Rpt. in *Apuntes para una biblioteca de escritoras españolas desde el año 1401 al 1833.* Ed. Manuel Serrano y Sanz. Madrid: Sucesores de Rivadeneyra, 1903-1905. 319-324.

Perry, Mary Elizabeth. "Deviant Insiders: Legalized Prostitutes and a Consciousness of Women in Early Modern Seville." *Comparative Studies in Society and History* 27.1 (1985): 138-158.

————. *Gender and Disorder in Early Modern Seville.* Princeton: Princeton Univ. Press, 1990.

Puig, Angelina, and Nuria Tuset. "La prostitución en Mallorca (s. XVI): El Estado un alcahuete?" *Ordenamiento jurídico y realidad social de las mujeres.* Ed. María Carmen García-Nieto. Madrid: Univ. Autónoma de Madrid, 1986.

Rahner, Hugo, S. J. *Saint Ignatius Loyola: Letters to Women.* Edinburgh: Nelson, 1960.

Rico-Avello, Carlos. *Vida y milagros de un pícaro médico del siglo XVI: Biografía del bachiller Juan Méndez Nieto.* Madrid: Cultura Hispánica, 1974.

Rossiaud, Jacques. "Prostitution, jeunesse et société dans les villes du sud-est au XV siècle." *Annales, E.S.C.* 31.2 (1976): 289-325.

Spierenburg, Pieter, ed. *The Emergence of Carceral Institutions: Prisons, Galleys and Lunatic Asylums, 1550-1900.* Rotterdam: Erasmus Univ., 1984.

Tractatus varii, et collectanea. British Museum, Egerton, 1873.

◆ Chapter 7

La bella malmaridada
Lessons for the Good Wife

Anne J. Cruz

May God give pleasure to the unhappily married woman, for she who is happily married has no need of it.

A la mal casada, déla Dios placer, la bien casada no lo ha menester.

—Correas, 1627

Cultured poetry has traditionally afforded contemporary society with paradigmatic attitudes toward relations between the sexes, mainly from the viewpoint of the male poet. From the medieval courtly love tradition to the sixteenth- and seventeenth-century Golden Age sonnets, the conventional poetic voice has celebrated woman's beauty, rejoiced in her love, or lamented her absence. Hardly, if ever, do these poems grant women a voice with which to register their own emotions. Until very recently, literary history thus inferred the status of high culture to the poetry of men, and limited female expression to the less-respected genre of "popular" poetry.[1]

Yet cultured and popular poetry did not exist in total isolation from one another; by the sixteenth century, popular poetry had been accepted by all levels of society. This interrelationship has given rise to a number of studies that point to the difficulties in attributing exact definitions to poetic styles. Margit Frenk studies the different periods of artistic valorization of popular poetry by court poets, calling their renovation "popularizing" rather than popular (*Entre folklore* 29-53). Américo Castro, noting the ballad's renewed popularity during this period, attributes this to what he terms the "rustification" of society—the growing significance of unlettered Christians in positions of power (186). Michael Nerlich, in an intelligent essay that takes issue with Ramón Menéndez Pidal's lucubrations on the distinctions between the popular and the traditional, explains that "if intellectuals . . . began to return to cultural forms then considered vulgar, it is because the society of that day had reached a state of development in which intellectual curiosity was directed toward everything unknown, alien, foreign, and exotic" (66).

What none of these critics takes into account, however—despite Nerlich's surprisingly apt choice of terms—is that popular poetry overwhelmingly voiced female concerns, while cultured poetry articulated male interests. It is with this gender distinction in mind that I consider the theme of the beautiful, unhappy wife—*la bella malmaridada*—unique in its development within both the popular and cultured traditions.[2] As I hope to show, the durability of the topic and increasingly harsh treatment of the unhappily married woman not only mirrored stricter societal expectations of women during this period but informed them, as the number of variants expanded from the Middle Ages to the Renaissance.

Believed by most critics to have expanded from its primitive beginnings in Romanic Maysongs to the French courtly *chansons*, the theme appeared in early Hispanic versions as part of the traditional lyrics voiced by women.[3] The theme, then, gains social significance because of its range of dissemination and the message it conveys: it emphasizes women's roles in medieval and early modern cultures as dependent primarily upon a husband, with little regard to their personal happiness or desires.

Nonetheless, the various representations of women in both popular and cultured lyrics underwent many transformations and prescribed differing social codes for them. These codes are especially notable in the diverse poetic forms of *la bella malmaridada's* lament—from its first lyric forms, to the popular ballads and cultured glosses, and finally, to the play of the same title by Lope de Vega—all of which reveal the increasing strictures placed upon women in Counter-Reformation Spain.

In its complex development, the ballad of *la bella malmaridada* exemplifies certain issues of origin and gender common to cultured and popular lyrics. While some critics have rejected the possibility of female authorship, others have attributed to women the cultured and traditional lyrics sung in the female voice.[4] Ria Lemaire has recently challenged the traditional view that cultured love lyrics were composed solely by male troubadours, positing instead that "women's songs" in general may have originated during the course of such women's occupations as spinning (87-114). To her, it is only good sense to attribute to a woman composer the poems' understanding of female psychology, and their freshness, spontaneity, and naturalness. Mary Gaylord Randel, in pointing to the traditional lyric's female persona, wishes not to identify a feminine "reality" behind it, but to posit a set of shared grammatical and rhetorical characteristics (115-124).

Whether the female persona of traditional oral poetry represents a poetic fiction, a "myth of female desire," as Gaylord Randel ascertains (124), and not a feminine reality, we must nevertheless attempt to understand how this poetry and its apparent opposite, the cultured lyric, functioned within (and through) the various levels of society. Thus, in her effort to recreate an accurate portrayal of women from the medieval epic and lyric poetry, Lucy Sponsler argues that the popular lyric offers a more "realistic" picture than the cultured courtly love poetry:

> [T]he erudite lyric not only centers totally on woman, but almost always views her in one fixed social position. Woman is now superior to man. . . . Even her physical appearance, stressed to a much greater extent than in epic or popular lyric, is regulated by convention. Now essential are aristocratic bearing, refined elegance, pristine, goddesslike beauty, courtly manners and learning. (120)

Sponsler points out that the cultured lyric's portrayal of women—its stress on an unvarying, stereotypical physical beauty—forms part of a literary representation in all likelihood historically inauthentic and, in any case, limited to the small minority of noble ladies, who are presented as objects of desire (46). The following poem by Villasandino, for example, lists many of the conventional feminine attributes admired through-

out the European courtly love tradition, such as the lady's elegant spirit (*donoso brío*) and crystalline hands (*manos de cristal*):

> God made you delicate,
>
> decorous, well-bred,
>
> your complexion lighter hued
>
> than the rose of a rose garden. (A. Alonso 82)[5]

To Sponsler, even when the lyric assumes the female voice,
the representation of women seems to be less the "true" depiction of experience than the insistence upon a Hispanic morality,
as in the following *albada* that clearly exalts married love:

> Kiss me and hold me,
>
> my husband,
>
> and in the morning I'll give you
>
> a clean garment. (A. Alonso 61)[6]

In contrast with the lady's cultivated charms of the courtly
lyric, popular poetry sings of the earthy attractions of peasant
girls:

> I, my mother, I am
>
> the flower of the village, I am.
>
> My mother will send me
>
> to sell bread in the village;
>
> Who saw me would say:
>
> "What a good-looking baker!"
>
> Good-looking was I,
>
> the flower of the village, I am.
>
> (Frenk, *Lírica* 117-118)[7]

While the female poetic voice informs the poem with a sense of
feminine selfhood reveling in her natural beauty, and suggests
that it was meant to be sung by a young girl, we do not know if
a real peasant girl composed the lyric, or whether its apparent
exaltation of peasant beauty was shared by the singer, since the
trade of *panadera* (baker) connotes a loose woman.[8] Similarly, the
medieval *morena* folk songs in which the female protagonists la-

ment their dark skin cannot be taken as reflections of real concern by their singers, but rather, evince the social stigma attached to dark women.[9]

Yet, what should be considered in the cultured poems as well as in the popular lyric is not whether the woman's depiction is realistic, but that the poetry establishes certain values for her—indeed, the poems convey certain messages to women, as well as about them. Sponsler notes that the cultured lyric (and, I would add, traditional poetry) responds to specifically Hispanic situations—which is seen in its treatment of topics such as rape and the restoration of honor—and, she observes, expresses a Christian view of Northern Spain (121). Despite their differences, the representation of women in both cultured and popular poetry addresses the social expectations of Spanish women in the countryside and at court.

The feudal economy required and encouraged the active involvement of women from both social classes: peasant women labored at home and in the field, while noble ladies held important positions as landowners and estate managers (Kelly-Gadol 137-164). The participation of women in society resulted in a poetry that spoke directly to women's concerns, one sensitive to the biological and social rhythms of female life—whether peasant or propertied—but most important, one that prescribed particular social attitudes, not only for women, but also for men. Although we cannot rely on this poetry to define the actual living conditions of medieval women, we agree with Sponsler that the poetry charts significant changes in women's social status from the eleventh through the fifteenth centuries. She points out that while the most radical change in women's roles may be seen in the learned lyric poetry, women in general remained dependent upon men:

> All genres reveal an elevated interest in woman's femininity, but . . . it is evident that among people of the more rustic society and of the middle classes woman remained basically subordinated to man. Probably in matters other than love this was also the case among the aristocracy as well. (121)

During the Counter-Reformation, and as their roles diminished outside the family structure, women's subservience was to manifest itself in literature by the increased silence, not only of female writers, but of their poetic voice. Heavily influenced by the novel Italianate style, both cultured and popular poetry adopted a masculine persona, converting the woman into a fetishized object of male desire. The female persona, whose own "voice of desire" imbued much medieval poetry with a feminine presence—however rhetorical or restricted—is thus voiced over by the male author who speaks through the poem to the audience to express his ideology.

Firmly entrenched in the collective memory of the people, however, popular lyrics and ballads continued to offer a rich source of themes to Golden Age writers, whose own new ballads (*romances nuevos*), lyrics, and plays documented the popular tradition. The revalorization of popular culture occurred at a time when Hispanic society itself was changing rapidly from a feudal, land-oriented economy to an urban population with a burgeoning middle class.[10] One significant outcome of such a change was the final disappearance of the earliest popular lyrics precisely due to their absorption by cultured verse.[11] The absorption of popular poetry into different genres thus corresponds to transformations in perceptions of literature and its social function; the diverse poetic voices are, as a result, accorded roles within the genres that reflect these perceptions.

Like the feminine voice of the lyric, the poetic persona of the ballad also suffers a transformation when the ballad is appropriated and converted into drama in the Golden Age.[12] Lope de Vega's plays testify to his talent for appropriating other literary and popular sources (Bradbury; D'Antuono). While *Peribáñez* and *El caballero de Olmedo* are perhaps the most famous of his plays to utilize traditional poetry, Lope had already expanded upon the popular theme of *La bella malmaridada* in an early play of the same name, written in 1596.

As we have seen, the play's theme of the unhappily married woman is conventional in both the European oral and written traditions, from the medieval French *chanson de la malmariée*, to the Italian *novella*, and the Hispanic popular lyrics. Indeed, the various poetic forms—*cuartetas*, refrains, ballads, and glosses—by which the theme was transmitted in Spain attest to its popularity: it has been glossed and cited with more frequency than any other poem, a fact that speaks eloquently to the situation of Hispanic married women.[13]

Gil Vicente mentions the ballad of La bella malmaridada in several of his works after 1515. Stating that its first lines were already well known in Portugal as a refrain at the beginning of the sixteenth century, he is among the first to make use of the second line, "de las más lindas que vi," in one of his poems.[14] In Spain, multiple variants of the ballad's first lines appear as cantares from at least the beginning of the sixteenth century:

> Beautiful, unhappy wife,
> the most beautiful I've seen,
> if you're going to take a lover,
> Love, don't ignore me.[15]

The poem in ballad form is first collected in Juan de Molina's Cancionero of 1527. This version is also the shortest: twenty lines long, it comprises an omniscient narrator, the female protagonist, and a male persona who offers himself as lover to the beautiful young wife, warning her of her husband's infidelities and of his threats against her. The wife begs him to take her with him, and the ballad ends when the husband returns to find them planning her escape:

> "Beautiful, unhappy wife
> the most beautiful I've seen
> I see you so sad and angry
> tell me the truth.
> If you are to take a lover
> don't abandon me for another,
> as your husband, my lady
> with other women I've seen
> kissing and gallivanting;
> he speaks poorly of you,
> he swore time and again
> that he would do you harm."

At this, the lady spoke,
she spoke, and said this:
"Take me, oh, knight,
take me from here.
Wherever you may go
I'd know to serve you well."
While they were thus engaged,
Lo, the husband appeared. (ll. 1-20)[16]

A much longer ballad of fifty-four lines appeared in Lorenzo de Sepúlveda's *Romances nuevamente sacados de historias antiguas de las crónicas de España*, published in Antwerp in 1551.[17] Basing himself on its length and its more complete narrative, Donald McGrady considers Sepúlveda's version the "definitive" one (Lope 21; McGrady 83-101). However, McGrady overlooks the fundamental fact that no one variant can ever be definitive since, in the felicitous words of Ramón Menéndez Pidal, traditional poetry "lives on in its variations" ("vive en variantes"). Rather, the additions to the ballad, which include the husband's accusation, the wife's admission of adultery, her wish that the husband punish her instead of the lover, and the final epitaph as appropriate ending for her transgression, reveal that Sepúlveda either reconstructed or recorded the longer ending based on contemporary aesthetic and moral valorizations (*Teoría general* 99-109). In effect, from its lighthearted beginnings in the thirteenth-century French *chansons*, the theme grows increasingly darker in the later Hispanic ballads, culminating in the Sepúlveda version:

"What are you doing, evil traitor?
Today you shall die!"
"Why, my lord, why?
I've never deserved this:
I've never kissed a man,
but one has kissed me.
The punishment he deserved,
my lord, give unto me:

with your horsewhips,
my lord, whip me.
With golden towropes
hang me alive;
in the orange grove
bury me alive.
In a golden sepulchre
sculpted in ivory
carve my epitaph,
my lord, saying this:
'Here lies the flower of all flowers,
here she died for love:
whoever dies for love
should be buried here.'
Wretched, I did as much,
I dishonored myself for love."[18]

Given the number of variants, it is impossible to determine which poetic form—ballad or lyric—appeared first, but as they continued to exist alongside the ballad versions, the various *cantares* and refrains functioned as lyrical indices to the longer narratives, and contributed to the creation of an atmosphere receptive to them (*Teoría general* 123-124). There are, however, significant differences between the *cantar* and the Molina and Sepúlveda ballads. In the ballads, the male persona is quick to mention the wife's emotional reaction to the husband, pressing her for a confession ("I see you so sad, so angry / come, tell me the truth" ["véote tan triste, enojada, / la verdad dila tú a mí"]). The *cantar* eliminates the third and fourth lines of the ballads, which bring the wife's actions into relief. By further limiting the poetic voice to that of the male, the *cantar* disallows any response by the wife to her predicament. Instead, it expresses a conditional situation that focuses the audience's attention on the wife's possible choice of action rather than on its cause, and underscores the rivalry between men ("if you're to take a lover / my love, don't abandon me for another" ["si habéis de tomar amores, / vida, por otro no dejéis a mí"]). Given the fact that the male viewpoint predominates, the audience remains fixated on the woman's seductive beauty and supposed free spirit, making no effort to understand her needs or the desire to avenge her husband's actions.

As we have seen, the ballad's male persona emphasizes the wife's emotions at the onset, and while he questions her regarding her true feelings, he confirms in graphic detail what she has probably suspected about her husband all along: "Your husband, my lady, / I saw with other women, / kissing and gallivanting, / he speaks poorly of you" ("que a tu marido, señora, / con otras dueñas lo vi, / besando y retozando, / mucho mal dice de ti"). Unlike the *cantar*, the ballad gives the wife a voice with which to express her fears. In the Molina ballad, the wife is depicted less as a temptress than as a frightened, battered woman. She promises to behave like a good wife to the lover if he, in return, will protect her from her husband. Despite the wife's resolve to flee with him, it is the lover who ultimately seduces the wife by convincing her of the husband's womanizing and repeating the latter's threats. Thus, although adultery was punishable by death according to Spanish law, the ballad takes an essentially sympathetic view of the woman. The impossible condition in which she finds herself—the wife must either remain with her cruel husband, or risk death by her unlawful behavior—is at the heart of the drama narrated in this version. That its truncated ending fails to expose the consequences that may befall the woman only heightens the Molina ballad's pathos, intensifying the audience's response by leaving the final resolution to the imagination.

In contrast, the Sepúlveda ballad renders a full account, not only of the wife's plea to the lover, but of her admission of guilt. While the Molina ballad briefly mentions the wife's offer to "bien servir" in return for the lover's protection, the Sepúlveda version dwells on the sensual aspects of her service:

> "I'd make up the bed nicely
> in which we would sleep.
> I'll cook you a good meal

for such a noble knight,
of chickens and capons
and a thousand other
things." (ll. 19-24)[19]

The details of the wife's expertise in bed and in the kitchen provide a more tempting offer to the lover and significantly alter her
image from hapless victim to that of a seductress similar to the
one offered in the *cantar*. The most damaging testimony of her
wrongdoing, however, is the wife's own admission of having
committed adultery, all the while weakly defending her virtue
("I never kissed a man / but one kissed me" ["nunca besé a hombre / mas hombre besó a mí"]). In a supreme gesture of forgiveness and repentance, she asks that her accomplice not be punished, but that she suffer in his stead, elaborating fully on the
forms of punishment she is willing to endure, ranging from being horsewhipped to being buried alive. To confirm without any
doubt that the wife will surely be murdered by the husband, the
Sepúlveda version has her read her own epitaph, which not
only states the reason for her death, but also serves as warning
to other would-be lovers:

"Here lies the flower of all flowers,
here she died for love;
whoever dies for love
should be buried here." (ll. 49-52)[20]

Despite the apparent courtly love style of the epitaph, its message is clear to all: "*amores*" should not be taken to mean *fin'a-
mors*, but rather an adulterous relation contravening law and religion.[21] Briefly hovering between the margins of the cultured
and the popular, the ballad returns firmly to its traditional roots
in its insistence upon the wife's guilt and her punishment. The
Sepúlveda version thus ends in a confirmation of the wife's
criminal and immoral behavior by restating her transgression:
"Wretched, I did as much, / I dishonored myself for love" ("Que
así hice yo, mezquina, / que por amores me perdí"). Regardless
of the historical accuracy of such a penalty, the wife's punishment for her crime serves as a normative measure for all

women.[22] In reinforcing the male-defined code of honor, her death ensures the triumph of traditional Hispanic values over those of the courtly love tradition.

It is important to note, however, that the cultured glosses on the *bella malmaridada* theme, unlike the Sepúlveda ballad, either play upon the desires of the woman and the poet, or defend the woman's position as one due to her extreme beauty. In the broadsheet gloss by Quesada, the poet, observing the *malmari-dada*'s beauty, informs her of her husband's philandering, and begs her to love him instead:

> Don't live so piteously
> nor suffer such torment
> don't be the cause of my death
> let me at least enjoy
> your sweet shyness
> since I long for your favors
> let me enjoy you
> as remedy to my pains
> if you are to take other lovers
> love, don't abandon me. (Chapbook version)[23]

In the 1554 gloss by Juan de Coloma, the musician-poet blames nature for having created such a perfect creature, whom nobody deserves:

> And so the husband's not to blame
> for having married unhappily.
> It's nature's fault
> For having fashioned you so
> That no one's worthy of you. (*Cancionero general* 509)[24]

With these different poetic versions of *La bella malmaridada* as backdrop, Lope de Vega appropriates the theme in his play of 1596. He takes his material more from the cultured glosses than from the ballads, as he has the presumptive lover Cipión gloss the *cantar* after seeing Lisbella for the first time:

If to be unhappily married
God made you so beautiful,
it's true then that you're
the beautiful, unhappy wife.
On seeing you, I gave you my soul,
my freedom, and my faith,
as you're from your head to your toe,
among the most beautiful I've seen.
Your husband mistreats you;
you need to be cherished:
and here you shall be,
by a soul of gold and silver.
I'm good among the very best
rich in noble blood and ancestry,
who could serve you well
if you're to take a lover.
I don't wish to convince you
to stop being who you are,
but if you wish to love,
don't leave me for another. (ll. 495-514)[25]

Cipión, a Spanish count, requests that Lisbella remain "quien es" (her own person), a term that discloses her social status as a worthy recipient of his own noble attentions. The play's subtitle, *La cortesana* (*The Courtesan*), contrasts the literal meaning of the epithet—a noble lady residing at court—with its homologue, the courtesan or high-class prostitute. Given her noble qualities, Lisbella conforms to the first meaning of the title. Her brother is later to comment on her courtly demeanor: "treat me courteously / since you yourself are so courteous" ("Trátame a lo cortesano / pues eres tan cortesana" [ll. 2308-2310]). From the beginning, then, Lisbella is pitted against her husband Leonardo's current mistress, the courtesan Casandra. In the first act, Lisbella, like Casandra disguised in the traditional cloak of a pros-

titute, goes out at night looking for Leonardo. While his friend
Teodoro courts Casandra behind his back, Leonardo—believing
that Lisbella is home praying for him ("I swear to you she's so
honorable / that at these hours / she's probably praying for me,
and has / her soul locked with a key" ["Que os juro que es tan
honrada / que a estas horas estará / rezando por mí, y tendrá /
con llave el alma guardada" ll. 371-374])—mistakes her for a
prostitute, and complains to her of his tiresome marriage:

> (Leonardo): I don't hate my wife,
> but seeing her always there
> tires me terribly.
> (Lisbella): Woe is me!
> You must not love her.
> (Leonardo): Yes, I do. But to find
> a wife at dawn,
> at noon a wife,
> a wife also at dinner,
> and afterwards in bed,
> and at all hours a wife,
> and to always have to protect
> my family and my honor,
> drives me crazy, by God! (ll. 342-355)[26]

Lisbella's apparent strength of character in risking her honor by
going out alone, at night, dressed as a prostitute, reveals instead
the desperate actions of a disconsolate woman. By comparing
the women's reactions to men's amorous attentions, the play reinforces the only two roles socially allowed to sexually active
women: the good wife and the whore. Rather than imitate Casandra's duplicitous behavior, Lisbella will remain faithful to
her husband, acknowledging that she has far more to lose than
he by taking revenge:

> I could take revenge upon you
> but I am honorable, you cur,

and such a mistake would be far worse
for me than for you. (ll. 467-470)[27]

Lisbella's love for Leonardo and her sense of honor are thus juxtaposed to Casandra's self-interested inconstancy. As an unhappily married woman, Lisbella can do little more than lament her
condition.

But the play encompasses more than the theme of the *malmaridada*.[28] It not only prescribes the actions of a noble woman, but
comments on the behavior of married men. Lope isolates in the
husband a vice that had become a particular target for Counter-
Reformation moralists: Leonardo returns to Lisbella in the third
act, but he is now a compulsive gambler. After he gambles away
her jewelry, she complains that this vice is worse than his philandering:

> And if with gambling you exchange
> such an unjust love,
> it's better that you return,
> Leonardo, to your past pleasures.
> Since, although gambling may seem
> less damaging than love,
> I believe it a far lesser evil
> that a man be blinded by love. (ll. 2170-2177)[29]

Thus, while Cipión's pursuit of Lisbella and Leonardo's false accusations are constants throughout the play, the plot is less a
tragic story of a potentially unfaithful wife than a quasi-bour-
geois family drama. In effect, the play's depiction of the family
can be compared to the bourgeois family structure developing
throughout most of Europe, as it incorporates the same value
system of social and financial interests. The values promulgated
by such influential treatises as Luis Vives's *Instrucción de la mujer
cristiana* and Luis de León's *La perfecta casada* no doubt accelerated the formation of bourgeois family values that entailed a
conflict between the preservation of capital and the value of individual choice (Poster 168). In Spain specifically, the edicts of

the Counter-Reformation stressed the male patriarchal role as head of family, and the maintenance of the wife's moral and economic subservience. Antonio de Guevara defines the respective roles of husband and wife:

> The husband's office is to accumulate finances, and the wife's is protect them. The husband's office is to earn a living out of doors, and the wife's to keep house. The husband's office is to earn money, and the wife's, not to misspend.[30]

In the play, Leonardo's obsessive gambling displaces his illicit passion for Casandra. Although betting as a mode of recreation was not considered a mortal sin, such Tridentine moralists as Fray Pedro de Covarrubias and Fray Francisco de Alcocer decried the many ills brought about by excessive betting. Realizing the disruptive effects gambling may have on the family, Alcocer notes that

> many times, cardsharpers and gamblers do not have money with which to gamble, and use jewelry and other valuables, which may belong to their poor wives, and they gamble everything or place partial bets on these valuables. (165)[31]

He concludes that those who bet on valuables are required to return them to their rightful owner.

The play thus intersects the wife's moral dilemma with the husband's vice. Because of his heavy gambling, Leonardo endangers the family economy: if in the first and second acts Lisbella is concerned with Leonardo's infidelity, in the third act she is more preoccupied with their precarious financial status. And, unlike the female persona in the *cantar* and the ballads, Lisbella is not only a wife, but a mother, and is doubly vulnerable through her children, since Leonardo threatens to send them away as punishment for her purported adultery. Again, this crucial difference opposes the play's courtly love elements with emerging bourgeois interests. As historian Mark Poster has noted, the increasing social pressures of the family imposed extensive psychological and moral strictures on the women:

> Children were re-evaluated by the bourgeoisie, becoming

important beings for the parents. . . . (Women) were encouraged to create a bond between themselves and the children so deep that the child's inner life could be shaped to moral perfection. Thus for a large part of their lives bourgeois women were confined to the home as never before; they were to nurture their children, maintain the home, and cater to their husbands, leaving aside the great transformations of politics and economics going on around them. (170)

After a miraculous intercession blocking Lisbella's attempted murder by Leonardo, and a practical joke on Cipión who, believing Lisbella had acceded to his advances, is tricked into sleeping with the go-between, the couple finally reconciles and the play ends happily. Not, however, without first reformulating the conditions a wife must meet in order to deserve a good husband:

(Leonardo): Let us prove our love today.

(Lisbella): I'm yours today, tomorrow, and always!

(Leonardo): I have an honorable wife:

From now on, I'll be a good husband. (ll. 3160-3163)[32]

Illustrating the interrelationship between genres, Lope's play conflates the *cantar*'s theme of the *malmaridada* with the honor code introduced in the Molina ballad, the condemnation of the wife in the Sepúlveda version, and the courtly attitudes of the cultured glosses. Although the play maintains the aristocratic origins of the protagonists, it crosses the dividing class lines between cultured and popular tastes by presenting them as both bickering spouses and Spanish nobles. The audience, comprised of the aristocracy, the urban classes, and the *vulgo*, could easily recognize the shifts in tenor. If Lisbella's noble origins and her courtship by Cipión form part of the courtly love convention, her worries regarding family and finances divulge an urban, middle-class mentality supported by the moral values of Counter-Reformation Spain. Moreover, the play's buffoonesque ending subtly parodies the desires of the upper classes, subverting the cultured gloss of the *cantar* by the aristocratic Cipión's bedding down, not with *la bella*, but with the old bawd who, when found out, cheekily blames the Count: "My lord, that serpent tricked me" ("Señor, aquesta serpiente me engañó" [l. 3146]).

However witty the parody, the play's message to its contemporary audience is deadly serious. Although the play exploits the comic scene from Bandello's *novella*, it accords a serious note to the hoax in keeping with Hispanic views on adultery. While not taking "full advantage of a source's rare comic potential" ("la oportunidad de aprovechar al máximo una fuente de rara potencialidad cómica"), the play adapts the comic situation to its own moral purpose (McGrady and Freeman in Lope, 15). Indeed, if we agree with Donald Larson, who views Lope's honor plays as exhibiting an increasing pessimism, it is only because of its early composition that the play ends happily at all.[33] Leonardo eschews his immoral behavior and gives up gambling; similarly, Lisbella—unlike the female protagonist of the *cantar*, the ballads, and the glosses—remains faithful to the end. Most important, while the Sepúlveda ballad in particular offers a negative model of behavior, the play sets forth socially accepted rules of conduct for the wife: it insists on her absolute fidelity; it requires her constancy in adversity, even when brought about by the husband; and, to preclude any vengeful actions on her part, it entraps her in a code of honor advantageous solely to men.

Yet the play could not function normatively without the audience's collective evocation of the other female voices of *malmaridada* poems. Blending popular poetry, cultured literature, and drama with moral intent, Lope's play exemplifies the ways in which different genres transform societal expectations of gender. From the *cantar*'s representation of the unhappily married seductress, to the Molina ballad's defense of the wife's unlawful escape, on to her despair as the adulterous wife in the Sepúlveda ballad, where she finally recites her own epitaph—and pointedly veering away from the cultured glosses—the popular poems vocalize the increasingly restrictive attitudes toward women. By the end of the sixteenth century the growing choruses of *malmaridadas* have set the stage for the exemplary Lisbella.

Notes

A shorter version of this essay appeared in *ARV Scandinavian Yearbook of Folklore* 43 (1987): 45-58. I am most grateful to Margit Frenk for generously commenting on an earlier version, and to the University of California-Irvine Focused Research Initiative in Women and the Image for research support.

1. The term "popular" is certainly controversial; I am in agreement with Michael Nerlich's definition of popular poetry as a category within the broader term "traditional."

2. Enrique Gastón's study on this same subject was published after my own research was concluded; I am gratified to see that we agree on a number of issues.

3. Dolly Lucero de Padrón subscribes to the theory of popular origins put forth by Gaston Paris, Joseph Bédier, and Alfred Jeanroy and sustained by later critics such as Pierre Le Gentil, Eugenio Asensio, and Peter Dronke, for both *La bella malmaridada*'s lyric and ballad forms. See her seminal article, "En torno al romance de 'La bella malmaridada.' " For a lucid study of the controversy over the origins of lyric poetry, see Frenk, *Las jarchas mozárabes* 69 + .

4. Theodor Frings believes that female poets may have written all love lyrics; however, see Aubrey F. G. Bell and Leo Spitzer, "The Mozarabic Lyric and Theodor Frings' Theories," *Comparative Literature* 4 (1952): 1-22, quoted in Frenk, *Las jarchas mozárabes* 80.

5. Unless otherwise noted, all translations are my own.

> Fízovos Dios delicada,
> honesta, bien enseñada,
> vuestra color matizada,
> más que rossa del rossal.

6.
> Bésame y abrásame,
> marido mío,
> y daros h'en la mañana
> camisón limpio.

7.
> Que yo, mi madre, yo
> que la flor de la villa me so.
> Enviaráme mi madre
> a vender pan a la villa;
> cuantos me vieron decían:
> "Qué panadera garrida!"
> Garrida me era yo.
> Que la flor de la villa me so.

8. The *Libro de buen amor* gives the most well-known example of this usage, where the term "bread" carries a sexual meaning.

9. The conviction that a feminine reality lurks behind the medieval *morena* folk songs in which the female poetic personae lament their dark skin, thus "persisting in their self-prejudicial prejudice," mars Bruce Wardropper's otherwise excellent analysis of these revealing poems (176-193).

10. Margit Frenk has documented the "first period" of valorization from 1450 to 1580, when such songbooks as the *Cancionero de Herberay des Essarts* and the Isabelline *Cancionero musical de Palacio* included poems based on traditional folk songs (Frenk, *Entre folklore y literatura* 29-45). According to Lucero de Padrón (311), the *Cancionero de Herberay des Essarts* included a *copla* beginning "Soy garridilla e pierdo sazon / por mal maridada" ("I'm very pretty but losing my looks / because I'm unhappily married") that most likely inspired the ballad.

11. Unlike the first period of valorization, which was carried out mostly by secondary poets, the second period (1580 to 1650) comprises a much more intense poetic activity. With the exception of traditional ballads that continued to be sung, the emergent poetry is a "modern" imitation of early folk songs; it then became popularized, displacing its sources (Frenk, *Entre folklore* 45-53).

12. Francisco E. Porrata gives an overview of ballads influencing Golden Age dramatists; he does not, however, include *La bella malmaridada*.

13. See McGrady and Freeman, "Introduction," in Lope de Vega, *La bella malmaridada* 22-23. Citations of the ballad are from this edition, which reproduces in its Appendix II (181-182) Lorenzo de Sepúlveda's version from his *Romances nuevamente sacados*, fol. 258. All citations of the play are also from this edition, and are indicated by line number.

14. The *cantar* appears in the *Cancionero general*, Suplemento, n. 288. We should add that the *cantar* itself belongs to a thematic nucleus including *villancicos* and *estribillos* (Frenk, *Lírica española* 145-148).

15.   La bella malmaridada,

         de las más lindas que vi,

         si habéis de tomar amores,

         vida, no dejéis a mí.

16.   "La bella malmaridada

         de las más lindas que yo vi,

         véote tan triste, enojada,

         la verdad dila tú a mí.

         Si has de tomar amores,

         por otro no dejes a mí,

         que a tu marido señora,

         con otras dueñas lo vi,

         besando y retozando,

         mucho mal dice de ti:

         juraba y perjuraba

         que te había de herir."

         Allí habló la señora,

         allí habló y dijo así:

         "Sácame tú, el caballero,

         tú sacáseme de aquí.

         Por las tierras donde fueres

         bien te sabría yo servir."

Ellos en aquesto estando,
su marido helo aquí.

According to McGrady and Freeman, the 1527 version from Molina's *Cancionero* coincides with lines 1-18 and 29-30 of Sepúlveda's version (Lope 21).

17. Of the eleven extant editions of this *Cancionero de romances,* only three include the ballad *La bella malmaridada* (Sepúlveda 1584, 149). Agustín Durán included the ballad in his *Romancero general* (Lucero de Padrón 308).

18.   "Qué hacéis, mala traidora?
    Hoy habedes de morir!"
    "Y por qué, señor, por qué?
    que nunca os lo merecí;
    nunca besé a hombre,
    mas hombre besó a mí.
    las penas que él merecía,
    señor, daldas vos a mí:
    con riendas de tu caballo,
    señor, azotes a mí.
    Con cordones de oro y sirgo
    viva ahorques a mí;
    en la huerta de los naranjos
    viva entierres tú a mí.
    En sepoltura de oro
    y labrada de un marfil
    póngasme encima un mote,
    señor, que diga así:
    'Aquí está la flor de las flores,
    por amores murió aquí:
    cualquier que muere de amores
    mándese enterrar aquí.'
    Que así hize yo, mezquina,
    que por amores me perdí."

19.   "Yo te haría bien la cama
    en que hayamos de dormir.
    Yo te guisara la cena
    como a caballero gentil,
    de gallinas y capones
    y otras cosas más de mil."

20.   "Aquí está la flor de las flores,
    por amores murió aquí:
    cualquier que muere de amores
    mándese enterrar aquí."

21. Lucero de Padrón has noted the double transgression implicit in the relationship: "The husband's vengeance distinguishes between two overlapping planes: the transcendent, which views Christian marriage as a sacrament; and the terrestrial, purely social, plane, where collective opinion weighs heavily" ("En la venganza del marido se pueden distinguir dos planos que se empalman: uno, el trascendente, que considera al matrimonio cristiano como sacramento; otro terreno, puramente social, en donde juega tanto el valor de la opinión colectiva" [344]).

22. Though husbands were legally permitted to murder their adulterous wives and their lovers (see the *Auténtica* added to the *Siete Partidas*, Título XVII, Ley XIII), critics disagree as to whether this law was effectively applied. Melveena McKendrick states that "there is little contemporary evidence that women lived in constant fear of blood-thirsty husbands, brothers, and fathers" (36), but historian María Helena Sánchez Ortega, on the other hand, citing the *Registro del Sello* of the Simancas National Archives (1492), comments that "the cases of husbands who sought royal pardon for having killed their wives because of their infidelity while the soldiers fought in the war of Granada, are so abundant as to not place [the issue] in doubt" ("Los maridos que se han acogido al perdón real por haber dado muerte a la esposa infiel mientras el interesado se marchaba a la guerra de Granada son casos tan frecuentes que no cabe lugar a dudas" [107]).

23.   "No vivas tan lastimera
        ni padezcas tal tormento
        no seas causa que muera
        dexame gozar si quiera
        de tu dulce acatamiento
        pues desseo tus favores
        dexame gozar de ti
        por remedio a mis dolores
        si has de tomar amores
        vida no dexes a mí."

24.   Y assi de haver mal casado
        No ha sido causa el marido.
        Naturaleza lo ha sido,
        por haveros tal criado
        que nadie os ha merescido.

Antonio Rodríguez-Moñino states that "this *cancionero* does not lack the normal thematics that had been appearing since 1500, that is, the glosses of the *Tristes lágrimas mías* or of *La bella malmaridada*" ("En este cancionero no falta la temática normal que venía arrastrándose desde 1500, es decir, glosas de *Las tristes lágrimas mías* o de *La bella malmaridada*" [79-80]). The *Cancionero gótico de Velásquez de Avila* also includes an anonymous gloss on the ballad.

25.   Si para ser mal casada
        tan hermosa os hizo Dios
        bien se dirá que sois vos
        la bella malmaridada.

En viéndoos, el alma os di,
la libertad y la fe,
que sois del cabello al pie
de las más lindas que vi.
Vuestro marido os maltrata,
regalo habéis menester:
aquí le podréis tener
con un alma de oro y plata.
Soy bueno entre los mejores
rico en sangre y deudos claros,
en quien podéis emplearos
si habéis de tomar amores.
Yo no os persuado aquí
que quien sois dejéis de ser,
pero si habéis de querer,
no dejéis por otro a mí.

26.   (Leonardo): No aborrezco a mi mujer
pero verla siempre allí
me cansa mucho.
(Lisbella): Ay de mí!
No la debéis querer.
(Leonardo): Sí quiero. Pero el hallar
mujer al amanecer,
a medio día mujer,
mujer también a cenar,
mujer después en la cama,
y a todas horas, mujer,
y aquel cuidado tener
de la familia y la fama,
loco me vuelve, por Dios!

27.   Vengar me puedo de ti,
pero soy honrada, perro,
y fuera mayor el yerro
contra mí que contra ti.

28. Besides its obvious borrowing from *La Celestina* in the figure of the go-between Dorotea, the play also borrows from Bandello's *Novella II*, 47 (McGrady and Freeman in Lope, 13-14).

29.   Y si de amor tan injusto
con el juego despicáis,
mejor será que volváis,
Leonardo, al pasado gusto.

Que aunque parezca que el juego
no es daño al amor igual,
yo tengo por menos mal
que esté un hombre de amor ciego.

30. "El oficio del marido es ganar hazienda, y el de la muger allegarla, y guardarla. El oficio del marido es, andar fuera a buscar la vida, y el de la muger, es guardar la casa. El oficio del marido es, buscar dineros, y el de la muger, no mal gastar los," Antonio de Guevara, "Letra para Mosen Puche Valenciano" (*Epístolas familiares*), quoted in Julia Fitzmaurice-Kelly (603).

31. "Los tahures y jugadores muchas vezes no tienen dineros que jugar y ponen algunas joyas y preseas y a las vezes son las tales joyas de las pobres de sus mujeres, las cuales juegan del todo o algunos dineros sobre ellas."

32. (Leonardo): Hoy nuestro amor confirmemos.

(Lisbella): Tuya seré, soy, y fui!

(Leonardo): Yo tengo mujer honrada:

de hoy más seré buen marido.

33. For Donald R. Larson, Lope's early honor plays attribute the ultimate responsibility of dishonor to the protagonist himself, and are disinclined to mete out extreme forms of vengeance; his middle and later plays, shifting considerably in tone, lack the sense of good conquering evil, and the feeling of life over death (159-162)

Works Cited

Alcocer, Francisco de. *Tratado del juego*. Salamanca, 1559.

Alonso, Alvaro. *Poesía de Cancionero*. Madrid: Cátedra, 1986.

Alonso, Dámaso. *Poesía de la Edad Media y poesía de tipo tradicional*. Buenos Aires: Editorial Losada, 1942.

"Aquí comienzan tres romances." Madrid: Biblioteca Nacional, R-9412. [Chapbooks.]

Bell, Aubrey F. G. *Da poesía medieval portuguesa*. Coimbra: Imprensa da Universidade, 1933.

Bradbury, Gail. "Lope Plays of Bandello Origin." *Forum for Modern Language Studies* 16 (1980): 53-65.

Cancionero general de obras nuevas. L'Espagne au XVIe et au XVIIe siècle. Heilbrunn, 1878.

Cancionero gótico de Velásquez de Avila. Madrid: Biblioteca Nacional, R-9428.

Castro, Américo. *De la edad conflictiva: crisis de la cultura española en el siglo XVII*. 3rd ed. Madrid: Taurus, 1972.

Covarrubias, Pedro de. *Remedio de jugadores*. Salamanca, 1543.

D'Antuono, Nancy L. *Boccaccio's "Novelle" in the Theater of Lope de Vega*. Madrid: José Porrúa Turanzas, 1983.

Fitzmaurice-Kelly, Julia. "Woman in Sixteenth-Century Spain." *Revue Hispanique* 52 (1927): 557-632.

Frenk, Margit. *Entre folklore y literatura*. México: El Colegio de México, 1st ed., 1971; 2nd ed., 1984.

_____ . *Las jarchas mozárabes y los comienzos de la lírica románica.* México: El Colegio de México, 1st ed., 1971; 2nd ed. 1984.

_____ . *Estudios sobre lírica antigua.* Madrid: Castalia, 1978.

_____ . *Lírica española de tipo popular.* Madrid: Cátedra, 1978.

Frings, Theodor. *Minnesinger und Troubadours.* Berlin: Deutsche Akademie der Wissenschaften zu Berlin, 1949.

Gastón, Enrique. "Malmaridadas en Lope de Vega." *Literatura y vida cotidiana. (Actas de las Cuartas Jornadas de Investigación Interdisciplinaria.)* Ed. María Angeles Durán and José Antonio Rey. Zaragoza: Seminario de Estudios de la Mujer, Universidad Autónoma de Madrid, 1987. 131-147.

Gaylord Randel, Mary. "The Grammar of Femininity in the Traditional Spanish Lyric." *Revista/Review Interamericana* 12 (1982): 115-124.

Kelly-Gadol, Joan. "Did Women Have a Renaissance?" *Becoming Visible: Women in European History.* Ed. Renate Bridenthal and Claudia Koonz. Boston: Houghton Mifflin, 1977. 137-164.

Larson, Donald R. *The Honor Plays of Lope de Vega.* Cambridge: Harvard Univ. Press, 1977.

Lemaire, Ria. "La lyrique portugaise primitive des 'Cantigas de Amigo.'" *Aspects of Female Existence. (Proceedings from the St. Gertrude Symposium "Women in the Middle Ages.")* Ed. Birte Carlé et al. Copenhagen: Gyldendal, 1980. 87-114.

Lope de Vega, Félix. *La bella malmaridada.* Ed. Donald McGrady and Suzanne Freeman. Charlottesville, Va.: Biblioteca Siglo de Oro, 1986.

Lucero de Padrón, Dolly. "En torno al romance de 'La bella malmaridada.'" *Boletín de la Biblioteca de Menéndez Pelayo* 1-4 (1967): 307-354.

McGrady, Donald. "Análisis de *La bella malmaridada,* de Lope." *Estudios sobre el Siglo de Oro en homenaje a Raymond R. MacCurdy.* Ed. Angel González et al. Madrid: Cátedra, 1983. 83-101.

McKendrick, Melveena. *Woman and Society in the Spanish Drama of the Golden Age: A Study of the 'Mujer varonil'.* Cambridge: Cambridge Univ. Press, 1974.

Molina, Juan de. *Cancionero.* 1527. Ed. Antonio Rodríguez-Moñino. Valencia: Castalia, 1952.

Nerlich, Michael. "Toward a Nonliterary Understanding of Literature." *Literature among Discourses: The Spanish Golden Age.* Ed. Wlad Godzich and Nicholas Spadaccini. Minneapolis: Univ. of Minnesota Press, 1986. 62-81.

Porrata, Francisco E. *Incorporación del Romancero a la temática de la comedia española.* Madrid: Playor, 1973.

Poster, Mark. *Critical Theory of the Family.* New York: Seabury Press, 1978.

Rodríguez-Moñino, Antonio. *Poesía y cancioneros (siglo XVI).* Valencia, 1968. (Discurso leído ante la Real Academia Española el día 20 de octubre de 1968.)

Sánchez Ortega, María Helena. "La mujer en el Antiguo Régimen: tipos históricos y arquetipos literarios." *Nuevas perspectivas sobre la mujer. (Actas de las Primeras Jornadas de Investigación Interdisciplinaria.)* Madrid: Universidad Autónoma, 1980.

Sepúlveda, Lorenzo de. *Romances nuevamente sacados de historias antiguas de las crónicas de España.* Antwerp, 1551.

_____ . *Cancionero de romances.* 1584. Ed. Antonio Rodríguez-Moñino. Madrid: Castalia, 1967.

Sponsler, Lucy A. *Women in the Medieval Spanish Epic and Lyric Traditions.* Lexington: Univ. of Kentucky Press, 1975.

Teoría general y metodología del romancero panhispánico: Catálogo general descriptivo (CGR). Dir. Diego Catalán. Madrid: Seminario Menéndez Pidal, 1984.

Wardropper, Bruce. "Meaning in Medieval Spanish Folk Song." *The Interpretation of Medieval Lyric Poetry.* Ed. W. T. H. Jackson. New York: Columbia Univ. Press, 1980. 176-193.

Chapter 8

Saint Teresa, Demonologist

Alison Weber

Teresa of Jesus (1515-1582) believed in the existence of an army of malevolent beings battling ceaselessly for the souls of God's creatures. The Devil as well as lesser demons are omnipresent antagonists in her work; they inflict physical pain and spiritual anguish, sow dissension and envy within the convent, and strive constantly to obstruct and discredit her efforts to reform the Carmelite Order. Teresa, very much a daughter of the Counter-Reformation, believed in the Devil as an extrapersonal presence with supernatural powers. Nonetheless, her conceptions of the demonic differ in important respects from those of her contemporaries; as a "demonologist" Teresa is often an original and occasionally a subversive thinker.

The Devil and his minions are named over two hundred times in Teresa's *Complete Works*, not including references to Lucifer, Satan, or his peculiarly Spanish sobriquet, Patillas.[1] The imposing presence of the Devil in the writings of a sixteenth-century nun is not surprising, considering that this was an era of heightened preoccupation with demonic powers. As Paul Delumeau has written, "The emergence of modernity in western Europe is accompanied by an incredible fear of the Devil. The Renaissance undoubtedly inherited concepts and images of the demonic that had been refined and multiplied in the course of the Middle Ages. But in the Renaissance they were given a coherence, emphasis, and diffusion that they had never before attained."[2]

Furthermore, it was a period that envisioned the Devil, increasingly, in sexual terms.[3] Of Satan's principal arms, pride and lust, it was the latter that more and more preoccupied theologians at the close of the Middle Ages. And woman (always more sensual and less intelligent than man), it followed, was the Devil's preferred victim. *Malleus Maleficarum*, the witch-hunting manual written in 1487, set forth a devastating picture of female susceptibility to carnal pleasures and diabolical seduction. The sixteenth-century demonologist Jean Bodin found it not at all unusual that forty-nine out of fifty witches and demoniacs were female; woman's bestial appetites, credulity, curiosity, spitefulness, and garrulousness made her an ideal satanic accomplice (Delumeau 331). The French witch-hunter Henri Boguet affirmed that the Devil could easily enthrall women with "agreeable provocations" since "there is nothing which makes a woman more subject and loyal to a man than he should abuse her body" (quoted in Klaits 68).

Spain, like the rest of Europe, was receptive to this new image of a monstrously erotic Devil with its corollary emphasis on women's fallen sexuality. In the first two decades of sixteenth-century Spain, women had participated enthusiastically in a variety of pietistic movements embracing humanist, Protestant, and illuminist tendencies, but by the 1530s more and more voices were raised against the religious egalitarianism that had granted women power, visibility, and active spiritual roles. In the subsequent period of renewed ecclesiastical antifeminism, the Church began to persecute vigorously not only the *heterodoxas*—the female evangelicals who gathered to read the New Testament in their kitchens—but also women associated with popular thaumaturgical enthusiasm—the visionaries and miracle workers. As the Franciscan Luis de Maluenda wrote in 1537, "With the fame of secret miracles secret sects are sown. Who knows how many deceptions have been sown with such fame: 'He's a saint, she's a saint who performs miracles'? In these times, the good Christian should make the sign of the cross upon seeing a miracle-working female reputed to be a saint."[4]

One notorious case, which had an immediate and lasting impact on Teresa's life, concerned a nun of the Poor Clare order, Magdalena de la Cruz. After several years of celebrity as a visionary and ecstatic, she was subjected to inquisitorial examination in 1546. Her sentence records that "from the time she was five years old, the Devil appeared to her in the figure of an angel of light and consoled her in various ways, and appeared as Christ crucified and moved her to devotion. . . . When she was twelve years old many demons appeared to her in the form of a handsome young man, one more gallant than the rest, and this one became her familiar and he appeared in the guise of Saint Jerome and Saint Anthony and other saints and angels to whom she was devoted."[5]

In Magdalena's case, the inquisitorial tribunal discovered particular relevance to the Scriptural warnings that the Devil could transform himself into an "angel of light." What was apparently accepted earlier in Magdalena's career as a beatific vision of Christ under questioning elicited a confession of nocturnal visits by a seductive and gallant Devil who offered pleasure, power, and prestige. Although Magdalena admitted to "carnal delights" with the Devil and attributed many of her supposed miracles to diabolic intervention, she also revealed that many others were simple acts of fakery.

From a doctrinal standpoint, a demoniac, as the unwitting victim of demonic deception, deserved solicitous concern, but Magdalena's examiners clearly held her responsible for deceiving the public. From the text of her sentence, it is impossible to determine whether they considered her fakery or her demonic alliance more pernicious, but whatever the case, they saw heretical implications in her behavior. Her sentence reads, "Today we command that she always be considered suspect in things regarding our holy Catholic faith and therefore it is our will that on the day this sentence is read, she should leave this tribunal's prison with a lighted candle in hand, a gag on her mouth, and a rope around her neck."[6] Magdalena escaped a death sentence, but was condemned to perpetual silence and life imprisonment.

The memory of Magdalena's spectacular fall was still vivid in the public imagination when, beginning in 1556, Teresa began to experience visions, voices, and raptures during periods of silent prayer. Repeatedly during her life, Teresa was accused by her enemies of being "another Magdalena de la Cruz." As certain as Teresa was of the beatific nature of her visions and locutions, her alarmed confessors, mindful of the many who had been "deceived" by Magdalena de la Cruz, reluctantly concluded that Teresa's favors were diabolical illusions. Accordingly, they advised her to limit her devotions to oral prayer and "resist" the experiences. At one point, Teresa writes that her confessors declined to hear her confession and were prepared to have her exorcized.

The Book of Her Life, Teresa's passionate apologia for mental prayer and the spiritual favors experienced through it, might also be considered a dissenting demonological treatise, defining the nature and limits of diabolical power.[7] Although Teresa admits the possibility of diabolical illusions, and concedes that women are more susceptible to them, she repeatedly insists— and here she is supported by Thomistic theology—on the superiority of divine powers. "Again I advise that it is very important to try not to let one's spirit rise, unless God raises it up. . . . This is especially bad for women, for the devil might cause some illusion, although I am certain the Lord does not let the devil harm anyone who approaches Him with humility; on the contrary she will benefit and end up winning where the devil thought to make her lose."[8] Humility is the cardinal virtue that provides protection and reassurance for the practitioners of mental prayer. Only those who remember that any divine favors are always unmerited can escape the Devil's snare of vainglory.

But with considerable daring she also suggests that the Devil can transform humility into a trap. "This was the most terrible deceit that the devil put before me in the guise of humility: I began to fear [mental] prayer, seeing I was so wretched."[9] As she warns her readers, "Do not let the devil tempt you, as he did me, to give up [prayer] out of humility"; "This was a false humility that the devil invented to upset me and see if he could bring my soul to despair."[10] More to fear than false visions themselves is the sense of worthlessness the Devil inspires in timid souls, tempting them to renounce their spiritual goals. As Jeffrey Burton Russell points out, the late medieval mystics also warned that the Devil was most dangerous when he tempted souls to despair of God's love (291-292). But although there were precedents within the mystical tradition, Teresa exploited this tenet to the full, making it the dramatic focus of her autobiography and the principal tactic in her defense of mental prayer.

Dryness, spiritual cowardice, disquiet, darkness, and finally, despair were the effects of the Devil on the soul.[11] Reading Teresa's descriptions of demonic power as manifested in terms of emotional turmoil, it is tempting to conclude that she shared the humanists' primarily metaphorical understanding of the Devil. Although Teresa may well have agreed with Erasmus's advice to consider the Devil "anything that deters us from Christ and his teachings,"[12] she does not *reduce* the Devil to a metaphor for spiritual distress. The Devil as an extrapersonal presence, capable of inflicting physical pain as well as inner anguish, is a continuing aspect of her thought.

In fact, Chapter 31 of *The Life* describes several "exterior representations" when the Devil and demons appeared to her in "physical form" as well as other "formless" visions.[13] Teresa learned to maintain her equanimity in the presence of these abominable visions, trusting in the particular efficacy of a sprinkling of holy water to frighten the demons away: "One night I thought that they were choking me; and when I had sprinkled much holy water on them, I saw a multitude of them flee as if they were plunging over a cliff. There are so many times that these wretched creatures torment me, and so little is my fear of them since I now see that they cannot budge an inch if the Lord does not allow it, that it would wear Your Grace out and I would tire myself if I told you about all of them."[14]

It is notable, moreover, that the Devil never appears in Teresa's writings in an attractive disguise, that is, as the "handsome gallant" that was appearing in so many confessional writings and inquisitorial records. Teresa's Devil, in contrast, is always hideous and repugnant, and therefore easily recognizable: "I saw next to me an abominable little black man, complaining desperately that he was losing where he had hoped to gain. When I saw him, I laughed and was not afraid."[15] Although medieval iconography may have provided Teresa with visual models, her repellent representation of the Devil is motivated by more than tradition. Teresa's hideous demons, her "medieval demons," might also be interpreted as a strategic attempt to displace the image of the beautiful and seductive Counter-Reformation Devil.[16]

Teresa further diminishes the prestige of the demonic with commonplace colloquialisms designed to evoke dismissive laughter: "[Demons] bother me no more than flies. They seem so cowardly to me that as soon as they see I don't think much of them, they lose their power."[17] The Devil, as Teresa would have it, is often more of a nuisance than a seducer. Delumeau has argued that the omnipotent Devil in the early modern period was primarily a creation of elite culture, whereas the Devil in popular culture "can also be a familiar person, human, much less formidable than the Church holds, and thus easily beaten."[18] Although some of her demonic representations are truly frightening, Teresa at times prefers to evoke, as a competing diabolical image, the familiar and less threatening *demonios* of popular culture. In short, as much as Teresa identified the Devil and demons with emotional states, her strategic skepticism questioned not the Devil's effective presence in the world, but the extent and nature of his powers to interfere with those who humbly sought God through prayer.

At considerable psychic expense, Teresa always exposed her experiences to the full scrutiny of her confessors, and obeyed the letter if not the spirit of their instructions. At one point, her confessors had ordered her to respond to her visions by "giving the fig," defined by the Renaissance lexicographer Sebastián de Covarrubias as follows: "It is a form of scorn that we display by making a fist and placing the thumb between the index and the middle finger; . . . previously, giving the fig was just an imitation of the male member, made by extending the middle finger and bending the index and little fingers."[19] Teresa vividly recounts her distress when faced with such an order: "The command to make this gesture when I saw a vision of the Lord gave me great pain, because when it was before me, I could not believe it was the devil, even if they tore me to pieces, and so it was a kind of great penance for me to obey."[20] She continues with words that resound even more unfavorably on her confessors: "I remembered the insults that the Jews had made to Christ and I begged Him to forgive me, since I was doing it only to obey the man He had put in His place, and I asked Him not to blame me, since they were the ministers that He had placed in His Church."[21]

Thus obedience to confessors and submission before their unwarranted suspicions is recast as a kind of *penance*. Furthermore, Teresa obliquely suggests that with their misguided orders, her confessors had unwittingly acted not as Christ's vicars but as his unredeemed persecutors. Confessors, rather than their spiritual daughters, become the locus of demonic deception: "A fig for all devils! They'll be afraid of me! I don't understand these fears, 'The devil, the devil!' when we can say 'God, God!' and make him tremble. For we all know that he can't budge an inch if the Lord does not permit it. Without a doubt I am more afraid of those who are greatly frightened by the devil than the devil himself; because he can't do anything to me, and the others, especially if they are confessors, can do a great deal of harm, and I have for several years suffered so greatly that I am amazed that I was able to stand it."[22] Teresa has effectively redefined the nature of the Devil's interference in terms of what she had suffered at the hands of uncomprehending confessors who attempted to turn her away from contemplation, deprive her of the sacraments of confession and communion, and "exorcise" from her the manifestations of God's love.

The idea that the Devil operates most successfully through spiritual intimidation is a reiterated theme of Teresa's second work, written for the eleven nuns of Teresa's first reformed convent, San José in Avila.[23] *The Way of Perfection* is full of reassurances for the members of the fledgling convent who, returning to the primitive rule of the Carmelite Order, wished to imitate their foundress in the practice of mental prayer. Urging the nuns to be steadfast in their new and more demanding devotions, Teresa mocks the kinds of objections to mental prayer they might have heard from confessors or family members: " 'It's dangerous,' 'So and so was lost,' 'Someone else was deceived,' 'Someone who prayed this way fell,' 'It's dangerous for virtue,' 'It's not for women, because it gives them delusions,'

'Let them stick to their spinning,' 'They have no need of these niceties,' 'It is quite enough to recite the Lord's Prayer and an *Ave María.*' "[24] Conceding the Devil's success in deceiving a few women who practiced mental prayer, Teresa nonetheless maintains that he reaped even more profit by frightening many away from the more arduous path of contemplation: "If anyone tells you that mental prayer is dangerous, consider him the main danger and flee from him. . . . It is dangerous if you don't practice humility and other virtues; but God forbid that the way of prayer should be dangerous! It seems that the devil has invented these fears, so he has been very clever in bringing about the fall of some who were following this path."[25]

To avoid subjugation by a timorous confessor, Teresa argues that nuns should be allowed to consult more than one confessor, and if need be, go outside the order to look for spiritual counsel. "When the devil tempts the confessor with some point of vanity, if he knows that she's dealing with other confessors, she'll slip through his fingers." In the revised Valladolid version, Teresa is more explicit: "When the devil tempts the confessor by deceiving him *about some point of doctrine*, if he knows she's dealing with other confessors, she'll slip through his fingers, and *he will watch what he's doing more carefully*" (emphasis added).[26] Presumably, the subject of the last two verbs is the Devil, but the sentence nonetheless leaves the impression that the confessor as well will "watch what he's doing," knowing that his doctrinal pronouncements will be subjected to a "second opinion." The tactic of consulting multiple confessors had worked to Teresa's benefit in the difficult days leading up to the reform, and she sought to institutionalize the practice in the new Discalced Carmelite Order.[27]

The Devil is also seen to operate within the convent by provoking scruples. In particular, Teresa seems anxious to assuage a nun's fear that she may have become too fond of a sympathetic spiritual director. Here, Teresa's advice might be seen as an attempt to counterbalance the kind of warnings found in one of Luis de Granada's sermons: "And although generally speaking, all obedience is good, this kind [of obedience to one's confessor] is very dangerous, because from it a familiar sort of friendship grows between the penitent and her spiritual father, which the devil little by little foments and stirs up, so that, as Saint Thomas says, 'Many times this spiritual friendship is transformed and changed into a carnal one.' "[28] Teresa's position is much less alarmist:

> For if those who practice [mental] prayer see that their confessor is a holy man who understands them, they begin to love him. And here is where the devil fires off a battery of scruples that disquiet the soul a great deal, and this is what he is trying to do; especially if the confessor is leading one's soul to greater perfection, the devil distresses the person so severely that she ends up leaving her confessor for another. And even if she goes on to one confessor after another, this temptation will still torment her. What you can do here is try not to think about whether you love or don't love your confessor, and love him if you want to; because, after all, we love those who treat our bodies well, why shouldn't we love someone who is always striving to benefit our soul? . . . Take this advice: if you see that all your conversations with your confessor are to the benefit of your soul, if you don't perceive any sort of vanity in him, . . . and if you understand him to be a God-fearing man, do not wear yourselves out over the temptation that you are too fond of him, and when the devil gets tired, the temptation will go away.[29]

It is significant that this passage is omitted in the Valladolid Codex, Teresa's second and more cautious version of the text.

Teresa does recognize a potential for danger if a *vain* confessor is *aware* of the nun's attachment. In this case she advises: "The best thing is to tell the Mother Superior that her soul is not at ease with him, and change confessor . . . and try not to deal with him at all, although it is terribly painful."[30] Teresa alludes here, I believe, to fears of a dangerous alliance by means of which the priest might use the nun's religious experiences to enhance his own power and prestige.[31] In this text, the Devil disrupts the confessor-penitent relationship, but in a very different way from that formulated by Luis de Granada. First of all, Teresa relocates potential danger (and the onus of responsibility) in the confessor rather than in the nun. Second, she clearly implies that the prospect of confessional seduction is much more imaginary than a practical danger. Once again Teresa downplays the erotic implications of the demonic. It is remarkable that Teresa managed to maintain such sangfroid on this issue during a period when the Inquisition was increasingly willing to give credence to charges of sexual misconduct in the confessor-penitent relationship.[32]

By the time she writes the first chapters of *The Book of Foundations* in 1573, Teresa has shifted her concern from spiritually timid nuns to those whose excessively zealous devotions had resulted in a proliferation of *arrobamientos* or suspect raptures. The case of a Cistercian nun is offered as an exemplary warning to her own Carmelites:

> There was a nun . . . who by dint of fasting and discipline became so weak, that every time she took communion or became inflamed with devotion, fell to the ground and lay there for eight or nine hours, and she and everyone else assumed it was rapture. . . . The fame of her raptures was spreading through the town: I was dismayed to hear it, because the Lord wanted me to understand what it really was, and I was afraid the whole affair would turn out badly. . . . I told her confessor that I understood what it was and that it was a waste of time, not rapture but weakness. I told him to have her give up fasting and discipline, and seek some distractions. She was obedient and did as she was told. As she soon gained strength she forgot completely about raptures.[33]

From her letters and the advice she gives prioresses in *The Book of Foundations*, we can assume that Teresa dealt with reports of rapture in the Discalced convents in a similar manner, without alarm, but with a certain degree of skepticism. Her criteria for the "discernment of spirits" was simple and direct. The affected nuns were to give up fasting and excessive penance; if the visions or locutions were false, they would disappear. If they were authentic, they would persist. With her pleas for moderation and her concern for the hallucinatory effects of fasting, Teresa clearly distinguishes herself from the medieval tradition of female spirituality, which was so closely identified with a theology of physical suffering.[34]

While never ruling out the possibility of divine ecstasy, Teresa warned her nuns and prioresses to be ever alert for the counterfeit effects of convent "melancholy," a humoral imbalance brought on by poor diet, isolation, and excessive acts of mortification. Although she conceded that the Devil could "take advantage" of melancholy, his role was incidental: "I believe that [the devil] doesn't do as much harm as our imagination and bad humors, especially if it is a question of melancholy, for women's nature is weak, and the self love that reigns in us is very subtle."[35] Teresa takes a position not dissimilar to that of the physician Juan Huarte de San Juan, whose *Examen de ingenios* was published two years after she had set forth her own ideas on melancholy in *The Book of Foundations*. Like Teresa, Huarte believed that some visions had a physiological origin: lengthy prayer and meditation caused the warm humors to cloud the brain. But he also attributed a role to the Devil: "The devil . . . when he wants to accomplish something of great importance to him, takes advantage of the corporeal qualities that help him achieve that end."[36]

It would appear that for Teresa, "demonic possession" was the diagnosis of last resort. Yet there is one piece of evidence that, at least initially, seems to contradict this hypothesis. In a letter dated May 1573 she writes to Mother Inés de Jesús: "I am distressed about Sister Isabel de San Jerónimo's illness. I am sending you Father John of the Cross to cure her, for God has given him the grace to cast out demons from persons who have them. Here in Avila he has just cast out three legions of devils from a person, and he ordered them in God's name to tell him their name, and they obeyed immediately."[37] Indeed, in that year, John had been called to examine an Augustinian nun who manifested the marvelous ability to explicate the Holy Scriptures without benefit of theological studies. Since the ability to speak and understand languages without study was considered one of the most unequivocal signs of possession, and vernacular translations of the Scriptures were prohibited after the Council of Trent, the nun was immediately suspect.[38] John reached a decision after his first interview with the nun and proclaimed, "Gentlemen, this nun is possessed." Crisógono de Jesús describes the exorcism sessions that followed:

With his first efforts at exorcism, Friar John made the
possessed nun confess that she had surrendered herself
to the devil at the age of six. . . . The surrender was
solemn: the girl used blood from her arm to sign a
document in which she stated that she surrendered
herself entirely to the devil. The exorcisms are
accompanied by terrible convulsions in the poor girl: she
furiously insults Friar John, foams at the mouth,
screams, thrashes about in a frenzy on the floor, and
even tries to attack the Friar and his companions. . . .
The young exorcist holds a cross before her. . . . The
demoniac throws the cross to the ground; but the friar
orders her to take it up and kiss it, and she obeys, while
bellowing. . . . At last, after months of exorcism, he
succeeds in destroying the document and freeing the
nun, who is utterly exhausted, as if she had just
emerged from a long and terrifying dream.[39]

Later in the same year when John was summoned by Teresa
to examine the nun at the Discalced convent in Medina, he arrived at a very different diagnosis: "This nun is not possessed,
but lacking in reason."[40] It seems quite possible that Teresa exerted some influence in this case to temper the young exorcist's
fervor, that she wanted to spare her own nuns the exorcist's
"long and terrifying dream." In fact, her correspondence regarding this troubled nun, for whom Teresa obviously felt both
exasperation and affection, provides a practical illustration of
her alternative treatment for suspect cases outlined in *The Book of
Foundations.*

In a letter dated October 23, 1576, Teresa again writes of her
concerns over the "possessed" Isabel de San Jerónimo, who had
apparently continued to experience visions: "As for San Jerónimo, she must eat meat for a few days and give up prayer, and
your grace should order her to deal only with him, or write to
me, because she has an unsteady imagination and thinks she
sees and hears whatever she meditates on; although sometimes
it may be true, and has been in the past, because she is a good
soul."[41] In the same letter, she writes cryptically, "It may be necessary to ask the 'angel' for freedom, although I would rather
drive 'Patillas' out of the house with the usual remedies."[42]
What Teresa appears to be saying is that it may be necessary to

call upon an exorcist (and alert the "angel" or inquisitor to problems within the convent), although she prefers to handle the matter in the usual way, that is, with the prescribed therapy of improved diet and rest.[43] On February 28, 1577, Teresa writes to the prioress of the Seville convent, "I wish I were [certain] about San Jerónimo. I am really concerned about the woman. She should never have left my side or gone where there was fear. Please God that the devil isn't up to something that will mean trouble for us. Tell the prioress not to let her write down one word, and tell Isabel—before she gets my letter—that I think she is suffering from a very bad humor, if not something worse."[44] Teresa's alarm is understandable given that any written account of visions or other extraordinary experiences was a potentially incriminating document.[45]

Once again on March 28, 1578, she writes the prioress, urging that Isabel and a companion not be allowed to commit their visions to writing: "I stress this because I understand the serious problems that can result when they start thinking about what they are going to write and I know what the devil might suggest to them. If it is something important, you can write it down without their knowing about it. If I had paid attention to the things San Jerónimo told me, I would never have heard the end of it, and although some of the things seemed genuine, I kept quiet about it."[46] She returns to the same preoccupation in a letter dated February 1, 1580, but this time in a lighter vein: "I find it amusing that you say that not everything San Jerónimo says must be believed, since that is what I have written you so often. . . . Still, she's a good soul . . . and if she goes astray it will be for lack of intelligence and not out of malice. Of course I may be wrong."[47] Although Isabel has obviously been a liability, Teresa frequently commends herself to her warmly at the end of her letters.

In sum, Teresa's attitude toward Isabel is at once tolerant and skeptical. Her "working hypothesis" is somatogenetic; the visions are probably the result of a humoral imbalance or an "unsteady imagination," although she does not rule out the possibility that they may be genuine, or even demonic ("something worse"). The Devil's role is seen as secondary—one might even say "political"—as he takes advantage of the unstable nun to stir

up trouble for the reform. Teresa does not fear "demonic possession" so much as the potential political repercussions should
the news get into the hands of the inquisitors or her enemies,
the Calced Carmelites, who had fought Teresa's reforms so
bitterly.

The Devil is evoked repeatedly in *The Book of Foundations* as
well as in the letters in this "political" sense. That is, Teresa attributes interpersonal conflict—especially the internecine
struggle with the Calced—to diabolical intervention: "The devil
cannot bear to see how much Discalced friars and nuns are serving the Lord. . . . Since we do not have our own governing
province, we have to endure countless trials and tribulations at
the hands of the Calced."[48] At times, as Teresa gives vent to her
animosity toward the Calced, the Devil seems less a disembod-
ied spirit of dissension than the real and formidable ally of her
enemies.

There was one other occasion on which Teresa seemed to lose
her characteristic equanimity regarding the demonic. She was
seriously alarmed that Jerónimo Gracián, her beloved disciple
and confessor, was becoming dangerously involved with a laywoman whom he had served as confessor. The situation, described in a letter dating from the beginning of November 1576,
merits quoting at length:

> As regards that girl or woman, I am quite convinced that
> it is not so much melancholy that has made her commit
> these frauds as the devil, and it is precisely so that he
> can deceive you too, now that he has deceived her. And
> so it is necessary for you to proceed with great caution
> in this business and never go to her house under any
> circumstances, or else what happened to Saint Marina (I
> think that's who it was) might happen to you: they said
> that she had produced a child, and she suffered a great
> deal. . . . Note that if she didn't give you that letter
> under the seal of confession, or during confession, it is a
> case for the Inquisition, for the devil lays a thousand
> snares. Another woman was put to death for the same
> thing, and I learned of it. The truth is I don't believe she
> gave the letter to the devil—for he would not give it back
> to her so soon—I really do not believe anything of what
> she says. I think rather she's a fraud (God forgive me)

and that she likes dealing with your Paternity. Perhaps she made the whole thing up; but I would like to see your Paternity far away from her, so that the matter can be over and done with.[49]

Although Teresa appears to prefer a demonic over a somatogenetic hypothesis in this letter, a closer reading reveals that her attitude toward the demonic is nonetheless one of "limited" skepticism. Although Teresa entertains the idea that the unidentified woman "has the devil in her," she comes to reject it and conclude that the woman is a charlatan, not the passive vessel of demonic power. Here, Teresa offers neither a physiological nor a supernatural model for "possession," but rather a *behavioral* one: the seducer is not the Devil, but the laywoman herself, who seems to crave Gracián's company and attention.[50] If it was a case of fraud, as Teresa believed, then the Inquisition was the proper authority to handle it.

The same dilemma of differentiating divine favors from diabolical delusions is a central concern of Teresa's masterwork, *The Interior Castle*, written in 1577. Again, her principal aim is to reassure her nuns against fears of demonic possession. She continues to protest the harm brought about by "inexperienced" confessors (those who have not had mystical experiences themselves), but nonetheless she insists on the need for her nuns to disclose all their supernatural favors in confession. She sets up a hierarchy of visions and locutions leading from the least to the most certain; that is, locutions are more deceptive than visions, and "imaginative" visions less reliable than "intellectual" ones.[51] In one of her more daring passages, Teresa goes so far as to assert that certain visions—even if they *are* demonic delusions—are not necessarily harmful:

Do not be disturbed or anxious, for even if the vision is not from God, if you are humble and have a good conscience, it won't harm you. His Majesty knows how to turn evil into good. You will profit by choosing the path the devil thought would lead to your perdition. . . . As a very learned man said, the devil is a great painter, and if he showed him a very realistic image of our Lord, it wouldn't bother him, because he would use it to quicken his devotion and wage war against the devil using the devil's own arms. And although a painter is very wicked, this doesn't mean that we must fail to revere the image that he creates, if it is of our every Good.[52]

At this point, she comes perilously close to advocating disobedience. Should a confessor order a nun to "give figs" to a vision of Christ, she writes, "My advice is . . . that you should humbly tell him these arguments and not accept his counsel."[53]

If in the early chapters of *The Book of Foundations* Teresa seems to be promoting a humoral explanation as an *alternative* to a determination of demonic possession, by 1577 when she pens *The Interior Castle*, she is aware of another problem: the danger that confessors might misjudge genuine raptures as the effects of melancholy. She begins on an undeniably truculent note: "Let us consider first the torment that comes from running up against a confessor so scrupulous but inexperienced that he doesn't accept any favor as genuine; he is afraid of everything; as soon as he sees anything out of the ordinary, he begins to doubt, especially if he sees some imperfection in the person who has such experiences (because they think that God must give these favors only to angels . . .) so everything is condemned as coming from the devil or melancholy." Yet in a more conciliatory tone she adds immediately, "And the world is so full of melancholy, that I am not surprised; there is so much of it about in the world just now and the devil works such harm using it, that confessors are very right to fear it and examine it closely."[54] As much as *The Interior Castle* constitutes an apologia for women's religious ecstasy and a protest against confessors' condemnation of that experience, it also reveals Teresa's continued adherence to a physiological concept of pseudoecstasy.

Using Teresa as a primary example, Steven Katz has argued that mysticism is essentially a conservative religious phenomenon and that its dissident character has been overemphasized. I would emphasize, however, that "dissident" and "conservative" are comparative terms. Teresa's mysticism is surely conservatively Christian in comparison with Eastern mysticism, but within the historical context of Counter-Reformation Spain, many of her beliefs were demonstrably marginal. The same arguments could be made about her demonological views. Teresa always insisted that she was a true daughter of the Holy Roman Church, and from the perspective of sixteen centuries of Church history, there is nothing radical about her central tenet: her belief in God's superior power over the Devil. But in Counter-Reformation Spain her confidence in women's capacity to experience and identify genuine mystical favors, as well as her skepticism regarding the frequency and perniciousness of demonic possession, made her a dissident demonologist. Teresa successfully distanced herself and her nuns from a myth that increasingly held sway over her contemporaries' imagination, which was the myth of woman as the Devil's compliant sexual partner. The fact that neither she nor her spiritual daughters were ever forced to submit to the ministrations of an exorcist is evidence of her persuasiveness. Her success, moreover, may well be attributed to the flexibility and adaptability of her thought. The three "hypotheses" that Teresa developed to interpret extraordinary phenomena—the supernatural, the physiological, and the behavioral—while conceding to the prevailing paradigms of interpretation and power, effectively protected and preserved a significant area of women's religious expression.

Notes

1. "Patillas" is the plural depreciatory diminutive of *pata*, or hoof. Edgar Allison Peers, Teresa's noted British translator, suggests "Hoofy" as an English equivalent (1: 317, n. 4).

2. "L'émergence de la modernité dans notre Europe occidental s'est accompagnée d'une incroyable peur du diable. La Renaissance héritait assurément de concepts et d'images démoniaques qui s'étaient précisés et multipliés au cours du Moyen Age. Mais elle leur donna une cohérence, un relief et une diffusion jamais atteints auparavant" (232). All translations throughout this essay are my own.

Jeffrey Burton Russell attributes the demonological fervor in the second half of the sixteenth century to the resurgence of scholastic realism and Augustinianism and the relative decline of the Neoplatonist and nominalist traditions that had tended to minimize the importance of the Devil (295-296).

3. On the sexualization of the demonic, see Delumeau 305-345; Cohn 263; and Klaits 51-58, 77, 118. As recent scholarship on the witch-hunts has shown, beginning in the fifteenth century, witchcraft became identified increasingly as a sexual pact with the Devil (Klaits 77).

4. "A fama de milagros secretos se siembran sectas secretas. ¿Quién podrá contar los engaños que se han sembrado con esta fama? Es un santo, es una santa que hace milagros. De hembra afamada por santa y que hace milagros se santigua el buen cristiano en estos tiempos" (quoted in Andrés 2: 558, n. 161). For additional background studies on women and religion in sixteenth-century Spain, see Andrés 2: 557-561; Ortega Costa; and Weber 17-41. As Bilinkoff's study on Mari Díaz shows, some charismatic holy women did continue to be revered.

5. "De cinco años . . . se le apareció el demonio en figura de ángel de luz y la consolaba en dichas maneras y se le aparecía como Cristo cruzificado y la movía a devoción. . . . Dixo mas que siendo de doze años se le aparecieron muchos demonios en forma de hombres galanes y uno más galán que todos y hera un familiar y aparecía en figura de San Jerónimo y de Santo Antonio y de otros santos y ángeles de los que ella tenía devoción" (Imirizaldu 53-54). For other examples of visions of the Devil disguised as an attractive young man, see Caro Baroja, Las formas complejas 62-66; Crisógono 187-189; and Perry, "Beatas" 156-158. Caro Baroja also notes that the Devil appears as an "elegant gentleman" in witchcraft testimonies (Vidas mágicas 2: 47).

6. "Hoy mandamos siempre sea tenida por sospechosa en las cosas tocantes a nuestra santa fe catholica y por tanto es nuestra voluntad que el dia de la publicacion desta sentencia salga de las carceles deste tribunal con una bela encendida en las manos y una mordaza a la lengua y una soga a la garganta" (Imirizaldu 61). Magdalena's sentence reveals how tenuous the distinction between possession and witchcraft could be in the early modern period. During the Middle Ages, witches were judged to be those who practiced maleficium, or maleficent magic. With the interjection of elite demonological theories at the close of the Middle Ages, a witch was defined as someone who had formed a sexual pact with the Devil, and who, by thus abjuring God, was a heretic. Although witches and the possessed theoretically formed separate classes (and the possessed were frequent witchcraft accusers), the distinction dissolved if the possessed were shown to have accepted the diabolical pact. See Cohn 174, 234-237; Klaits 50-51, 118; and Midelfort 20-25.

7. Teresa practiced a form of silent or meditative prayer that was the object of considerable debate in sixteenth-century Spain. A number of theologians feared that it could lead to a disdain for vocal prayer and other exterior works, or to illuminist heresies. For an excellent summary of the controversy, see Andrés 2: 562-569.

Teresa's autobiography was repeatedly reworked and expanded. A first draft, now lost, dates from 1562; the extant version was probably completed near the end of 1565.

8. "Torno otra vez a avisar que va mucho en no subir el espíritu, si el Señor no le subiere. . . . En especial para mujeres es más malo, que podrá el demonio causar alguna ilusión; aunque tengo por cierto no consiente el Señor dañe a quien con humildad se procura llegar a El, antes sacará más provecho y ganancia por donde el demonio le pensare hacer perder" (V 12: 52).

For all of Teresa's works, I have used the edition of Efrén de la Madre de Dios and Otger Steggink. The abbreviations for her works are as follows: V—El libro de la vida (The Book of Her Life); C—Camino de perfección (The Way of Perfection: Escorial

Codex); M—*Moradas del castillo interior* (*The Interior Castle*); F—*El libro de las fundaciones* (*The Book of Foundations*); Cta—*Cartas* (*Letters*). The Arabic numerals refer to chapter and page. For *The Interior Castle*, Roman numerals refer to the sections called *moradas* and the subsequent Arabic numerals to chapter and page. All translations are my own.

9. "Este fue el más terrible engaño que el demonio me podía hacer debajo de parecer humildad: que comencé a temer de tener oración, de verme tan perdida" (V 7: 31).

10. "Y no le tiente el demonio por la manera que a mí, a dejarla por humildad" (V 8: 38); "Esta es una humildad falsa que el demonio inventava para desasosegarme y provar si puede traer el alma a desesperación" (V 30: 121).

11. Agnes Moncy's article examines many of Teresa's descriptions of demons in *The Book of Her Life* and rightly points out the way in which they are associated with internal emotional states and human evil. However, I am unable to agree with Moncy's conclusion that Teresa rejected the traditional concept of the Devil as a "specific being" (156).

12. Quoted in Russell 295. Regarding the humanists' attitudes toward the Devil and demons, Russell adds, "Their existence is not denied, but it is thrust into the background in a system that has no real use for them" (295).

13. "I have seen the devil a few times in physical form, and many times without physical form" ("Pocas veces le he visto tomando forma, y muchas sin ninguna forma" [V 31: 127]).

14. "En este tiempo también una noche pensé que me ahogavan; y como echaron mucha agua bendita, vi ir mucha multitud de ellos como quien se va despeñando. Son tantas veces las que estos malditos me atormentan y tan poco el miedo que yo ya los he, con ver que no se pueden menear si el Señor no les da licencia, que cansaría a vuestra merced y me cansaría si las dijese" (V 31: 126).

15. "Vi cabe mí un negrillo muy abominable regañando como desesperado de que adonde pretendía ganar perdía. Yo, como le vi reíme, y no huve miedo" (V 31: 125).

16. Aurora Egido has observed that the grotesque Devil of medieval literature and iconography was gradually replaced on the Spanish Golden Age stage with the vision of the Devil as a beautiful, seductive gallant—Don Juan in many different guises (20).

17. "Que no se me da más de ellos que de moscas. Parécenme tan covardes que en viendo que los tienen en poco, no les queda fuerza" (V 25: 103). Russell observes that the English mystics Walter Hilton and Julian of Norwich also recommended laughter as a defense against the devil (292). Whether or not Teresa derived this particular defense from the European mystical tradition, it was one well suited to her personality. All her works are pervaded by a sense of irony, and there are numerous personal testimonies of her sense of humor.

18. "[Le diable populaire] peut être aussi un personnage familier, humain, beaucoup moins redoutable que ne l'assure l'Eglise—et cela est si vrai qu'on arrive facilement à le rouler" (242).

19. "Es una manera de menosprecio que hazemos cerrando el puño y mostrando el dedo pulgar por entre el dedo índice y el medio; . . . La higa antigua era tan solmente una semejanza del miembro viril, estendiendo el dedo medio y encogiendo el índice y el auricular."

20. "Dávame este dar higas grandísima pena cuando vía esta visión del Señor; porque cuando yo le vía presente, si me hicieran pedazos, no pudiera yo creer que era demonio, y ansí era un género de penitencia grande para mí" (V 29: 117).

21. "Acordávame de las injurias que le havían hecho los judíos y suplicávale me perdonase, pues yo lo hacía por obedecer a el que tenía en su lugar, y que no me culpase, pues eran los ministros que El tenía puestos en su Iglesia" (V 29: 117). The alternation between singular and plural can be explained because Teresa consulted a group of five priests and laymen during this period.

22. "¡Una higa para todos los demonios!, que ellos me temerán a mí. No entiendo estos miedos; ¡demonio! ¡demonio!, adonde podemos decir: ¡Dios, Dios!, y hacerle temblar. Sí, que ya sabemos que no se puede menear si el Señor no lo primite [sic]. ¿Qué es esto? Es sin duda que tengo ya más miedo a los que tan grande le tienen a el demonio que a él mesmo; porque él no me puede hacer nada, y estotros, en especial si son confesores, inquietan mucho, y he pasado algunos años de tan gran travajo que ahora me espanto cómo lo he podido sufrir" (V 25: 104).

23. The first redaction of *The Way of Perfection*, known as the Escorial Codex, was written sometime between 1562 and 1566. The second, extensively revised (and censored) version of the Valladolid Codex was probably begun around 1569.

24. " 'Hay peligros', 'fulana por aquí se perdió', 'el otro se engañó', 'dañan la virtud', 'no es para mujeres, que les vienen ilusiones', 'mijor será que hilen', 'no han menester esas delicadeces', 'basta el Paternóster y Avemaría' " (C 35: 249).

25. "Quien os dijere que éste es peligro, tenedle a él por el mesmo peligro y huid dél; . . . peligro será no tener humildad y otras virtudes; mas camino de oración camino de peligro, nunca Dios tal quiera. El demonio parece ha inventado poner estos miedos, y ansí ha sido mañoso a hacer caer a alguno que llevava este camino" (C 36: 250).

26. "Cuando el demonio tentase al confesor en alguna vanidad, como sepa que tratan con otros, iráse a la mano" (C 5: 202 Escorial Codex); "Que cuando el demonio tentase al confesor en engañarle en *alguna doctrina*, como sepa trata con otros, iráse a la mano y *mirará mijor en todo lo que hace*" (Valladolid Codex, emphasis added).

27. As the reform movement grew, however, Teresa came to prefer that her nuns confess only with Discalced priests.

28. "Y aunque generalmente hablando, toda obediencia sea buena, pero ésta es muy peligrosa, porque de ella nace una familiar amistad entre el penitente y el padre espiritual, la cual suele el demonio poco a poco fomentar y atizar de tal manera, que, como Santo Tomás dice, 'muchas veces esta amistad espiritual se transforma y muda en carnal' " ("Sermón contra los escándalos de las caídas públicas" in Imirizaldu 201-263, quoted 259).

29. "Que personas que tratan oración si le ven santo y las entiende la manera del proceder, tómase mucho amor. Y aquí da el demonio gran batería de escrúpulos que desasosiega el alma harto, que esto pretende él; en especial si el confesor la trai a más perfeción, apriétala tanto que le viene a dejar. Y no la deja, con otro ni con otro, de atormentar aquella tentación. Lo que en esto pueden hacer

es procurar no ocupar el pensamiento en si quieren u no quieren, sino si quisieren, quieran; porque, pues cobramos amor a quien nos hace algunos bienes al cuerpo, quien siempre procura y travaja de hacerlos al alma, ¿por qué no le hemos de querer? . . . Lleven este aviso: si en el confesor entendieren que todas sus pláticas es para aprovechar su alma, y no le vieren ni entendieren otra vanidad . . . y le entendieren temoroso de Dios, por ninguna tentación que ellas tengan de mucha afeción se fatiguen; que de que el demonio se canse se le quitará" (C 7: 199).

30. "Y lo mijor sería decir a la madre no se halla su alma bien con él y mudarle . . . y poner lo que pudiere en no tratar con él, aunque sienta la muerte" (C 7: 199).

31. Years later, Teresa would be faced with just such a scenario. In the Seville convent, the prioress was convinced that two nuns had formed a dangerous alliance with their confessor, who was inciting his confessional daughters to believe suspect visions and locutions. Teresa felt torn between her suspicion and affection for all parties involved, and vacillated considerably in her judgments on this case. See also Weber 152-153 and Perry, "Subversion and Seduction."

32. The topic of confessional seduction, and sexual phobias in general, is treated humorously in El cerro, a satire written by Teresa's disciple Jerónimo Gracián (and with Teresa's collaboration, it is now believed). Accusations of orgiastic sexual activity between confessors and female penitents was the cornerstone of the campaign against the alumbrados in Extremadura in the 1570s and in Andalucía from 1575 to 1590 (see Huerga's two-volume study). As Perry points out, charges of sexual misconduct also figured prominently in trials against Sevillian beatas at the turn of the seventeenth century ("Beatas and the Inquisition").

33. "Estaba una monja que . . . con muchas disciplinas y ayunos vino a tanta flaqueza, que cada vez que comulgaba y hacía ocasión en encenderse en devoción, luego era caída en el suelo y ansí se estava ocho o nueve horas, pareciendo a ella y a todas era arrobamiento. . . . Andava por todo el lugar la fama de los arrobamientos: a mí me pesava de oírlo, porque quiso el Señor entendiese lo que era, y temía en lo que havía de parar. . . . Yo le dije [a su confesor] lo que entendía y cómo era perder tiempo y imposible ser arrobamiento sino flaqueza; que la quitase los ayunos y disciplinas y la hiciese divirtir. Ella era obediente; hízolo ansí. Desde a poco que fue tomando fuerza no havía memoria de arrobamiento" (F 6: 514).

34. For an analysis of fasting within the medieval ascetic tradition of female spirituality, see Bynum. Early in her career Teresa was greatly influenced by the Franciscan ascetic Pedro de Alcántara, but I believe that she moved toward a more moderate position in the course of the reform movement. In their convent satire El cerro, Gracián and Teresa deride nuns who persist in excessive penance.

35. "Creo no hace tanto mal [el demonio] como nuestra imaginación y malos humores, en especial si hay melencolía, porque el natural de las mujeres es flaco, y el amor propio que reina en nosotras muy sutil" (F 4: 506). For a more extensive discussion of Teresa's theory of melancholy, see Weber 139-146.

36. "El demonio no solamente apetece lugares alterados con calidades corporales para estar en ellos contento, pero aún, cuando quiere obrar alguna cosa que le importa mucho, se aprovecha de las calidades corporeales que ayudan para aquel fin" (184-185).

37. "Mucho me pesa de la enfermedad que tiene la hermana Isabel de San Jerónimo. Ahí la envío al padre fray Juan de la Cruz para que la cure, que le ha hecho Dios merced de darle gracia para echar los demonios de las personas que los tienen. Ahora acaba de sacar aquí en Avila de una persona tres legiones de demonios, y les mandó en virtud de Dios le dijesen su nombre, y al punto obedecieron" (Cta: 685).

38. In addition, Counter-Reformation Spain was an especially inhospitable place for women who presumed to make theological pronouncements. Teresa herself describes the dilemma she frequently found herself in when called upon to explain her supernatural experiences: "They asked me questions; I answered plainly and without concern; then it seemed to them that I was teaching and I thought I was wise. They told everything to my confessor . . . and he ended up scolding me" ("Preguntávanme algunas cosas; yo respondía con llaneza y descuido; luego les parecía los quería enseñar y que me tenía por sabia. Todo iva a mi confesor . . . él me reñía" [V 28: 115]). For a fuller discussion of ecclesiastical misogyny in Counter-Reformation Spain, see Weber 17-41.

39. "A los primeros conjuros, [el fraile] hace confesar a la posesa que se ha entregado al demonio a la edad de seis años. . . . La entrega se hizo solemnemente: la niña se sacó sangre de un brazo y con ella escribió una cédula en la que hacía constar que se daba por entero al diablo. Los exorcismos son acompañados de terribles convulsiones de la pobre endemoniada: insulta furiosa [al fraile], echa espumarajos por la boca, grita, se revuelve frenética en el suelo, hasta intenta abalanzarse sobre el descalzo y sus acompañantes. . . . El joven exorcista pone una cruz sobre ella y continúa exorcizándola. La endemoniada arroja la cruz contra el suelo; pero el fraile le manda cogerla y besarla, y ella obedece, aunque bramando. . . . Al fin, después de meses de exorcismos, logra arrancar al diablo la cédula y dejar libre a la monja, que queda rendida, como salida de una pesadilla larga y atormentadora" (108-110). The "document" seems to refer to a diabolical "pact," one of the cornerstones of witchcraft beliefs.

40. "Esta hermana no tiene demonio, sino falta de juicio" (Crisógono 111).

41. "De la San Jerónimo será menester hacerla comer carne algunos días y quitarla la oración y mandarla vuestra paternidad que no trate sino con él, u que me escriva, que tiene flaca la imaginación y lo que medita le parece que ve y oye; bien que algunas veces será verdad y lo ha sido, que es muy buena alma" (Cta: 773).

42. "Bien es pedir esa libertad al 'ángel', aunque yo holgaría que se procurase echar 'Patillas' de esa casa, con los remedios que se suelen tomar para eso" (Cta: 773).

43. Teresa urges the prioress to have Isabel eat meat in two other letters, March 2, 1577, and June 4, 1578.

44. "Aun ansí lo estuviera yo de San Jerónimo. En forma me da pena esa mujer. Crea que no havía de salir de cabe mí u adonde tuviese temor. Plega a Dios que no nos haga alguna cosa el demonio que tengamos que hacer. Vuestra reverencia avise a la priora que no la deje escrivir letra, y a ella le diga—mientra va mi carta—que entiendo anda con gran mal humor, y si no lo es, es peor" (Cta: 827).

45. Indeed, it was dangerous for women to write on any religious subject. Counter-Reformation theologians interpreted St. Paul's command that "women

be silent in the churches" with particular rigor, proscribing in effect all forms of women's writing that presumed to "teach" in any sense. See the comments by Milagros Ortega Costa on the trial of Isabel Ortiz, a laywoman whose works were burned by the Inquisition, not because of doctrinal error but because of their female authorship (100-103, 117, n. 85).

46. "Porque entiendo los inconvenientes que hay en andar pensando en qué han de escrivir y lo que las puede poner el demonio, pongo tanto en esto. Si es cosa muy grave, vuestra reverencia lo puede escrivir aun sin que lo sepan. Si yo huviera hecho caso de cosas de San Jerónimo, nunca acabara; y con parecerme algunas ciertas, aun me lo callava" (Cta: 870)

47. "En gracia me cai decir vuestra reverencia que no se ha de creer todo lo que dijere San Jerónimo, haviéndoselo ya escrito tantas veces. . . . Con todo digo que es buen alma, . . . que errará por falta en entendimiento, mas no por malicia. Ya puede ser que yo me engañe" (Cta: 955-956).

48. "El demonio no puede sufrir cuán de veras estos descalzos y descalzas sirven a nuestro Señor. . . . Como no está hecha provincia por sí, son tantas las molestias y trabajos que se tienen con los 'del paño', que no se puede escrivir" (Cta: 897-898). The letter is dated October 4, 1578.

49. "En lo que toca a esotra doncella u dueña, mucho se me ha asentado que no es tanto melancolía como demonio que se pone en esa mujer para que haga esos embustes, que no es otra cosa para si pudiese en algo engañar a vuestra paternidad, ya que a ella tiene engañada; y ansí es menester andar con gran recato en este negocio y no ir vuestra paternidad a su casa en ninguna manera, no le acaezca lo que a santa Marina (creo era), que decían era suyo un niño y padeció mucho. . . . Advierta, mi padre, que, si esa carta no le dio debajo de confesión u en ella, que es caso de Inquisición, y el demonio tiene mil enredos. Ya otra murió en ella por lo mismo, que vino a mi noticia. Verdad es que yo no creo que ella se la dio al demonio—que no se la tornara a dar tan presto—ni todo lo que ella dice, sino que deve ser alguna embustera (Dios me lo perdone) y gusta de tratar con vuestra paternidad" (Cta: 776). Teresa refers to the woman as a "dueña," a word that had acquired unsavory sexual connotations by the late sixteenth century. The specific woman has never been identified. The letter mentioned in the passage appears to refer to a written "pact" with the Devil, similar to the one signed by the Augustinian nun exorcized by John of the Cross.

50. Nearly forty years later, Miguel de Cervantes would explore the fictional possibilities of possession as a form of theatrical behavior. See Wilson, Chapter 10, "The Histrionics of Exorcism" (223-247).

51. An intellectual vision was one without external or internal image. The imaginative vision, considered less perfect but nonetheless spiritually beneficial, produced a transitory but vivid internal image. In her Life, Teresa asserted that she had never experienced the most dangerous type, the "corporeal vision," which is seen with "the eyes of the body" (V 28: 111).

52. "Y con esto no andéis turbadas ni inquietas, que aunque no fuese de Dios, si tenéis humildad y buena conciencia no os dañará, que sabe Su Majestad sacar de los males bienes, y que por el camino que el demonio os quería hacer perder, ganaréis más. . . . [Q]ue como decía un gran letrado, que el demonio es gran pintor, y si le mostrase muy al vivo una imagen del Señor, que no le pesaría, para con ella avivar la devoción y hacer a el demonio guerra con sus mesmas

maldades; que aunque un pintor sea muy malo, no por eso se ha de dejar de reverenciar la imagen que hace, si es de todo nuestro bien" (M VI, 9: 412).
53. "Si el confesor le da este consejo, . . . el mío es que aunque os le dé, le digáis esta razón con humildad, y no le toméis" (M VI, 9: 412).
54. "Comencemos por el tormento que da topar con un confesor tan cuerdo y poco espirimentado que no hay cosa que tenga por sigura; todo lo teme, en todo pone duda como ve cosas no ordinarias, en especial si en el alma que las tiene ve alguna imperfeción (que les parece han de ser ángeles a quien Dios hiciere estas mercedes . . .), luego es todo condenado a demonio u melencolía. Y de ésta está el mundo tan lleno, que no me espanto, que hay tanta ahora en el mundo y hace el demonio tantos males por este camino, que tienen muy mucha razón de temerlo y mirarlo muy bien los confesores" (M VI, 1: 386-387).

Works Cited

Andrés, Melquíades. La teología española en el siglo XVI. 2 vols. Madrid: Católica, 1977.

Bilinkoff, Jodi. The Avila of Saint Teresa: Religious Reform in a Sixteenth-Century City. Ithaca, N.Y.: Cornell Univ. Press, 1989.

Bynum, Caroline Walker. Holy Feast and Holy Fast: The Religious Significance of Food to Medieval Women. Berkeley: Univ. of California Press, 1987.

Caro Baroja, Julio. Vidas mágicas e inquisición. 2 vols. Madrid: Taurus, 1967.

————. Las formas complejas de la vida religiosa. Religión, sociedad y carácter en la España de los siglos XVI y XVII. Madrid: Akal, 1978.

Cohn, Norman. Europe's Inner Demons. New York: Basic Books, 1975.

Covarrubias, Sebastián de. Tesoro de la lengua castellana o española. 1611. Madrid: Turner, 1977.

Crisógono de Jesús y Matías. "Vida de San Juan de la Cruz." Vida y obras de San Juan de la Cruz. Ed. Luciano Ruano. 6th ed. Madrid: Católica, 1972.

Delumeau, Paul. La Peur en occident. Paris: Fayard, 1978.

Egido, Aurora. "Sobre la demonología de los burladores (De Tirso a Zorrilla)." Iberoromania 26 (1987): 19-40.

Gracián de la Madre de Dios, Jerónimo. El cerro. 1582. Appendix I in Ana de Jesús y la herencia teresiana. Ed. Ildefonso Moriones de la Visitación. Rome: Edizioni del Teresianum, 1968.

Huarte de San Juan, Juan. Examen de ingenios para las ciencias. Ed. Rodrigo Sanz. Madrid: Imprenta La Rafa, 1930.

Huerga, Alvaro. Historia de los Alumbrados. 2 vols. Madrid: Fundación Universitaria Española, 1978.

Imirizaldu, Jesús, ed. Monjas y beatas embaucadoras. Madrid: Editora Nacional, 1977.

Katz, Steven. "The 'Conservative' Character of Mystical Experience." Mysticism and Religious Traditions. Ed. Steven Katz. London: Oxford Univ. Press, 1983. 3-60.

Klaits, Joseph. Servants of Satan: The Age of the Witch Hunts. Bloomington: Indiana Univ. Press, 1986.

Midelfort, H. C. Eric. Witch-Hunting in Southwestern Germany 1562-1684. Stanford: Stanford Univ. Press, 1972.

Moncy, Agnes. "Santa Teresa y sus demonios." *Papeles de Son Armadans* 10.107 (1965): 149-166.

Ortega Costa, Milagros. "Spanish Women in the Reformation." *Women in Reformation and Counter-Reformation Europe.* Ed. Sherrin Marshall. Bloomington: Indiana Univ. Press, 1989. 89-119.

Peers, Edgar Allison, trans. *The Letters of Saint Teresa of Jesus.* 2 vols. London: Burnes, 1951.

Perry, Mary Elizabeth. "Beatas and the Inquisition in Early Modern Seville." *Inquisition and Society in Early Modern Europe.* Ed. and trans. Stephen Haliczer. London: Croom Helm, 1987. 147-168.

_____ . "Subversion and Seduction: Perceptions of the Body in the Writings of Religious Women in Counter-Reformation Spain." *Religion, Body, and Gender in Early Modern Spain.* Ed. Alain Saint-Saëns. San Francisco: Edwin Mellen Research Univ. Press, 1991 (forthcoming).

Russell, Jeffrey Burton. *Lucifer: The Devil in the Middle Ages.* Ithaca: Cornell Univ. Press, 1984.

Teresa de Jesús. *Obras Completas.* Ed. Efrén de la Madre de Dios and Otger Steggink. Madrid: Católica, 1962.

_____ . *Libro de la vida.* Ed. Otger Steggink. Madrid: Castalia, 1986.

Weber, Alison. *Teresa of Avila and the Rhetoric of Femininity.* Princeton: Princeton Univ. Press, 1990.

Wilson, Diana. *Allegories of Love: Cervantes's "Persiles and Sigismunda."* Princeton: Princeton Univ. Press, 1991.

Chapter 9

Woman as Source of "Evil" in Counter-Reformation Spain

María Helena Sánchez Ortega

(translated by Susan Isabel Stein)

Since ancient times, woman has been the object of accusations that have essentially transformed her into the source of all suffering. Both classical and Judeo-Christian traditions associate her with the appearance of sudden illnesses, death, accidents, and even metaphysical malaise. Eve, Lilith, Delilah, Pandora, and Helen are names that immediately bring to mind the misfortunes befalling the men who trusted these women. Humanity in general is said to have suffered because of woman's imprudence, her frauds, her cunning, as well as her capacity to distract and seduce even the strongest and most God-fearing of men. Traditionally, women have also been regarded as the repositories of supernatural powers, which they have used to aid their lovers, but which they have often also used against them, as was the case with Circe and Medea.

Man's distrust of woman is thus based upon a lengthy tradition converting her into the bearer of both physical and spiritual ailments. This pejorative view is not allayed by the existence in the Greco-Latin pantheon of female deities, nor is the rejection of women abated through the cult of the Virgin Mary, by which means Christianity attempts to emphasize woman's importance as mother "without blemish," that is, distanced from any sexual contact or experience. Throughout the Middle Ages, women were suspect in the eyes of the Church, which always feared that Satan would use women as the most accessible and adequate means of setting his traps.

In Spain, the view of women as the supreme embodiment of carnality, promulgated by the Church fathers compelled to wage a war against women, was inherited by the Hapsburg Regime. The Inquisition trials contain many examples of this juxtaposition of classical and Christian ideas, which transforms many women into objects of suspicion because of their evil powers, especially since society believed them to be endowed with sexual energies capable of weakening, effacing, or corrupting men's wills. According to Inquisition documents, these women reveal an entire array of evil powers that paradoxically were viewed with more tolerance by the inquisitors than by the women's neighbors. These presumed powers were the source of much suffering to single or older women, especially those singled out for their scandalous or bad temperament. Women were not always innocent victims in these situations, however. Sorcery was not only an occupation that some easily fell into, but also a relatively lucrative profession freely chosen by many.

In spite of Henry Charles Lea's conclusion that the proliferation of cases of superstition in Spain was the result of racial intermixing during the medieval period,[1] most of the magic practices mentioned in the laws promulgated from the twelfth to the seventeenth centuries have their origins in classical times, at least as far as the most common and widespread practices of "love magic" are concerned. This magical repertoire, mainly practiced by women, is derived from its essential connection to the classical world, as well as to the Christian rites of the Middle Ages. The women of Thessaly, famed for their magical practices, find their immediate heiresses in the disillusioned, solitary, or seductive women encountered in the inquisitional trials. In the Toledo tribunal alone more than 75 percent of the sorcery cases were against women, the majority of whom had practiced amorous or erotic rituals or spellcasting.[2] Any attempt to study the history of women during the Hapsburg Regime would be incomplete without a systematic attempt to understand these trials, where woman appears as the source of evil.[3]

In both city and country, collective fears could be inspired by the most trivial circumstances. Isabel Maesso was tried in 1670 after a neighbor accused her of keeping a small horn-box with some suspicious contents (AHN, Inq. Leg. 90, n. 3). The contents might be used to cast a spell: two pieces of heart-shaped wax, one pierced from top to bottom with three pins, and the other pierced through the thickest part with a needle; and another piece of wax in the shape of a stomach, with a hole. All of these pieces were covered with an oil-soaked rag. There is no indication in the trial of how the box had been discovered, but somehow the neighbor had entered Isabel's house and taken the box from the chest where she kept it. This simple accusation led Isabel to the Holy Office, where she testified that her cousin had found the suspicious box in the street, and that she herself was unfamiliar with the contents when she put it away. The accused sorceress categorically denied that she was the owner of the contents or that she had knowledge of their purpose, but under the commissioner's authority she was condemned to exile by the tribunal.

A similar case occurred in 1632 when Roque Fernández from Puebla de Montalbán made an accusation against Isabel López, "the storekeeper" (AHN, Inq. Leg. 89 [2], n. 13). Roque suspected that she was attempting to cast a spell on him; he testified that someone had sewn a small taffeta bag inside his doublet, over the right sleeve, containing a powder that caused him to experience strange bouts of dizziness. A little while later he discovered that someone had placed another bag on the left side, over his heart. Roque explained that he had felt "weak in the head and of a disposition unlike what he usually felt" ("desvanecido de la cabeça y con diferente disposición de la que solía tener"). He asked his wife who had sewn the bags in his clothes and was surprised to discover that she herself had done so on the advice of a neighbor, Isabel López, who had assured her that she would spare herself vexations. The results had been less than positive for Roque, however, who worriedly explained to the inquisitors the symptoms of the spell. His suspicions were aroused because of his relationship with Isabel López, and he was obliged to confess Isabel's response when he asked her to relieve him of his sufferings: "She told him that she would set things right as soon as he recommenced his relationship with her." Isabel López, in spite of the evidence against her, was luckier than Isabel Maesso and the case was suspended. As we have just seen, both men and women through the early modern period and beyond, firmly believed in the possibility of physical harm inflicted by their enemies' wishes. The necessity of responding somehow to the situation was channeled through accusations made at the Holy Office.

The types of spells we have just examined were apparently familiar to many, and judging by the testimonies made at the tribunals, those who employed them trusted in their power as much as the victims feared their effects. Neither beliefs nor circumstances had altered significantly since the classical period: mysterious powders, little sacks with magical effects, figurines made of wax or metal, pierced hearts, and herbs with extraordinary powers all contributed to the repertory of what is known as "sympathetic magic," utilized all over Europe as well as on other continents. The spells, as we will see in the following cases, gained as diverse and dangerous a reputation as the women who employed them.

The possibility of suffering some mysterious ailment unresponsive to either science or prayer constituted a daily threat to the men and women of the Hapsburg Regime. Whoever had the misfortune of incurring the anger of some neighbor who either possessed or had recourse to this hermetic knowledge might begin to suffer strange personal or material afflictions or disgraces. This threat was capable of bridging the space between desire and deed; potential victims faced an enigmatic reality fraught with evils affecting all aspects of daily life. Misfortune, illness, and material ruin were interpreted as the results of powerful spells cast upon the victims and their most precious possessions. The fears of the rural population, constantly aware of the ephemeral nature of prosperity, are quite evident in the inquisitorial documents.

For the largely rural population of early modern Spain, the death of a domestic animal represented not only an important material loss, but the symbol of greater misfortunes to come. In

1625, an accusation was made against a woman known only as "Doña Angela, who lives on Madera Street" (AHN, Inq. Leg. 82, n. 12). The accusation was made by María Ruiz Romero, a thirty-one-year-old married woman acting as an intermediary, or simply as a scrupulous individual wishing to inform the inquisitors of suspicious occurrences. The case concerned the sudden death of a small dog and a black cock-pigeon owned by the informant's friend. Extremely concerned about these losses, the friend interpreted them as a sign of bad luck and ill will, and she feared she was the victim of Doña Angela, the alleged local sorceress and expert in spells.

María Ruiz's testimony was apparently based on a trivial circumstance, but one hardly insignificant for contemporary men and women whose accusations and trials reveal a constant fear of harm befalling their domestic animals. In 1630 a long trial was held for Ana García, a woman from El Campillo, who was supposed to have "scandalized the entire area of El Campillo with her evil way of living, doing great harm to the residents, both to their persons and to their livestock, for anything she asks for and is denied" (AHN, Inq. Leg. 86, n. 16).[4] Ana García had, in effect, terrorized a substantial number of people by the aggressive behavior she usually exhibited when she was with her daughter and her daughter-in-law. The three of them comprised a family of women capable of casting spells on whomever they chose.

According to the witnesses, Ana García caused numerous damages to livestock. On one occasion she had fought with some neighbors regarding the concession of acreage; she had arrived late, and when she saw that they had no intention of assigning the plots to her, she threatened that "they would pay for it." When one of the neighbors returned home, he found one of his calves and three goats dead. Ana had argued with this witness's wife, whom she had threatened by drawing a cross on the floor and repeating that she would pay. A few days after this encounter, a calf began "wandering away from its mother, hurling itself against the rocks until it died in great agony." Obviously the presence of Ana García, her daughter, or her daughter-in-law provoked extreme anxiety among their neighbors, who believed their threats to be of supernatural origin. A married couple who had also had an altercation with them explained that these women were surely responsible for the losses they had suffered, "when their cows had suddenly died in great agony." With their threats and behavior, these three women had convinced the entire town that they had made a pact with the Devil.

The loss of domestic animals thus represented a major catastrophe for most peasants, who associated any threat followed by sudden illness directly with the neighbors employing this kind of threat to obtain favors. When the loss of a domestic animal was accompanied by the sudden disappearance of a child, fear and superstition increased accordingly, as occurred in Ana García's case. These incidents acquired a significance far beyond any dispute among neighbors involving merely strong words or threats. Any woman associated with the illness or death of a child attracted the Holy Office's attention much more directly, as we shall see.

While the rural population was justifiably concerned with material well-being, the preoccupation with one's own physical and mental state was of equal significance, and the peasants were convinced that good health was attributable to powerful forces or strange faculties that were too often in the hands of women. The testimonies or trials related to cases of illness brought on by magic are numerous. Ana García, held responsible for damage to the material wealth of her neighbors, was also accused of having caused illness in some of her neighbors as well as in people from other areas (AHN, Inq. Leg. 86, n. 16). She was supposedly responsible for an entire family's illness; the witnesses swore that the curse had entered the house under the door and had individually attacked everyone who lived there.

The inexplicable death of an infant or small child represented, however, a very special problem. The accusations and testimonies reveal a special concern on the part of adults, in spite of the high incidence of infant mortality and the thousands of unwanted illegitimate children characteristic of the period.

Suspicions were easily aroused when a child fell ill after a visit by someone of dubious reputation, as was the case of a woman named Gerónima who worked as an aide in the hospital of San

Bartolomé in the township of Toledo (AHN, Inq. Leg. 87, n. 15). Sebastián Bautista, the alderman from the village of Tor de Inguna, where the woman worked, made the accusation in 1616; he suspected that Gerónima's visit to his house had some connection to his daughter's subsequent poor health. It seemed that the alderman had had to leave his home, and during his absence Gerónima had visited his wife, asking her for a pitcher of water. When the visitor left, his wife had fallen into an abnormally deep sleep; she awoke very frightened and began to call for the maid and one of her relatives who lived there. They then found her daughter on the floor, covered with bruises. A few days later, Gerónima returned to the village accompanied by another woman, and once again the little girl was found covered with bruises. The parents' suspicions grew when the wife saw a large, unfamiliar black dog in one of the rooms. When she exclaimed, "Jesus, what is this!", the dog opened one of the windows with his paws and left. That day the little girl again appeared covered with bruises.

For various reasons—such as their evil temperament, their disputes with the neighbors, and their failure to follow community norms—some women were viewed with suspicion by most of their neighbors. Once suspected, any of their gestures could appear questionable. In some cases, near relatives formed a common front against someone; in others, those who shared the same occupation or interest in magic did so. María Estevan and her sister, tried in 1701, were known as "spellcasters using ingredients to ruin health" (AHN, Inq. Leg. 85 [2], n. 14). Their spells consisted of practically the entire repertory of feminine magic practices: illnesses, divinations, spells to induce impotency, and even curing impotency caused by spells. The Holy Office carefully studied the case of the two women and condemned María Estevan, a married woman, to two years in exile.

In general, the women who cast spells on livestock, crops, or on their neighbors were not professional sorceresses. There were, however, cases in which the specialists in "love magic," whose objective was to obtain the love of a scornful man, truly revealed a professional character. These magic practices did not always achieve the desired effects, and the request would then turn to vengeance, rendering the man impotent, incapable of having relations with the woman responsible for separating him from his lover. Love magic included spells capable of provoking strong fears and concerns in the young Don Juans of the period.

One frequent concern in the trial documents dealing with superstition and magic was the man who had abandoned a sexual partner. Often, these were married men carrying on "illicit" relations or marrying someone other than their lovers. These men apparently believed as fervently as the women who carried out the conjurations and rites in the possibility of losing their sexual capacity as a result of some spell. They would appear in desperation before the inquisitors after having tried various remedies, believing finally that only the Church had the power to neutralize their ex-lover's influence upon them. The formulas, treatments, and testimonies concerning impotency spells appear intermingled for the most part with other types of magic, but there are cases of an exclusively amorous nature.

María López, nicknamed "La Potencia," was accused in 1638 of having rendered her lover impotent prior to his decision to marry the accuser's sister (AHN, Inq. Leg. 89 [2], n. 16). Shortly before the wedding, Potenciana had sought out her ex-lover, begging him not to marry, and threatening him if he abandoned her. Shortly thereafter, she followed him to a church and, as he was praying, she cautiously approached him and cut off a piece of his cloak. When he returned home and realized that someone had taken a piece of his clothing, he immediately suspected his former lover. He became so frightened that he told a relative who then accompanied him to María López's house. They discovered the missing pieces of his cloak, but María assured them that she had no intention of causing him any harm; her only desire was to make him "detest" the woman he was to marry.

In general, men would go to the same sorceresses who had cast the spell on them in hopes of obtaining a cure. In María Estevan's trial we find the formula she gave to a young man who was impotent for the same reasons as Potenciana's lover (AHN, Inq. Leg. 85 [2], n. 14). In order to cure the young man, recently married and unable to have relations with his wife because he had been rendered impotent, María Estevan asked him for a black hen that had not been washed or plucked. She boiled it in holy water and threw the broth over a sword that she then gave to the sick man, telling him to go to church and attend mass with the sword at his side. Each time that the priest faced the parishioners, he was to recite the Apostles' Creed, and when the mass was over, he was to wrap "three quarters of a green silk ribbon" around the sword's handle. Then he was to drop the sword on the floor and leave it there, even if people said something to him. Finally, he must walk all around the church; in this way he would be cured. As we can see, María Estevan chose an appropriate phallic symbol for curing the recently married man's ailment; she had merely added to this a religiomagical ritual corresponding to the general love-magic procedures.[5]

The masculine fear of falling under the influence of a powerful woman, one capable of keeping a man against his will, is frequently in evidence in the testimonies and accusations made against both sorceresses and their clients. The men's testimonies convey both fascination and fear inspired by a force superior to their own. Isabel Martín personifies this type of woman; she was arraigned before the Toledo inquisitors on charges made by her ex-lover, an anguished twenty-five-year-old potter named Juan de la Casa. His testimony exemplifies the risks a man took if he fell into the hands of a woman whose attraction and fascination could only be explained through recourse to magic:

> He said he had come to ease his conscience by reporting that he had been bewitched by a woman named Isabel Martín, the wife of a man nicknamed Lagaña whose proper name he did not know, a fisherman from Puebla de Montalbán. Three years ago he had had carnal relations with this woman, and had been rendered impotent in such a manner as to be able to have relations exclusively with her; when he was away from her, he suffered from heart palpitations and felt as if his liver would fall out of his body. Recently he had moved to Toledo and married, and has barely been able to have relations with his wife, thus revealing that he is indeed under the spell of Isabel Martín, because he still suffers from heart palpitations and when he goes to her, he is able to have relations, but separated from her, with his wife or any other woman, he is unable to achieve any results. (AHN, Inq. Bk. 1149, fol. 474)[6]

The culmination of amorous magic, the dreaded impotency spell, makes it quite clear that Isabel Martín had no reason at all to envy Circe, whose destiny and circumstances would be tragically altered as the historical period would transform her avatars into characters completely different from the Homeric heroine.

The people most susceptible to spells were those who for physical or emotional reasons found themselves in a vulnerable position: lovers, women, and children whose total vulnerability was, in theory, irresistible to evil beings. Women were the most frequent objects of suspicions, and their behavior and attitudes were understood—at times even by their closest relatives—in terms of satanical influence. Testimonies against them reveal the difficulties they continually faced, both socially and psychologically, as well as their extreme dependence upon surroundings that could so easily turn hostile. The case of María Florín, a resident of Villaseca from 1778-1779, illustrates this type of situation (AHN, Inq. Leg. 86, n. 18).

María Florín was accused by her own husband, José Fernández de Julián, after he had consulted his confessor, a priest from Toledo who helped him draw up the accusation. Married for fourteen years, he had only begun to be aware of what he considered suspicious occurrences for six or seven years. The first thing that had caught his attention was María's apparent ignorance of Christian doctrine. As he explained in the document:

> I only desired, according to my obligations, to instruct
> my children in Christian doctrine, and so I called her,
> telling her I was going to ask her some questions. "What
> is attrition?" I asked her. Barely had she heard the word
> before she fell to the floor, which angered me, so I asked
> her, "So you're a Jew, are you? So you don't want to
> hear what's good for you." All she said was, "Go ahead
> and talk; I can hear you perfectly well."[7]

From that moment, his suspicions continued to increase, especially after having found the fragments of a saint's statue, which he respectfully picked up while his wife looked on with complete indifference, saying only, "Don't be silly." The situation became unbearable, however, after he witnessed a scene one night that left him terrified:

> A month had gone by when, seeing how badly she acted with me, I struck her a few times; in the middle of the punishment, she said, "Look at the face of the image I am holding (which was extremely ugly), and know that it is not you who hits me, but the demons and enemies that you have inside your body." Two days later she said to me, "Tonight Jesus Christ will show you what kind of wife you have." That night she asked me for an engraving of God which I had with me, and which I still have, and she circled it around her head a few times, she scratched it, and she made a hole in the shoulder and another one on top of the head of Jesus on the cross with a needle . . . Afterward, she told me, "Take your Christ and wear it on your chest where you must ask me for forgiveness, so you may know what type of wife you have." I put it on my chest, begging God not to let me fall asleep. As I remained awake, I could see a great number of wild boars, some big and some little, enter the kitchen, and sitting up, I said that with the blessing of Jesus Christ, whoever could ask for or grab something here would be a witness to this infamy. I reached out my hand to grab one and I grabbed a shoe, which I threw violently to the floor, realizing I had been tricked. After this, I saw what appeared to be a man, wearing my blue cape and hat, with the same braid and cockade I have, but I really don't know what he was, and he soon disappeared.[8]

José Fernández's nightmares and fears did not end with these diabolical apparitions; they continued to confirm his wife's strange powers and temperament. Evidently, José felt such an aversion toward her that he was psychologically disposed to testify to practically anything:

> I hadn't quite gotten over the shock when I felt something—I don't really understand what it was—; all I can say is that it suddenly rose from my ankles and rested on my tongue. Without being able to help myself, I arose with a strange impulse from the bed, and on my knees I called her. She answered me as if she had been in a deep sleep, asking me what I wanted. I said to her,

"Woman, I beg your pardon, do whatever you want
with me; you were right when you said you were an
honorable woman, and that is all I have to say." She
then said to me, "Lie down and go back to sleep; you
will rest now." I got back in bed, and before I had lain
down, I was asleep (and thus her damned prophecy
came true).[9]

Apparently, José was so frightened or tired of his wife, that
any gesture of hers intimidated him and convinced him of her
diabolical temperament. He therefore went to the priest who advised him to present the document we have just examined—
where he furnished many other details regarding María Florín's
strange nature—so that the inquisitors could intervene immediately in such a dangerous situation. The Holy Office put the suspect on trial, but we do not know how benevolent or severe the
inquisitors were with her, since the case records are incomplete.

In the same way that María Florín's husband feared the Devil's presence, whose existence had been readily affirmed and di-
vulged by the Church, many others believed that their problems
were proof of the constant threat he presented through women
as the main cause of human suffering.

One trial that demonstrates even more clearly the social pressure experienced by women whose character or conduct
shocked their peers, took place in 1648 against Ana García, "La
Lobera," accused by her pastors and neighbors of having a pact
with the Devil (AHN, Inq. Leg. 86, n. 17).[10] "La Lobera" was a
twenty-five-year-old woman who looked much older. Ashamed
because the father of her child did not want to marry her, she
lived a semisavage life in the wild, with a pack of wolves controlled by her commands. It was rumored that she had had "li-
centious" relations with the shepherds, and whenever they or
the owners would not give her what she needed, she would un-
leash her animals against them. The witnesses swore that she
had been seen making circles and casting spells in the wild, and
that she had made a pact with the Devil. The woman herself was
convinced that she had witnessed diabolical apparitions, as she
declared before the judges at her trial. According to her version,
the Devil had appeared on more than one occasion and had
treated her badly, asking her to give him her arm. The woman's

tormented state can be evinced by her own explanation to the inquisitors:

> Talking alone with the aforementioned Catalina González, the woman who initiated her pact with the devil and who was sick with an illness from which she later died, she was told that if she wanted to be with the wolves and cast a spell on them, she had to give her right arm to the devil, and then by making a circle in the dirt with her hands and whistling, the wolves would be under her spell, and that she could create any trouble she desired with them, only she should leave all livestock and people alone.[11]

Advised by her lawyer, Ana García readily confessed her guilt, although she denied the charges of having made a pact with the Devil, and she was treated benevolently by the inquisitors because of this attitude. She was absolved "ad cautelam" and released under the guidance of a "scholarly" individual from whom she would receive religious instruction for a few months.

In spite of the fact that the inquisitors' attitudes toward these women were frequently much more benevolent than those of their neighbors and relatives, it was the Church's intolerance toward women that was responsible for converting them into witches. Thus, when a case involved a child's accident, many inquisitors were tempted to explain the events as a diabolical pact. Their attitudes became even more rigid and stern. Ana García was condemned in 1656 to submit to torture because of her neighbors' accusations; apparently, it was the inquisitors' desire to intimidate the prisoner, and the following scene is frightening indeed (AHN, Inq. Leg. 18, n. 18).

Ana was led to the torture chamber at nine o'clock in the morning, where she was cautioned, "for the love of God," to tell the truth, "in order to extricate herself from the present difficulties." The same question was repeated many times, yet she had nothing to add to her previous declarations. The torturer—"minister," in the inquisitorial document—entered, and swore to "carry out his duties to the best of his abilities." Ana was again warned that she should confess; when she maintained that she had nothing more to say, she was ordered to undress.

When this moment arrived, she began to weaken, exclaiming, "I am blameless. Justice cannot command that I say what is not true. Blessed be God for putting me in this situation." The judges insisted once more that she tell the truth, but she replied, "Sir, I have sinned. I will not testify. My Father and Savior, I will not testify." Maintaining her innocence and refusing to accept responsibility for the children's accidents, she said, "If their kids died, so did my little ones. Sirs, don't press me and don't force me to say what I do not know."[12] Once again the question was posed and the prisoner admonished to tell the truth, but as Ana firmly maintained her innocence, she was finally ordered to dress and return to her cell because it was too late in the day to continue with the interrogation. Ana García's integrity throughout this ordeal was probably decisive in the tribunal's handing down a less severe verdict than had been anticipated at the beginning. In spite of the suspicions falling on her, the inquisitors only rebuked and warned her about her behavior.

On many occasions, old age and solitude appeared to provoke the neighbors' suspicions and fears. Among the women accused of spellcasting at the Toledo tribunal of this period, the cases of Juana la Izquierda, Catalina Matheo, and some others stand out; they first appeared before the curate and were afterward harshly judged by the inquisitors (AHN, Inq. Leg. 88, n. 13). The basic accusation concerned the deaths of some children who appeared to have been mysteriously maltreated. Undoubtedly advised by her lawyer, Juana la Izquierda presented the following statement of exoneration in which the real drama of these trials is evident:

> Juana la Izquierda, widow of Pedro Izquierdo, resident of Casar, in response to five witnesses' statements given to me and the accusation made by the Holy Office's prosecutor in which I am accused of being a witch, of having a pact with the devil, of teaching in company with another woman to a third how to be a witch, of meeting with other women in the house of a witch, where we smeared an ointment all over our bodies, and left the house flying naked, and went to kill infants, that one night we went to Joan Vaquerizo where we took a little girl and placed her upon the fireplace coals, which

killed her, and that another night we went in the same manner to Joan García the blacksmith's house, where we took a little boy from his bed, pulling him by the penis, pinching and mistreating him until he finally died.[13]

Juana continued listing the accusations of injuries inflicted on the neighbors' children in order to refute them and deny categorically the charge of witchcraft. She denied the prosecutor's accusations on the grounds that they went beyond her own declarations, as she had denied all criminal charges against her, and she also rejected the final witness's testimony on the grounds that there was no proof:

> Because all the proof against me consists of five witnesses and the judicial confession I made, they say, before the Alcalá curate [Juana had also been tortured, on this occasion by the bishopric] and because the third of the five witnesses has said nothing of substance, and the other three . . . said extrajudicial things in their confessions, saying they heard me saying things I never said nor could I ever say them.[14]

Her lawyer's flawless argument and the Inquisition's benevolence allowed Juana and her friends to escape relatively unscathed, with the exception of the torture episode, the appearance before the judges, and public opinion. Juana and the other "witches" abjured *de vehementi* their guilt, appearing at the 1591 *auto de fe* at which Philip II was present.[15]

The gallery of feminine portraits we have just analyzed illustrates that the role of women who practiced the magical arts was subject to continual transformation since the establishment of the prototype of Circe and her followers until the sixteenth and seventeenth centuries. The women capable of seducing and retaining a man by inexplicable means—Circe, Medea, Delilah, and even the beautiful Nausicaa and her followers, the "innocent seductresses"—are slowly replaced by negative figures converted by the ecclesiastic institutions into beings whose powers could only be explained through demonic intervention. Feminine characters such as Melusine, one of the fairies of popular tradition, and especially the nocturnal and ambiguous Lilith, became part of the diabolic entourage that, according to the

Church elders, wandered the earth in order to scourge the living. As we have seen, the *ctónicas* deities and the women of their cult suffered the greatest transformation, perhaps because they all shared an explicitly sexual image in classical literature as well as in popular folklore. There occurred an increasing demonization of female sexual energy not directly and exclusively linked to maternity or the general submission of the mother/wife. Lilith the seductress is ultimately converted into a nocturnal child-killing black bird, her figure leaving a shadow over the inquisitorial trials of the supposed witches. Even the animals of these women acquired sinister connotations: owls, cats, serpents, and, at times, dogs were seen as demonic apparitions.

While most people feared the possibility of a spell or a visit from a nocturnal guest, others viewed the problems realistically. The creation of the prototype belongs once more to the literary world, and Cervantes presents it better than anyone else in his *El Coloquio de los perros* (*The Dogs' Colloquy*). Here, Berganza describes to his friend his encounter with the witch Cañizares, who believes him to be a son of her old friend Montiela, whose children had been turned into dogs by Camacha, a witch envious of her powers. The old witch takes him to her home, explains his supposed origins to him, and tells him of the friendship she shared with his mother and her reasons for the kind of life she has chosen. La Cañizares is a woman accustomed to dissimulation and feigned virtue. She has kept up all the appearances of religious devotion and she is employed as a hospital aide just like our friend Gerónima. Berganza, impressed by her arguments on the convenience of simulating what is not real and of feigning virtue, exclaims indignantly, "Who made this damned old woman so discreet and so evil?" When his protectress anoints herself in preparation for her witchcraft, he grabs her by the leg in order to expose the truth to all her neighbors. Cervantes's version of Cañizares remains the best description of how witches were perceived at the time:

> She was more than seven feet tall; her bones stuck out
> all over, covered with dark, hairy, hard skin; her private
> parts were covered with the folds of skin from her
> stomach which was like a sheepskin and hung half-way
> down her thighs; her nipples were like the udders of

wrinkled, dried-up cows; her lips were black, her teeth worn down and her nose hooked and all askew. With her staring eyes, her dishevelled hair, her hollow cheeks, her shrunken neck and shrivelled breasts, she was as hideous and repulsive as could be. (Cervantes 236)[16]

Above all, La Cañizares is a solitary old woman who had most likely been involved in love magic and "illicit relations" all her life. "But this has passed, as everything does pass; memories fade. You can never live your life over again, people's tongues get tired of gossip, new things make one forget the old ones," she tells the son of her friend.[17] When her beauty fades, her powers to attract men are permanently affected, and her relation with the Devil becomes explicit. The seductress Lilith uncovers her true character, and even the dogs forming the entourage of the queen of the witches are repulsed by her. After such a sinful life, the only alternative is to surrender body and soul to the Devil.

Notes

1. "Spain was the classic land of magic whither, during the Middle Ages, resorted for instruction from all Europe those who sought knowledge of mysteries, and the works on the occult arts, which were circulated everywhere, bore for the most part, whether truly or falsely, the name of Arabic authors" (Lea 4: 180). Lea is correct in drawing attention to the importance of the cultural influences of the Spanish Jews as well as the Muslims, especially in astrology, *geomancia*, or "cult magic," as Caro Baroja calls it, but popular tradition in general relied on other elements that we must not ignore. I emphasize these elements in the present essay.

2. According to the data gathered by Sebastián Cirac Estopañán, the Toledo tribunal tried sixty-six men and two hundred women for sorcery during the sixteenth, seventeenth, and eighteenth centuries.

3. I have utilized the sources from the Toledo tribunal conserved in the National Historical Archive of Madrid. The summaries that follow are taken from the files 82-89 (A through L), including the case files of twenty-eight men and ninety-two women. Among these women, thirty-seven were dedicated to practices related fundamentally to amorous magic, twenty-four were denounced or tried for having cast spells, nineteen were specialists in curative practices, seven files concern amorous spells, and four concern possible witches.

For this essay, I have been exclusively concerned with the documental sources for the Toledo tribunal, although my perspective on the issue has been verified by the study I have been carrying out during the past few years about various Spanish tribunals.

4. "que tiene escandalizado el dicho lugar y tierra de el Campillo de Ranas con su mal modo de bivir, aciendo en los vecinos del dicho lugar grandes daños, assí en sus personas como en sus ganados por qualqier cossa que les pide y se le niega."

5. Regarding the special "synchretism" between superstition and religion achieved by women practicing love magic, see the chapter "La hechicería de los no-gitanos" in Sánchez Ortega, *La Inquisición y los gitanos*, 97-246.

6. "Dixo que viene a decir y manifestar por descargo de su conciencia que sabe que le tiene hechizado una mujer que se llama Isabel Martín, mujer de un hombre que por mal nombre llman Lagaña, que el nombre propio no lo sabe, de oficio pescador, vecino de Puebla de Montalbán, de donde es natural, habrá que trató carnalmente con esta mujer más de tres años y a este le ligó de suerte que cuando estaba con ella podía usar de hombre y después de ningún género ni modo, y cuando estaba fuera de ella se le afligía el corazón y los hígados parece que se le querían salir del cuerpo. Y últimamente se vino a Toledo y se casó, y no ha podido ni puede tampoco casi tener acto carnal con su mujer con lo cual echa de ver que la dicha Isabel Martín le tiene a este hechizado por lo que él siente en su corazón y porque cuando va al dicho lugar si quiere tratar con ella está bueno y sano, y en apartándose della ni con la mujer propia ni con otra puede tener acción ninguna." These testimonies occurred between 1618-1652. A detailed analysis of the sociocultural character of these testimonies can be seen in Sánchez Ortega, *La Inquisición* and *La mujer*.

7. "Quise . . . según mi obligación, instruir a mis hijos en la doctrina christiana, para esto la llamé diciéndola, vamos muger a hazer algunas preguntas. Qué cosa, dime, es atrición. Apenas oyó esta palabra se dejó caer en el suelo, con cuya acción yo enfadado la dije, con que eres judía? Con que no quieres oir lo bueno. A que solamente respondió: 'habla, que bien te oigo.' "

8. "Un mes se habría pasado, quando viendo lo mal que conmigo se portaba, la dí algunos golpes; en medio de este castigo decía: 'mira esta cara de ymagen que tengo (siendo en extremo horrible) advierte que no me das tú, sino los demonios o enemigos que tienes en el cuerpo.' Pasados dos días me dijo, esta noche te revelará a Jesuchristo la muger que tienes. En esta misma noche pidióme un divino Señor estampado que conmigo trahía, y traygo, y dándole varias bueltas por la cabeza, lo arañó luego, y con un alfiler le hizo un agugero en un hombro, y encima de la cabeza que es de Jesus con la cruz. . . . Pasado este, me dixo, toma tu Christo, y métetelo en el pecho que te has de levantar a pedirme perdón, para que entiendas la muger que tienes. Metímelo en el pecho suplicando a este Señor no me permitiese el que me quedase dormido. Estando assi despierto vi entrar en la cozina multitud de javalíes, chicos i grandes, e incorporándome dixe con el favor de Jesuchristo aquello que pide o coja aquí se quedará para testimonio de esta infamia; alargué la mano a cojer uno y agarré un zapato el que tiré con gran fuerza contra el suelo, viendo después mi engaño. Pasado esto vi uno como hombre, que trahía puesta mi capa azul y sombrero, con el mismo galón y escarapela que yo tengo, lo que fuese no lo se, ello desapareció muy en breve."

9. "No bien me había recobrado del susto, quando sentí una cosa (que no comprehendo lo que fuese) sólo puedo dezir que me subió repentinamente desde los tobillos y fijándoseme en la lengua, sin poder resistirme, me levanté con

estraño impulso de la cama, y puesto de rodillas a vozes la llamé, y respondién-dome como quien sale de un profundo letargo me dixo: 'qué quieres?' Y yo: 'Mu-ger, te pido perdón, haz de mí lo que quieras, dices bien que eres muger hon-rada, i buena.' Al punto me dixo: 'échate, échate a dormir que tú descansarás ya.' Assí q lo hize y fue esto de manera que antes de tender mi cuerpo ya estaba dormido (cumpliéndose de este modo su maldita profecía)."

10. Cirac Estopañán is the first to mention the trial against Ana, "La Lo-bera." Julio Caro Baroja refers to it as a case of "lycanthropy" (*Vidas mágicas*).

11. "Estando a solas parlando con la dicha Catalina González, que estaba mala de una enfermedad murió—la mujer que la inició en su trato diabólico—la dixo a esta que si quería andar con los lobos y encantarlos que abia de dar el brazo derecho a el diablo y que haziendo un zerco con las manos en la tierra y dando un silbo vendrían a su mandado y los encantaría y si querí hazer mal con ellos lo podría hazer y sino que podría guardar el ganado de ellos y hazer que no les hiziesse mal a los ganados ni a persona ninguna."

12. "y no se quiera ber en tanto trabaxo"; "hacer bien su oficio"; "estoy sin culpa. La justicia no manda que diga lo que no es. Bendito sea Dios, y alabado que a este estado me a traydo"; "Señor, pequé. Yo no he de lebantar testimonio. Padre mio, redentor, yo no he de lebantar testimonio"; "Si se les murieron sus chibatos, también a mis chiquitos. Señores, no me aprieten no me agan decir lo que no sé."

13. "Juana la Izquierda, viuda muger que fue de Pedro Izquierdo, vecina del Casar, respondiendo a la publicación de cinco testigos que me fue dada y a la acusación que por parte del fiscal de este Santo Oficio me fue puesta por la qual en efecto me acusa que soy bruxa, y como tal tengo pacto con el demonio, y que yo y otra muger bruxa enseñamos a cierta muger a ser bruxa, el que muchas no-ches yo y otras nos juntamos en casa de una muger bruxa, donde nos untávamos los cuerpos con cierta untura y salíamos desnudas en queros por el ayre y yvamos a matar niños criaturas, e una noche fuimos en casa de Joan Vaquerizo a donde tomamos una niña y la asentamos en las asquas de la lumbre, de lo qual vino a morir, e otra noche fuimos en casa de Joan García, herrador de la misma forma y le sacamos de la cama un niño y le tiramos de su miembro, y le pelliz-camos e hizimos tan mal tratamiento que quedó muerto."

14. "[P]orque toda la probanza que ay contra mi son cinco testigos y la con-fesión judicial que dicen que hice ante el vicario de Alcalá, e quanto a los cinco testigos el uno dellos que es el tercero no dice cosa de substancia, e los otros tres . . . dicen de confesiones cosas extrajudiciales que dicen me oyeron todas las quales cosas yo nunca dixe ni puedo decir."

15. From the beginning, the Spanish Inquisition placed special emphasis on obtaining concrete proof of witches' declarations—and recommended that the judges act with the expected prudence and assurances during the interroga-tions. See the 1554 document mentioned in Sánchez Ortega, *La Inquisición* (103). The inquisitor Salazar y Frías who allowed the Supreme Council to express a de-finitive judgment in this respect is not an isolated case but rather, the right man at the right place.

16. "Ella era larga de mas de siete pies; toda era notomía de huesos, cu-biertos con una piel negra, vellosa y curtida; con la barriga que era de badana se cubría las partes deshonestas, y aún le colgaba hasta la mitad de los muslos; las

tetas semejaban dos vejigas de vaca secas y arrugadas, denegridos los labios, traspillados los dientes, la nariz corva y entablada, desencasados los ojos, la cabeza desgreñada, las mejillas chupadas, angosta la garganta, y los pechos sumidos; finalmente, toda era flaca y endemoniada" (Cervantes, *Coloquio* 297-305).
   17. "Pero esto ya pasó, y todas las cosas se pasan; las memorias se acaban, las vidas no vuelven, las memorias se cansan, los sucesos nuevos hacen olvidar los pasados" (234).

Works Cited

Archivo Histórico Nacional (AHN), Sección Inquisición. Various documents.
Caro Baroja, Julio. *Las brujas y su mundo*. Madrid: Alianza Editorial, 1966.
_____. *Vidas mágicas e Inquisición*. 2 vols. Madrid: Taurus, 1976.
Cervantes, Miguel de. *Novelas exemplares*. Ed. Francisco Rodríguez Marín. 2 vols. Madrid: Espasa Calpe, 1975.
_____. *Exemplary Novels*. Trans. C. A. Jones. Rpt. 1984. New York: Penguin, 1972.
Cirac Estopañán, Sebastián. *Los procesos de hechicería en Castilla la Nueva: Tribunales de Cuenca y Toledo*. Madrid: Consejo Superior de Investigaciones Científicas, 1942.
Henningsen, Gustav. *The Witch's Advocate*. Toronto: Toronto Univ. Press, 1980.
Lea, Henry C. *A History of the Inquisition of Spain*. 4 vols. New York: Ams Press, 1966.
Russell, Jeffrey B. *Witchcraft in the Middle Ages*. Ithaca, N.Y.: Cornell Univ. Press, 1972.
Sánchez Ortega, María Helena. *La Inquisición y los gitanos*. Madrid: Taurus, 1988.
_____. "La Inquisición Española como fuente para la vida cotidiana." *Homenaje a Luis Sánchez Belda*. Madrid: Ministerio de Cultura, Archivo Histórico Nacional, forthcoming.
_____. *La mujer y la sexualidad en la perspectiva inquisitorial* (in press).

◆ Chapter 10

On the Concept of the Spanish Literary Baroque

John R. Beverley

Like one of its major figures, Janus—"el bifronte dios" in Góngora's exact characterization (one face peering perhaps at the sunset of feudalism, the other at the dawn of capitalism)— the Baroque has been seen an ambivalent phenomenon as has its "reception." The debate over its nature and value has been perennially on the agenda of modern European literary and cultural criticism, indeed was in a sense the issue that founded this criticism as such. What is at stake here is not only the Baroque as a "style-concept," but also its articulation as a cultural signifier, with a correspondingly variable set of signifieds, in the long history of ideological class conflict that accompanies the transition from feudalism to capitalism in Europe.

It is reductionist to argue, like Werner Weisbach, that the Baroque was the cultural form of the Counter-Reformation (among other reasons because there was a Protestant Baroque), but perhaps not too much so. The pejorative connotation the term acquired in European art history came from the Enlightenment attack (Boileau, Luzán) on the Baroque as a decadent and irrational style; in the case of Spain, the aesthetic correlative, as it were, of the Black Legend. The Romantics resurrected some figures associated with the Baroque (e.g., Bach and Calderón), but did not revise the negative vision of the epoch as a whole. For an emerging and still combatted liberalism on the Hapsburg-Latin periphery of European development, the Baroque was seen as an essentially reactionary phenomenon (by, for example, Galdós, Clarín, and Antonio Machado in Spain; by Croce and Gramsci in Italy). Consequently, its revalorization, initiated by Heinrich Wölfflin's influential *Principles of Art History*, would be contingent precisely on the crisis of liberalism that accompanied World War I and the Russian Revolution. In turn, the emerging ideology of aesthetic Modernism in its fascist (D'Ors, Spengler, Pound), neoliberal (Eliot, Ortega, and the Spanish Generation of '27), and Marxist (Walter Benjamin) variants would recuperate the Baroque—and invert the Romantic hierarchy of symbol over allegory—in its own "invention of tradition" (to borrow Eric Hobsbawm's phrase).

One point of contact with Modernism was that the Baroque was by antonomasia a "difficult" style. The Italian Mannerists had advanced in the sixteenth century the idea of difficulty as such—*difficoltà*—as an aesthetic property. They held that a special pleasure was to be gained through the ability of mind (*acutezza*) to experience the artwork as an intricate space of signification. The point was related to a Neoplatonic argument in favor of intuition and artistic freedom that amounted to a kind of formalism. What counted for the Mannerists was the *dispositio*, not the *materia*. By contrast, the leitmotif of Góngora's *detractores* in the seventeenth century—post-Tridentine humanists like Francisco de Cascales, who claimed to represent an Aristotelian "discipline of the rules" in literature—was that the cultivation of difficulty for its own sake betrayed a contradiction of the Scholastic entailment of *res* and *verba*, of language and that which language represents. By seeming to posit conceptual wit (*ingenio*) as the primary basis for aesthetic pleasure, they felt that Góngora and his followers produced a discourse that was nugatory and functionally atheistic (see Collard, and Smith, "Barthes").

The element of difficulty and excess in Baroque writing in particular links to the question of reading and "reading formations," to use a term Tony Bennett has done much to develop (and by which is meant those *historically* and *socially specific* determinations that bear on how a reader reads a text, as opposed to phenomenological reader-response theory of the sort associated with Gadamer or Fish). Who read in Golden Age Spain and its colonies, and what does this have to do with our notion of the literary Baroque? Early modern texts are ubiquitously disfigured by the sort of linguistic modernization favored by formalist philologists like, in Spanish literary criticism, Dámaso Alonso.[1] In like fashion, there is a natural tendency to misrecognize their nature and function as cultural artifacts by considering them as if they were in their initial moment of production and circulation the same thing that they are when we encounter them today as part of an academically defined and sanctioned enterprise like "Spanish literature."

The notion of literature as something available to a "reading public" at large is historically linked in Europe to the commodification of literary production and distribution, and to the growth of mass public education, particularly in the nineteenth century. As the cases of both the *comedia* and *Don Quijote* suggest, such a commodification was well under way in seventeenth-century Spain. The book industry was one of the first forms of capitalist production and merchandising in Spain and in Europe generally. In one of his last adventures, Don Quijote visits in Barcelona — then as now the most highly developed capitalist enclave on the Iberian Peninsula — a factory where books like *Don Quijote* are composed, printed, and bound. That, for all practical purposes, is the end of Don Quijote, both the hero and the novel. It is not until the period of triumphant liberalism in the late eighteenth and nineteenth centuries, however, that the virtual monopoly of the Church and the aristocracy on higher education and literacy (of the sort required for the "appreciation" of complex literary works) is decisively broken, and that something like a large, socially diverse reading public emerges.

By contrast, we know that certain forms of Baroque literature were in fact designed to resist even the already existing possibilities of commercial publication and distribution in seventeenth-century Spain, since their instrumentality was not at all to "reach" a mass audience but rather to intervene in discrete circuits of aristocratic power and patronage. The mode of existence of literature and literary texts in precapitalist societies—even in a transitional, late feudal (or, if you prefer, early modern) society like Golden Age Spain, already marked by a flourishing book trade—is in several respects quite different than it is in our own, something that should lead us to regard with suspicion the notion of literature itself as an unchanging essence.

To begin with, there is the fact that probably some 80 percent of the population of Golden Age Spain could neither read nor write at all (and that this was regarded as *normal*, as compared to our contemporary anxiety over illiteracy). This did not mean that this section of the public was necessarily barred from literature altogether. Wlad Godzich and Nicholas Spadaccini have drawn attention to the emergence in the sixteenth century of a mass-oriented "auditive culture"—the concept comes from the Brazilian critic Luiz Costa Lima—that differed both from traditional oral poetry and narrative, dependent on recitation from memory, and from the written/published text produced for the private consumption of a reader or readers. Such a culture might involve, for example, the *comedia* itself, which could engage its audience in extremely complicated word play, or the common practice of reading books aloud alluded to several times in the *Quijote*, or the *poesía de cordel*—texts that could be orally delivered but were composed in written form and published cheaply in some form or other (one of the earliest forms of the Top 40 hit is the *pliego suelto* or printed song sheet). Such discursive forms and practices are characterized, in Godzich and Spadaccini's words, "by a high level of rhetorical fabrication" dependent on the new possibilities of expression developed in Renaissance vernacular literature. "Although orally delivered, [they do] not seek to establish a dialogical relation with the audience but instead to leave the audience dumbfounded: *boca abierta*" (47). The Baroque penchant for difficulty which was supposed to be a mark of its differentiation from the *vulgo* produced paradoxically a popular taste for extravagant syntax and images.[2]

The most influential theorist and one of the most important practitioners of Baroque *écriture* in Spain was the Jesuit Baltasar Gracián. Readers of Gracián are familiar with the extreme artificiality of his writing. This involves not only its elliptical *conceptista* syntax and its very dense play of intertextuality but also its extremely intricate structural design, sometimes hidden by its aphoristic surface form. What is curious is that such an intensely and explicitly literary writing could be seen as effective, as Gracián certainly intended it to be, in forming a guide to statecraft or "mirror of princes"—particularly in a situation of imperial *descenso* where new forms of political imagination and practice were urgently needed. In part, of course, this claim had something to do with the discovery of the nonreferential, generative properties of language by what Noam Chomsky has called Cartesian linguistics. In part too, however, the claim fits with what we know about the nature of aristocratic dictatorship itself as a power system. In Maravall's well-known thesis, the Spanish Baroque represents a "lyrical engineering of the human world" by the absolutist state. This is not a case of cultural activity directing itself to a power center from the outside, in the way both mass and elite cultures are related to the state in contemporary liberal societies (see *La cultura del barroco*). In the Spanish Court and the colonial viceroyalties of the Golden Age, art and politics are not yet clearly separate disciplines and activities. That is why for Gracián an *arte de agudeza* based on the study of literary conceits (*conceptos*) could be seen as a prerequisite for the formation of the Baroque man of affairs, the *político*.[3]

This extreme dependence on cultural production for securing and developing rule also entailed what in contemporary philosophy would be termed an "antifoundationalist" conception of politics and power. This is implicit in Gracián's theory of the conceit itself, which as A. A. Parker stressed, begins with the distinction between *agudeza de artificio*—literary wit, justified by aesthetic criteria—and *agudeza de perspicacia*—philosophical intelligence, the ability to see relations that are logically and objectively true. In his famous definition of the *concepto* as "an act of the will that expresses the relationship that exists between objects" ("un acto del entendimiento, que exprime la correspondencia que se halla entre los objetos" [*Agudeza y arte de ingenio*, Discurso II, 240]), Gracián was not proposing a symbolist poetics of correspondence of hidden essences, Parker argued, but stressing precisely the arbitrary and formalistic character of linguistic signification.

What is continually deferred in Gracián is the resolution of the indeterminacy between a rhetorical notion of the discursive construction of power and meaning—what Nietzsche must have admired in his work—and the notion of power as an expression of an innate quality (*quilate rey*, to use one of his characteristic expressions) demanded both by aristocratic caste assumptions and Counter-Reformation political theory. As is well known, Gracián sustained this deferral by substituting a logic of appearances for a logic of essences. As he notes in one of the central maxims of *El héroe*, "This first rule of greatness advises that, if not infinite, to appear so, which is not an ordinary subtlety" ("Esta primera regla de grandeza advierte, si no el ser infinitos, aparecerlo, que no es sutileza común" [7]). The means of this deferral is the practice of literature or writing itself.

Jean-Cristophe Agnew has recently argued that the development of Elizabethan and Jacobean theater in England coincided with the onset of market society in the context of the primitive accumulation of capital. Where the *marketplace* was a necessary but liminal institution in feudal society, the *market* came to seem as coextensive with (and determinant of) society itself. The expansion of exchange relations and the increasing importance of money disrupted traditional hierarchies of social status and privilege, producing what Agnew calls a crisis of representation that the emerging secular theater both reflected and deepened. As in the Calderonian topic of the "great theater of the world," the Spanish Baroque is similarly aware of the "semiotic" or arbitrary and contingent character of social authority and roles; on the other hand, it will also insist on the necessity of these remaining as they are.

Clifford Geertz has written of the "semiotic of power" that underlies the "theatre state" of seventeenth-century Bali:

> The stupendous cremations, tooth filings, temple dedications, pilgrimages, and blood sacrifices, mobilizing hundreds and even thousands of people and great quantities of wealth, were not means to political ends: they were the ends themselves, they were what the state was for. Court ceremonialism was the driving force of court politics; and mass ritual was not a device to shore up the state, but rather the state, even in its final gasp,

was a device for the enactment of mass ritual. . . . The
ritual life of the court, and in fact the life of the court
generally, is thus paradigmatic, not merely reflective, of
social order. (13)

Geertz's vision of the "theatre state" is intentionally formalistic (he does not trouble to explain the forms of feudal extrac-
tion that provided among other things the revenues for such
spectacles). But it does help us understand the Baroque's sense
of the autonomy and centrality of cultural practice (see Apostolidés, and Marin on French absolutism). The Baroque's major institutional and ideological form is in fact the spectacle of the city
itself, whose rise all over Europe as an international, national,
and/or regional corporate *seigneur* involved, as John Merrington
has noted, "not only a massive shift of human and material resources in favor of urban concentrations, but also a *conquest* over
the countryside, which becomes ruralized, since it by no means
represented in the past an exclusively agricultural milieu" (171).
As an urban cultural form, the Baroque implies a taste for the
new and the artificial, for example fireworks (*fuegos de artificio*),
which, Maravall notes, "were an adequate sign of the splendor
of whoever ordered them because of their very artifice, their difficulty, the expense in human labor and in money that they implied" (*Culture* 246).

But the taste for the artificial also carries with it for a Baroque
sensibility the fear of moral or ecological perversion—the transgression of the Horatian golden mean—and a consequent nos-
talgia for "the simple life" represented in idealized form by the
pastoral. Góngora has elaborate fireworks scenes in both the *Soledades* and the *Panegírico* for the Duke of Lerma, his last major
work. In the *Soledades* (I, 642-658) an old man who witnesses the
spectacle fears, however, that, on the analogy of Phaëthon's
chariot, an accident will happen ("and miserably / the village
that greeted the night / will make at dawn a sterile field" ["y mis-
erablemente / campo amanezca estéril de ceniza / la que ano-
checió aldea"]).

This same cult of (and anxiety about) the artificial character-
izes those elite forms of Baroque culture that are internal to the
life of the court represented, say, by Góngora's poetry or Veláz-

quez's paintings. These embody the aristocratic fetish of a highly wrought art form, which is seen as noble or sublime to the extent that it eludes the comprehension of the masses and situates itself outside the nascent bourgeois value system of money and market exchange as determinants of power and status. In Baroque representation, for example in the key symbol of the cornucopia, wealth and power appear as uncoerced reflexes of some providence built into Nature itself, rather than as products of human labor carried out under exploitative and in the case of the colonies, genocidal relations of production. This is part of its service as an ideological practice for and of a seigneurial, Catholic ruling class that needs to differentiate itself from the sordid world of commerce and manual labor at the same time that it depends on the gold and silver exports from the Americas. Metaphorical and mythological decor, the Baroque's peculiar verbal and iconographic alchemy, constitutes a kind of "theory of magic accumulation" that masks the real primitive accumulation of capital in the colonies and in the confiscation of Jewish and *morisco* property, making it appear harmonious with the religious and aristocratic assumptions of the state's imperialist ventures. Such a procedure works to affirm the hegemony not by its *coincidence* with the official representations of power and authority but precisely by its "defamiliarization" of these. A poem like the *Soledades* or a novel like *Don Quijote* sets up a sphere of private experience that was distinct from but not (necessarily) in contradiction with the public sphere and the public identity of the reading subject as a social agent.

Maravall's basic thesis is that the Spanish Baroque is a culture of reaction against the ideological and social mobility in both Spain and Europe that threatened to break down both the hierarchical order of feudal estates and the authority of the Church: as a "historical formation" it represents a feudalism that has incorporated and recontained the emerging energies of both a nascent bourgeois and plebeian humanism and capitalism. Such a vision, however, entails a number of paradoxes. First, as J. H. Elliott, among others, has observed, Maravall's concept of the absolutist state which he derives from Weber's characterization of the modern state bureaucracy is too monolithic, and assumes too great an identity of interests between Crown, nobility, and

Church and too great a degree of centralization and functional rationalization of the state apparatus itself ("Concerto"). Elliott does not make the point, but it would perhaps be more pertinent to see representation of the state in Baroque culture more as an *imaginary*—in the Lacanian sense of a projection of desire that systematically misconstrues the real—of absolutism than as an expression of its actual coherence and authority.

Second, if Baroque culture indeed seeks to reassert the principle of seigneurial authority it cannot do this on a *purely feudal* or, what amounts to the same thing in culture, on a Scholastic basis, as we noted previously apropos of Calderón. The Spanish literary Baroque is at least in part the product of the Jesuits' insistence that the suspect new genres of Renaissance vernacular literature, many of which had been placed on the Index of prohibited books in the wake of the Council of Trent, could be recuperated and mobilized in the service of Catholic orthodoxy and the defense of Spain's overseas empire.[4] Among the products of the relative liberalization of literary policy that follows the death of Philip II in 1598 are *Don Quijote,* Góngora's *Polifemo* and *Soledades,* the *comedia,* and the body of novels known in Spanish literature as the Baroque picaresque. What this implies, however, is that the literary forms the Baroque will mobilize against an emergent bourgeois and artisanal culture are precisely those provided by that culture: the Petrarchan lyric, the pastoral and picaresque novel, the essay, the autobiography, the "history," and the plebeian-humanist drama of the sort represented by the *Celestina* or Juan del Encina. Far from restoring the Scholastic principle of *comunitas,* based on the natural reciprocity of the hierarchically differentiated orders of society, Baroque culture tends precisely to interpellate the human subject as a solitary individual. Maravall notes that "in the baroque world individuals appear on the level of morality as monads," something confirmed by the picaresque novel or the "baroque anthropology" of Shakespeare's or Calderón's characters (*Culture* 203).

Third, the Baroque is a profoundly historicist cultural form. But its representation of history has a problematic dimension, since it addresses not only an apotheosis of empire but also a growing sense that Spain itself has entered its Iron Age, a period of irreversible crisis and decay. Elliott voices the question that must have inevitably confronted the Baroque *letrado:* "If all the great empires, including the greatest of them all, had risen only to fall, could Spain alone escape?" "The idea of an infinite cyclical process by which all living organisms were subject to growth, maturity and decay was deeply embedded in European thinking," he continues. "The organic conception of the state in the sixteenth century reinforced the analogy, and history confirmed it" ("Self-Perception" 48). To represent history is to be aware of the possibility of change, but change is precisely something the Baroque—as an affirmation of the conservative sectors of Spanish society—wants to resist. How to deal with a situation in which history is seen both as a necessary ("epic") condition for sublimation and authority, and as a force of decay or entropy that will reduce the architectonic consolidation of state and ecclesiastical power to the status of a ruin (or what is perhaps even more frightening and incomprehensible, bring to the fore in its further course new forms of human community and culture, i.e., a new dominant class). From this aporia derives the Baroque's peculiar fascination with ruins, disillusion (*desengaño*), and death.[5]

What is entailed in Baroque spiritualism is the paradoxical conjunction of the principle of submission to authority with the practical and theoretical ideal of the self-willed, independent individual. The quality of mind that is to synthesize these two aspects is *ingenio*—wit. Wit is what allows both for *desengaño*, a sense of the ultimate vanity of history and human desire, and for effective invention and innovation in what Gracián called a *"mundo trabucado,"* a world turned topsy-turvy. Wit is ultimately a political virtue and necessity, but it is to be learned primarily in the laboratory of poetic or artistic conceits. The artist is himself (much less herself) an *hidalgo* or gentleman, yet at the same time aware of the ambiguous nature of his or (problematically) her social position as a kind of artisan producing (and sometimes making a living at it) a specific knowledge artifact. Góngora speaks of the *trabajo* or labor involved in both the creation and reading of his poetry; Cervantes makes self-deprecating jokes about copyrights and royalties; a favorite Baroque term is *fabricación*, making (the Spanish word for factory is *fábrica*; for a mechanically powered mill, *ingenio*); the image of Nature in Baroque representation anticipates Newton's mechanics and Enlightenment deism. Partly as a consequence of a new sense of mastery and freedom, but partly also as a way of disassociating the artist from the sphere of "ordinary" labor and language, there arises something close to the modern ideology of the aesthetic, with its concepts of "genius" and aesthetic autonomy, which are tied in turn to the promotion of art by the ruling class as witness to its rule.

The "other" of the Baroque is consecutively Neoclassicism, liberalism, and bourgeois revolution. Spain was, like Russia or the components of the Austro-Hungarian empire, a country that represented an impasse in the transition from feudalism to capitalism: hence the Black Legend and the anti-Baroque stance of the emerging bourgeois aesthetics. Gramsci observed that in seventeenth-century Italy "humanism assumed the aspect of a restoration. Yet like every restoration, it assimilated and developed, better than the revolutionary class it had politically suffocated, the ideological principles of the defeated class, which had not been able to go beyond its own corporate limits and create the superstructures of an integral society" (234). Hence the split between intelligentsia and people that marks subsequent Italian cultural history. Glossing this point, David Forgacs remarks that "[w]hereas in the other European countries the exported Renaissance produced a progressive scientific intelligentsia, which played a crucial role in the formation of the modern national states, in Italy itself it led to the involutionary Counter-Reformation and the ideological triumph of the Catholic intellectual hierarchy" (90).

This does not exactly fit Spain, because of the populist and "national" character of Baroque culture, Maravall suggests, although the point about the cooptation and involution of a potentially democratic and secularizing force by a Catholic and aristocratic intelligentsia is certainly relevant. Elliott warns against the tendency (in, among others, Maravall) to "overestimate the passivity of seventeenth-century societies and to exaggerate the capacity of those in authority to manipulate those societies for their own ideological ends. . . . [T]he works of Spain's Golden Age contain sufficient ambiguities to suggest that subversive subtexts are there for the reading" ("Concerto" 28).[6] On the other hand, part of the literary Baroque's effectiveness as an ideological practice may have been precisely its ability to engage, through ambiguities and possibilities of plural readings, the attention and conviction of its audiences. As Michel Foucault reminds us: "If power were never anything but repressive, if it never did anything but say no, do you really think one would be brought to obey it?" (*Power/Knowledge* 119).

But the Baroque is also, as Spengler argued, already partly the *modern*. The contemporary "man [*sic*] of letters" and contemporary literatures are, in effect, carryovers from the Baroque into bourgeois-liberal culture, as is also the literary critic, who was brought into being by the demand for exegesis posed by the difficulty or aesthetic radicalism of the Baroque text. To reflect, as we have been doing here, on the concept of the Spanish literary Baroque is thus in some sense to reflect on the modern institution of literature and literary criticism itself in its condition as an ideological apparatus of the state, that is, on the activity represented in part by this collection of essays.

Notes

This essay is based on ideas developed in a review article that originally appeared in *boundary* 2 (Spring-Fall 1988) under the title "Going Baroque?" (subsequently translated and revised for *Revista de crítica literaria latinoamericana* 28 [1988]) and in a new article on Gracián and the Baroque concept of literature forthcoming in a collection of essays on the Latin American Baroque edited by Mabel Moraña for Ediciones del Norte. I am grateful to Paul Bové, Margaret Ferguson, Anne Cruz, and Mary Elizabeth Perry for their comments and suggestions.

1. This is an issue similar to the revival of Baroque instruments and performance practices in early modern music; i.e., it involves attention to *ideologies* of textual determination and interpretation. For a discussion of Alonso's modifications of the text of Góngora's *Soledades* see Beverley, *Soledades* 9-13.

2. Apropos the "neobaroque" poetry of Ungaretti, Gramsci observed: "We might note, however, that the classical baroque, sadly, was and is popular (it is well-known that the man of the people likes the acrobatics of images in poetry), while the current baroque style is popular among pure intellectuals. Ungaretti has written that his comrades in the trenches, who were 'common people', liked his poems, and it may be true: a particular kind of liking to do with the feeling that 'difficult' (incomprehensible) poetry must be good and its author a great man precisely because he is detached from the people and incomprehensible" (272-273).

3. On the knowledge/power axis in Baroque representation see in particular the opening chapters of Foucault's *Les Mots et les choses;* Beverley, "The Production" and "Sobre Góngora"; and Hildner 47-67.

4. On the role of the Jesuits in fomenting the literary Baroque, see "La barroquización de la *ratio studiorum*" and "Gracián y la retórica barroca" in Batllori 101-114, and Wittkower.

5. On the theme of entropy in Baroque representation, Walter Benjamin commented: "This is the heart of the allegorical way of seeing, of the baroque, secular explanation of history as the Passion of the world; its importance lies solely in the stations of its decline. The greater the significance, the greater the subjection to death, because death digs most deeply the jagged line of demarcation between physical nature and significance. But if nature has always been subject to the power of death, it is also true that it has always been allegorical. Significance and death both come to fruition in historical development, just as they are closely linked as seeds in the creature's graceless state of sin" (106).

6. On this point, see, e.g., the acts of the 1981 University of Toulouse colloquium (*La Contestation*); Hildner; Ruth El Saffar's deconstruction of figures of gender in Calderón's theater; and Smith, "Barthes" and "Writing Women." Perhaps the strongest case for the potentially contestatory power of Spanish Baroque culture has been made by Walter Cohen for the *comedia*, which had usually been regarded in previous Hispanism of both the right and the left as ideologically conformist.

Works Cited

Agnew, Jean-Cristophe. *Worlds Apart: The Market and the Theater, 1500-1750.* Cambridge: Cambridge Univ. Press, 1986.

Apostolidés, Jean-Marie. *Le Roi-Machine: Spectacle et politique au temps du Louis XIV.* Paris: Editions de Minuit, 1981.

Batllori, Miguel. *Gracián y el barroco.* Rome: Edizioni di Storia e Letteratura, 1958.

Benjamin, Walter. *The Origin of German Tragic Drama.* Trans. John Osborne. London: New Left Books, 1977.

Bennett, Tony. "Texts in History: The Determinations of Readings and Their Texts." *Journal of the Midwest Modern Language Association* 18, 1 (1985): 1-16.

Beverley, John. "The Production of Solitude: Góngora and the State." *Ideologies and Literature* 13 (1980): 23-41.

———. "Sobre Góngora y el gongorismo colonial." *Revista Iberoamericana* 114-115 (1981): 33-44.

Chomsky, Noam. *Cartesian Linguistics.* New York: Harper, 1966.

Cohen, Walter. *The Drama of a Nation: Public Theater in Renaissance Spain and England.* Ithaca: Cornell Univ. Press, 1985.

Collard, Andrée. *Nueva poesía: conceptismo, culteranismo en la crítica española.* Madrid: Castalia, 1967.

La Contestation de la Société dans la Littérature Espagnole du Siècle D'or. Toulouse: Université de Toulouse, 1981.

Elliott, J. H. "Self-Perception and Decline in Early Seventeenth Century Spain." *Past and Present* 74 (1977): 41-61.

_____. ed. *Poder y sociedad en la España de los Austrias*. Barcelona: Editorial Crítica, 1982.

_____. "Concerto Barroco." *The New York Review of Books*. April 9, 1987: 26-29.

El Saffar, Ruth. "Reason's Unreason in *Life Is A Dream*." *Plays and Playhouses in Imperial Decadence*. Ed. Anthony Zahareas. Minneapolis: Institute for the Study of Ideologies and Literature, 1986. 103-118.

Forgacs, David. "National-Popular: Genealogy of a Concept." *Formations of Nations and People*. Ed. Tony Bennett. London: Routledge, Kegan and Paul, 1984. 83-97.

Foucault, Michel. *Power/Knowledge. Selected Interviews and Other Writings*. New York: Pantheon, 1980.

_____. *Les Mots et les choses*. Paris: Gallimard, 1986.

Geertz, Clifford. *Negara: The Theatre State in Seventeenth Century Bali*. Princeton: Princeton Univ. Press, 1980.

Godzich, Wlad, and Nicholas Spadaccini, eds. *Literature among Discourses: The Spanish Golden Age*. Minneapolis: Univ. of Minnesota Press, 1986.

Góngora y Argote, Luis de. *Soledades*. Preface by John Beverley. Madrid: Ediciones Cátedra, 1979.

Gracián, Baltasar. *Agudeza y arte de ingenio*. In *Obras completas*. Madrid: Aguilar, 1960.

_____. *El héroe*. In *Obras completas*. Madrid: Aguilar, 1960.

Gramsci, Antonio. *Selections from Cultural Writings*. Ed. David Forgacs and Geoffrey Nowell-Smith. London: Lawrence and Wishart, 1985.

Hildner, David Jonathan. *Reason and the Passions in the Comedias of Calderón*. Amsterdam: John Benjamins, 1985.

Hobsbawm, Eric, and Terence Ranger, eds. *The Invention of Tradition*. Cambridge: Cambridge Univ. Press, 1983.

Kagan, Richard. "Las universidades en Castilla, 1500-1700." *Poder y sociedad en la España de los Austrias*. Ed. J. H. Elliott. Barcelona: Editorial Crítica, 1982. 57-89.

Maravall, José Antonio. *La cultura del barroco: Análisis de una estructura histórica*. Barcelona: Ariel, 1975.

_____. *Culture of the Baroque: Analysis of a Historical Structure*. Trans. Terry Cochran. Minneapolis: Univ. of Minnesota Press, 1986.

Marin, Louis. *Le Portrait du Roi*. Paris: Editions de Minuit, 1981.

Merrington, John. "Town and Country in the Transition to Capitalism." *The Transition from Feudalism to Capitalism*. Ed. Rodney Hilton. London: New Left Books, 1976. 170-195.

Molho, Maurice. "Dissolution et Subversion dans la Culture Espagnole du Siècle d'Or." *Les Langues Neo Latines* 270 (1989): 5-13.

Parker, A. A. *Polyphemus and Galatea: A Study in the Interpretation of a Baroque Poem*. Austin: Univ. of Texas Press, 1977.

Smith, Paul Julian. "Barthes, Góngora, and Non-sense." *PMLA* 101.1 (1986): 82-93.

_____. "Writing Women in Golden Age Spain: Saint Teresa and María de Zayas." *Modern Language Notes* (1987): 220-240.

Weisbach, Werner. *Der barock als kunst der gegenreformation*. Berlin: P. Cassirer, 1921. (A Spanish translation is available from Gredos.)

Wittkower, R. *Baroque Art: The Jesuit Contribution*. New York: Fordham Univ. Press, 1972.

Wölfflin, Heinrich. *Principles of Art History*. 1916. Trans. M. Hottinger. New York: Dover, 1962.

◆ Afterword
The Subject of Control

Anthony J. Cascardi

In a 1946 essay entitled "An Introduction to the Ideology of the Baroque in Spain," Stephen Gilman advanced the view that the artistic style characteristic of the late sixteenth and early seventeenth centuries in Spain was the reflection of a series of doctrinal premises that had come into power beginning roughly with the Council of Trent, whose "ideological" force could best be measured by the degree to which the art of that period succeeded in communicating Counter-Reformation ideas to the public at large. For evidence of his views, Gilman drew on some of the more dramatic representations of Counter-Reformation ideology in Spanish Baroque literature and thought. By examining the controversial area of the theology of free will and grace (as exemplified in the *de auxiliis* debate), as well as the literature of asceticism as represented in the works of Malón de Chaide (*La conversión de la magdalena*), Luis de Granada (*Guía de pecadores*), Ignacio de Loyola (*Ejercicios espirituales*), and Hernando de Zárate (*Discursos de la paciencia cristiana*), Gilman described how the "ideological" threats of a sacred infinity and eternity exerted a disorienting pressure on representations of space, time, and substance, transforming the placid Renaissance scenes of Garcilaso's swains into a Baroque landscape of theological doom and gloom. Turning finally to the literature of moral repentance and to the figure of the "caído en la cuenta," Gilman described the spiritual model of the Spanish Baroque as "ascetic" in the sense that it idealized a repressive "victory over self" in the moral battle of the soul against the world;[1] as such, the spirituality characteristic of Counter-Reformation Spain could be placed in contrast both to the asceticism that developed in conjunction with the Protestant ethic described by Max Weber as well as to the measured worldliness of the *honnête homme*, for whom meaningful intercourse with the world could be rationally regulated and the seductions of the senses thereby resisted and controlled.

Already in 1946 Gilman recognized the poverty of the concept of "ideology" when taken in its literal sense as the simple study of ideas and their cultural effects:

> No rigid sequence of cause and effect can be traced between the religious movement and its ultimate artistic expression, since innumerable economic, sociological and political changes interweave themselves into the texture of the period. (83)

Gilman continues:

> The term "ideology" is poorly chosen here. By it I mean not only a system or complex of ideas but also a cohesive system of values. This latter, alone, could perhaps be referred to by using the technical term "axiology," but this, also, would not carry the full meaning desired. Actually the thought lying behind "ideology" is something corresponding to the German *erlebnis*, that is to say, a living totality of points of view, attitudes toward life, and patterns of thought occurring in those generations of *men actively partisan to the Counter-Reformation*. (98; emphasis added)

Yet, as this final phrase perhaps all too clearly reveals, an awareness of the depth to which ideology penetrates all levels of cultural life and, similarly, any strongly defined notion of Counter-Reformation culture in relation to the problems of ideological power or control remained external to his approach. Indeed, Gilman himself abandoned his interest in "ideology" in ex-

change for the views of Américo Castro on the decisive importance of caste values in the formation of Spanish culture. And
perhaps equally as important for assessing the direction of this
work, the study of "ideology" was conceived as constituting the
merely preparatory labor necessary for the kind of biographical
and existentialist criticism whose supervening goal was to uncover the relationship between the artist qua individual and the
social values that provided the "vital context" for the creative
act.

Indeed, only in recent years has a new understanding of ideology made its way into studies of the history and literature
of the Spanish Baroque. Through the work of critics associated
with the Prisma Institute and the journal *Ideologies and Literatures*, and now with the regularized publication of *Hispanic Issues*, ideological analysis of the culture of the Golden Age has
moved increasingly to the fore. The difference between the understanding of "ideology" reflected in this recent work and that
of Gilman's 1946 essay is clear. Whereas the concept of "ideology" functioned for critics of Gilman's generation largely as a
means to relate the doctrinal pronouncements of the Catholic
bishops at Trent relevant to the issues of free will, salvation, and
the theology of grace to a series of stylistic tendencies prevalent
during subsequent years in Spain, the work of more recent critics has been strongly shaped by an awareness of the fact that
ideas do not, in and of themselves, play a causal role in culture
and so can of themselves serve as the basis for interpretive
claims of a relatively limited scope. For those historians of Spanish culture who have come to take their bearings by Marx, Max
Weber, and Foucault, the challenge is rather to relate ideology,
conceived as the symbolic dimension of power, to the material
level of historical life. By focusing on shifts in economic modes
of production (as in Marx), on the mediating power of social institutions (as in Max Weber), and on practices directed toward
the body (as in Foucault), these critics allow us to see ideology as
involving all the varied means through which symbolic forms of
power are brought to bear on the material plane of cultural life.

It is thus not altogether surprising to see that contemporary
interests in the study of ideology have turned toward the questions of culture and control in Counter-Reformation Spain, for of

all the phenomena associated with the Spanish Golden Age none offers as varied and dramatic a demonstration of the social, political, and aesthetic means through which the symbolic effects of power were brought to bear on material life, and none offers as many challenges to the views that would see Spanish culture of the Golden Age as the simple reflection of the conservative doctrinal positions originally mapped at the Council of Trent. The present collection of essays assembled by Anne J. Cruz and Mary Elizabeth Perry is a case in point. While attempting to bridge the disciplinary gap between the fields of history and literature by placing the work of social and cultural historians alongside that of literary critics sensitive to the historical embeddedness of texts, the collective ambition of these essays is to redefine our understanding of the Counter-Reformation in Spain by a rereading of culture in terms of the "control mechanisms" that govern human behavior and, we might add, that serve to channel power's material effects.

On the one hand, these essays suggest that cultural control in Counter-Reformation Spain was produced by the literal inscription of orthodox beliefs, in such a way that material culture served to reproduce a series of canonical Church positions. For instance, Jean Pierre Dedieu argues that the growing concern of the Church in religious education served to promote an orthodox ideology among the masses and thus to "socialize" a heterogeneous population; Sara T. Nalle shows how the municipal government and cathedral of Cuenca together used Baroque celebrations of power to popularize the cult of San Julián, which had been all but abandoned since medieval times; and Jaime Contreras suggests that inquisitorial authority was used (and, if this can also be said, abused) in order to marginalize New Christians by excluding them from positions at all levels of power. Yet it is precisely in the face of examples such as these, where the evidence for control is so explicit and direct, that the constellation of problems described under the heading of "culture and control" is vulnerable to the effects of a theoretical collapse, by virtue of a premature identification of Counter-Reformation culture with its orthodox religious base; at the very least, such a conception of control suggests a more or less unquestioned faith in the relationship between religious doctrine and the patterns of behavior that such doctrine was used to encourage and support.

On the other hand, the work of critics like Alison Weber, Gwendolyn Barnes-Karol, and María Helena Sánchez Ortega suggests that an empirical analysis of culture must be supplemented by an understanding of culture's symbolic basis as well as by an investigation of the psychological mechanisms of control and of power's sometimes contradictory effects. Thus Sánchez Ortega shows how the frequent associations of women with the Devil created an atmosphere of fear and dread whose effects were at least as disturbing as the allegedly demonic powers attributed to women over livestock, crops, and men. Alison Weber suggests how in the case of Saint Teresa the conditions of an authoritarian and patriarchal culture produced a contradictorily rational defense of the authenticity of mystical experience. Weber describes Saint Teresa as a "dissident demonologist" within an orthodox culture and, in this respect, as occupying a position that was both conservative *and* marginal with respect to the dominant ideology of her day; in Weber's analysis, Teresa adopts a full-blown skepticism toward mystical claims in order to *preserve* a confidence in women's capacity to identify and experience a genuinely mystical spirituality. As these and other examples suggest, it would be hazardous indeed to form categorical associations between particular modes of consciousness (whether orthodox, mystical, or demonic) and any class or gender of individuals, even within a culture as apparently authoritarian and closed as that of Counter-Reformation Spain.[2]

When taken as a group these essays raise at least as many questions as they may answer, if only because they create the semblance of a cleavage between the empirical level of culture and the symbolic means through which cultural "power" was sustained. By identifying culture with its (literal or symbolic) "mechanisms of control" these essays suggest the need for a corresponding analysis of the "subjects of control," which they themselves do not provide. For if culture can indeed be defined in terms of its "control mechanisms" then it is necessary also to ask: who were its subjects and how did they become *subject to* control? Thus I would suggest that if we are to understand the complex relationship between "culture" and "control" in

Counter-Reformation Spain we will need to voice a series of questions about the relationship between the organized resources of power and the formation of the (social, historical, psychological) subjects of control. The question "Who is in control?" (which may be given a summary "ideological" answer by reference to the Church and the State) must be supplemented by another, less easily answered question: "Who is controlled?" Only in this way, I think, can we use recent advances in Hispanism's understanding of "ideology" as a way to go beyond the tasks of locating the material consequences of ideas or of describing the various mechanisms of psychological control to a deeper understanding of the various modes of agency through which individuals achieved a cultural identity as subject-selves.

While my approach to these issues shares with critics like John Beverley and Gwendolyn Barnes-Karol certain of the perspectives on the crisis-structure of the Spanish Baroque first put forward by José Antonio Maravall, my principal thesis nonetheless differs from Maravall's in some significant respects. Maravall regards the phenomenon of the Spanish Baroque as bound up with the urbanization of life and with the creation of a "sociedad de masas" that is dependent on the increasingly capitalistic environment of the sixteenth and seventeenth centuries. Those who follow Maravall's thesis tend to agree that the culture of the Spanish Baroque must be understood as a conservative formation whose ideological support of the status quo was produced in response to the economic crisis resulting from the transition from feudalism to capitalism. To wit, Beverley sees the Baroque, not implausibly, as Janus-like, with one face turned toward the "sunset of feudalism," the other looking out onto the "dawn of capitalism," and Maravall himself argues that "the baroque was a culture . . . consisting in the response given by active groups within a society that had entered into a severe crisis in association with *critical economic fluctuations*" (*Culture* 19; emphasis added). By contrast, I would suggest that any attempt to align the doctrinal groundwork of the Counter-Reformation with the cultural practices commonly identified as "baroque," or to account for the lasting influence of Counter-Reformation ideas, must articulate the problem of cultural control in terms of the crisis of subject formation in early modern Spain. To introduce the category of subjectivity in this debate is not to suggest that we should return to a theory of the individual as freely constituting its world, or that we should analyze the problem of self-consciousness in relation to the history of ideas; indeed, it is precisely such notions that a concept of subject *formation* would be used to argue against. But by focusing on the category of the "subject" we may be able to articulate the links between structures and agency in a way that Maravall's focus on the "baroque" as a motivating category may not allow. Moreover, in addressing subjects *as formed* we may be able to link large-scale transformations in historical structures with the changing modes of psychology and shifting patterns of belief that determined the nature of social relations in early modern Spain.

On one level, the crisis of subjectivity in early modern Spain can be described as the product of a conflict between two distinct value systems, each with its own psychology and each with modes of recognition proper to it. On the one hand a hierarchical society, in which actions were evaluated according to a series of naturalistic principles, and in which social functions and roles were sedimented into near-static patterns, was confronted with modes of thinking, feeling, acting, and evaluating based on the premises of a psychologizing "individualism," in which the social order was dominated by what Weber described as "rationalized" structures, and in which the dominant cultural ethos was that of autoregulation or *self*-control. In what are sometimes taken as the paradigmatic instances of subject formation—in England, Germany, and France—this conflict is generally conceived as having been "successfully" resolved; at the very least, the "legitimacy" of the modern age is staked on claims of the independence of subjects from the historical questions they may in fact have been invented to answer. Elsewhere I argue that this understanding lends a semblance of false necessity to the pattern of modernization taken as representative for the West;[3] here I would point out that the case of Spain is inherently more complex. On the one hand, social conditions in early modern Spain generated a new class of individuals who could be imagined and had to be addressed as subject-selves; as Barnes-Karol's study of religious oratory helps makes clear, Counter-Reformation ideology counted on the existence of subjects who would be responsive to relatively "modern" methods of psychological persuasion and control (she cites a stunning passage from Fray Angel Manrique: "You will hear a preacher's Sermon . . ."). And yet the cumulative effect of this psychology was to close off the resources of subjectivity, in effect reinforcing the ideological essentialism of the Counter-Reformation by creating in subjects a willingness for subjection to the principles of a "higher" rule. (A case in point is Lope de Vega, who supplies this authority when he addresses the audience of his plays in the "Arte nuevo de hacer comedias": "since the common people pay for them, it is right / to address them like fools if that will please them" ["como las paga el vulgo, es justo / hablarle en necio para darle gusto" vv. 47-48].) As we shall see in relation to Gracián, it is thus only through an internalization of authority that the "modern" subject could represent itself as autonomous and free.

In political terms, this reinvestment in authority means that an understanding of the process of subject formation in early modern Spain requires interpretation in terms of the relationship between the subject and the absolutist state. From the point of view of the State, the crucial problem of legitimation cannot be resolved without an understanding of the psychological mechanisms of subjection, for given the weakening of "naturalistic" premises about the social world, the authority of the State could only depend on its ability to establish a willingness for subjection among those who were submitted to its rule. To understand the effects of the Counter-Reformation in terms of the (political) resistance to subjectivity may thus enable us better to locate what Maravall calls the "motivating forces" (*resortes*) that allowed the proponents of a conservative religious program to secure a position of dominance and control, in part because the crisis of subjectivity as reflected in the Counter-Reformation's drama of free will, sin, salvation, and grace, provided the means through which the State was able to defend itself against the modernizing "threats" to its legitimacy presented by the desires and wills of those same subject-selves. As I hope also to suggest, these questions will enable us to move from a description of the means and mechanisms of control *as imposed* to a calculation of the motives by which a heterogeneous "public" came willingly to submit to the State's political force.[4]

This much having been said, I would add that any discussion of the issue of cultural control must make room for a deeper understanding of the possibility of *resistance* to control than has so far been the case in studies of early modern Spain. While traditional historians like J. H. Elliott have warned that any description of the Golden Age in homogeneous or totalizing terms is bound simply to falsify the empirical facts, it is not inconceivable that now dominant perspectives on power may present an even greater risk. Indeed, if there is a danger in adopting the views on power put forward by Marx, Weber, and especially Foucault— who sees power as so deeply bred into the social body that no position can be thought of as immune to its effects—it is that we will come to read *absolute* power absolutely, thus yielding to the seduction that sometimes ascribes to the thesis of culture the sum of power's effects.

To continue these arguments, I want to turn first to the question of the Counter-Reformation's philosophical basis, for it is with reference to a certain orthodoxy of belief that the Counter-Reformation is customarily conceived as having had regressive ideological effects in Spain. For example, it is often argued that what became visible as a "Counter-Reformation" ideology had its origins in Spain's theocentric reaction to the progressive philosophical rationalism emergent in England and France during the late Renaissance and early modern age. Indeed, literary critics and historians of ideas have long argued that while philosophy outside of Spain took a decisively modern and rationalist turn, the climate of opinion in Spain remained conservatively theocentric, in large measure because it remained subordinate to the premises of neo-Scholastic belief. For instance, it is often pointed out that while the *Disputationes metaphysicae* (1597) of the Spanish Jesuit Francisco de Suárez played a decisive role in the development of modern subjectivity insofar as they served to stimulate the thinking of Descartes, the Spanish response to skepticism took a theocentric, rather than a rationalist turn (see Gilson, *Etudes sur le rle de la pensée médiévale dans la formation du système Cartésien*). In the face of evidence like this, a series of comparative questions inevitably comes to mind. Given prevailing tendencies to relocate the centers of consciousness, agency, and value in the rational capacity of the subject-self, what can explain persistence of neo-Scholasticism, and its resistance to subjectivity, in early modern Spain? Given the strategic linkages between an emergent capitalism and liberal political theory elsewhere in Europe, what can account for the continuing Spanish defense of the absolutist state?[5] In works like Suárez's *De legibus ac Deo legislatore* (1612) and Quevedo's *Política de Dios y gobierno de Cristo, nuestro señor* (1626), the discourse of legitimation proceeds from a defense of the *religious* basis of the absolute monarch's power, rather than from a recognition, as in Hobbes, of absolutism's "rational" core.

If we are to address questions like these we will need to abandon the idea that the role of ideology in Counter-Reformation Spain was simply to reinforce a series of orthodox religious beliefs. To be sure, it might initially seem that Counter-Reformation beliefs presented an obstacle to the kind of subjective self-consciousness that developed elsewhere in Europe during the sixteenth and seventeenth centuries; Counter-Reformation culture was indeed authoritarian and repressive. But I would hasten to add that the customary description of early modern Spain in terms of the power of its reactionary position with respect to modernizing institutions and ideas may tempt us to underestimate the relationship between subjectivity and subjection *tout court*. Indeed, the thesis of a fully autonomous subject-self (whether sacred or secular, masculine or feminine), wholly free from control, must also be regarded as an "ideological" construct of the early modern world, belief in which leads at best to a systematic denial of the individual's political position as *subject to* a higher authority or rule. Moreover, it may conceal the ways in which the disciplinary techniques learned in Counter-Reformation Spain were later subsumed and incorporated by secular writers like Gracián into the psychology of *self*-control.

In the case of Spain, it would initially seem that the effect of Counter-Reformation beliefs was to align a neo-Scholastic understanding of the nature of the self with a series of hierarchical principles of social values, centering around the accessibility to the good by those who could prove themselves to be of truly noble birth. The neo-Scholastic philosophy invoked to reinforce Counter-Reformation practices and beliefs customarily identified three innate faculties—memory, understanding, and the will—and related each to a particular dimension of the human soul. The final goal of the philosophy, as witnessed for example in the growth and change of Segismundo over the course of Calderón's well-known play, *La vida es sueño*, was to integrate and balance these faculties in the service of moral ends; the image of their successful integration was the figure of the ruler-prince. In a neo-Scholastic reading, which takes the play as the structural mapping of this moral psychology, Segismundo's opening complaint ("Oh, miserable and unhappy me! / You heavens above, I demand to know, since you treat me this way, / what crimes I've committed against you" ["¡Ay, mísero de mí, y ay, infelice! / Apurar, Cielos, pretendo, ya que me tratáis así, / ¿qué delito cometí?" 502a]) represents the action of memory, as Segismundo recalls his vexed origins and recognizes the conditions of his own spiritual displacement from the world. Segismundo's famous second monologue ("let us repress this beastly nature, this fury and ambition" ["reprimamos / esta fiera condición, / esta furia, esta ambición" 522a]) is in turn seen to display the work of the reflective intellect or "understanding," as he comes to recognize remarkable transformations in his material circumstances. Segismundo's second speech demonstrates the skepticism characteristic of one who has experienced the full force of the Counter-Reformation's ascetic warnings against the deceit of the senses and who has come to adopt an ethical denial of the external world. Yet the neo-Scholastic point of this reading would be lost if it were not also to say that neither memory nor understanding when taken alone can lead to the kind of moral action expected of the truly "noble" soul.

The process of moral development as imagined by Calderón culminates in the creation of the "magnanimous prince," whom we may provisionally describe as an essentialist, neo-Scholastic version of the "generous soul"[6] theorized by Calderón's contemporary, Descartes. (Descartes writes in *Les passions de l'âme* that "Those who are generous . . . have complete command over their passions. In particular, they have mastery over their desires, and over jealousy and envy."[7]) Indeed, the neo-Scholastic interpretation of Calderón's play centers on the crucial point that the work of the memory and understanding would remain unfulfilled without the intervention of the will, which begins with self-control. As the events of Act III suggest, the structural allegory of Segismundo's moral development can be made complete and the moral "profit" of the inherited Counter-Reformation lessons about the contingency of life fully received only when the prince freely wills to renounce his own circumstantial power and agrees to restore his father's rule. Calderón's hero makes the point well when he remarks that the course of events overwhelms the powers of his intellect and virtually *requires* the intervention of the will: "Heavens, if indeed I'm dreaming, / suspend my memory, / for in a dream so many things could not occur" ("Cielos, si es verdad que sueño, / suspendedme la memoria, / que no es posible que quepan / en un sueño tantas cosas" 530a). The will serves thus to "complete" what memory and understanding could not by themselves perfect.

And yet it might be more accurate to say that the will represents the "unpresentable" element of Baroque persuasion and control. Indeed, all of the more overt and explicit mechanisms of "control"—whether in religious oratory, meditative practice, or catechesis—are dependent on the action of the subject's inscrutable "will." Hence, Calderón's recourse in other plays to the intervention of wonder-working magicians, to near-miraculous conversions, and to the astonishing power of the saving angels of the Lord. None of these means succeeds in representing the response of the will as such, but all of them have calculated *effects upon* the will, as if in the experience of the *arrebatos* of wonder and "disbelief" the subject could somehow come to perceive the will *as will*. Hence, also the Counter-Reformation's effort to represent in demonic forms those forms of agency that could *act upon* the will and Loyola's effort to represent the will, in meditation, as *under control*. All of these efforts, and many more, were designed to make explicit and confirm what remained in fact the unpresentable element of persuasion itself.

Whether the will is ultimately imagined as "free" or "controlled," it seems equally clear that a work like *La vida es sueño* represents something still more complex than a reflection of the Counter-Reformation attempt to represent what is unpresentable in the work of persuasion itself, albeit fortified by the intervention of a neo-Scholastic interpretation of the progress of the soul toward the moral "good." While the moral "goal" of the play is the production of the virtuous prince, Segismundo's development begins from a subjective psychology that the orthodox reading finds difficult to accommodate and, indeed, that Counter-Reformation theology found necessary to repress. More accurately, Calderón mirrors the crisis of subjectivity in Spain by staging the encounter of neo-Scholastic perspectives about the innate faculties of the soul with a series of relatively "modern" discoveries about the contingent existence of the self. In the process, he allows us to uncover the genealogy of the "moral psychology" of absolutism and to understand the crisis of legitimation in a society of increasingly disgregated individuals, albeit "resolving" the latter in favor of a neo-Scholastic defense of the inherent goodness of order, authority, and control. For a writer like Calderón, the purpose of glossing a fundamentally political action in moral terms, or of turning secular plots *a lo divino,* as in the *autos sacramentales,* was to relate neo-Scholastic moral psychology with absolutist politics, and by so doing to model the creation of subjects who would in principle be unable to resist control. In this context, the confirming power of orthodox beliefs was to bridge moral psychology and politics in order to present the image of culture as a unified, seamless whole. In the process, the resistance to subjectivity became an essential ingredient in the task of political subjection, and so served to help resolve the legitimation crisis of the State.

Phrased in other terms, Calderón's view of Segismundo not simply as the subject of an ideal moral itinerary but as *subject to* the "passions of the soul" mirrors a crisis of subjectivity that leads to a vision of the self as *requiring* (political) control. Indeed, it could be said that a work like *La vida es sueño* provides one of the best examples of the ways in which an encounter between the inherited principles of psychology and the problem of the legitimacy of authority leads to manifestly conservative ends, for what is ultimately at stake in Calderón's play can best be described in terms of the relationship between Segismundo's subjective self-consciousness and the need to restore authority in his father's State. Counter-Reformation ideology served in this context as the means by which the State could reassert, reassure, or legitimize its rule, not so much by dominating subjects as by producing subjects who would not wish to escape its control.

As epitomized in Calderón's play, the problem of subject formation in early modern Spain begins with the discovery, characteristic of the antinaturalism of the Baroque, that the existing political order is no longer entitled to draw on the legitimizing authority of nature itself. But rather than begin from a historical interpretation of his hero's fate, Calderón reads the excruciating "difficulty" of Segismundo's situation in terms of the moral psychology of sin and guilt.[8] Not unlike the pilgrim hero of Góngora's *Soledades*, and not unlike Hamlet, who finds that the time is "out of joint," Segismundo believes that the order of nature has been rendered inscrutable to the human gaze, and that his own condition has been rendered unintelligible and seemingly without cause in naturalistic terms; accordingly, it requires interpretation in psychological terms:

> To have been born, I know, / is itself a crime; / your punishment is sufficiently just, / since man's worst crime / is to have been born. / I should only wish to know / in order to relieve my doubts— / leaving aside, oh heavens, / the crime of birth— / what more could I have offended you / so to have punished me more?

> si nací, ya entiendo
> qué delito he cometido;
> bastante causa ha tenido
> vuestra justicia y rigor,
> pues el delito mayor
> del hombre, es haber nacido.
> Sólo quisiera saber,
> para apurar mis desvelos
> —dejando a una parte, cielos,
> el delito de nacer—,
> ¿qué más os pude ofender,
> para castigarme más? (502a-b)

Whereas his father Basilio could once employ "subtle calcula-
tions" ("matemáticas sutiles") to fathom the "difficulty" of the
world, Segismundo's task is to recover—and if not to recover,
then to invent or impose—the "reason of nature" through the
resources of prudence, *ingenio,* and the will.

Given the confrontation of neo-Scholastic beliefs about the innate capacities of the soul with the "antinaturalistic" perspec
tives characteristic of the Baroque, it was perhaps to be expected
that a vision of the subject as an entity shaped by the desires or
"passions," and a vision of desires as requiring political direction and control, would emerge as central elements in the formation of the subject-self.[9] Ostensibly, the Baroque hero's work
is to find a solution to the problem of subjective desire, a problem that is mirrored as a crisis in the reason of nature itself; because the subject believes that the authority of nature has been
withdrawn, he is confronted with the imperative of a reactionary political task, one that requires the reinforcement of the Father's rule as legitimate and just, but that recognizes as well that
any authority must be heterogeneous to nature, external to the
subjects, and *imposed.* In other words, the Baroque crisis of subjectivity could only be resolved through repressive politics.
Thus Segismundo's moral "progress" only begins with the
Counter-Reformation's work of ascetic self-repression (e.g., "let
us repress this bestial nature" ["reprimamos / esta fiera condición" 522a]); as we shall see in relation to Gracián, that self-repression was brought forward and incorporated as part of a
more "rationalized" model of the self. What is important to see
in the case at hand is that the hero's development must conclude
with the work of political self-repression and control, as he pardons his father and imprisons the rebel soldier. In this respect,
Segismundo is not unlike Tirso's Don Juan, who exemplifies the
distinctively modern problem of a desire that must be repressed
if the subject is to be incorporated into cultural life.

As I argue elsewhere, the myth of Don Juan consistently appears to acknowledge the subjective basis of a desire that seems
to welcome the contingent multiplicity of its objects and ends,
while at the same time it seems to forfeit that vision to a more
powerful demand for cultural authority and control. In his role

as a libertine Don Juan would seem at first to prove the *failure* of the Counter-Reformation efforts to immunize subjects against desire through the psychological imposition of guilt; but perhaps seen more accurately, Don Juan attempts to answer the Counter-Reformation's moralizing threats of impending spiritual doom with a Baroque extension of time, brought about by means of repeated appeals to the will: "Trust me a while longer!" ("¡Tan largo me lo fiáis!"). Accordingly, a more appropriate model for the psychology of Don Juan would be one in which the moral problem of desire is both created and "resolved" by modes of persuasion available to subjects of the Baroque, but in which that "resolution" is itself the source of a "higher" authority (whether of society or of God) and its principles of control.

To be sure, it would be easy to read the story of Don Juan as a story of male aggression and female deception, answered by the forces of cultural repression and control. But rather than simply reinforce the standards of moral psychology, the myth of Don Juan may more profitably be seen as confronting what Catherine Clément has described as the "emptiness of the soul,"[10] but also as closing this awareness off, thus advancing the values of traditional, patriarchal society as a *response* to the pressures of subjectivity. This interpretation no doubt bears some resemblance to Maravall's claim that the seventeenth-century Spanish theatre played an essentially conservative social role. In Maravall's judgment, seventeenth-century society developed an affinity for the theatre because of its need to lend an appearance of legitimacy to a structure of social relations that was founded on illegitimate practices of domination and, in so doing, to avoid the ethical questions that situations of domination are bound to raise.[11] Yet it is precisely an ethical principle, that of social control, that establishes the possibility of closure and organizes the psychological "content" of Tirso's play. Indeed, the stabilizing function of the theatre, its exceptional resourcefulness in the work of cultural "control," may be attributed to the *desire for* control initiated by a prior loosening of the constraints on the attachment of subjects to preestablished ends. Without an explanation such as this, it would be nearly impossible to account for those features of the play that critics like Maravall have described as crucial for an understanding of the impact of the theatre in Golden Age Spain, most notably its ability to control and direct those who were on the surface unlikely to benefit from the politics of conservatism—the *vulgo*.[12]

In describing the society of early modern Spain as a "guided culture" (*una cultura dirigida*) and a "mass culture" (*una cultura masiva*) Maravall has also argued that it was increasingly "bourgeois": "it is absurd to deny the baroque a bourgeois character," he says, "simply because it failed to exhibit a complete process of rationalization" (*Culture* 63). Indeed, the same can be said of the psychological "subject" of early modern Spain, whose development has been portrayed (when it is indeed portrayed at all) as damaged, truncated, regressive, or incomplete with respect to the seemingly homogeneous models of "rational" self-consciousness theorized by thinkers like Descartes and Locke. In Don Juan's case, as in Segismundo's, the psyche is better seen as internally split rather than undeveloped: as divided historically between the seignorial values of nobility and prestige on the one hand and a newly mobile individualism on the other; as cleaved metaphysically between the attractions of the finite *siglo* and the moral threats of the everlasting world; and additionally as split psychologically between the conditions of subjective desire and the various resistances to desire that we have begun to see in the preceding essays.

On the one hand, these divisions would appear to stand as evidence against the identification of the subject with the bourgeoisie, for one of the defining traits of bourgeois consciousness was its ability to deny any fractures or contradictions in its own social and historical formation, and hence to represent itself as free from external control. In attempting to address these issues, I want to turn to Gracián, who elevates the "subjective" virtues of sincerity and authenticity to the basis for a new social rationality (e.g.: "Believe your heart. . . . Never contradict it, for it usually predicts what matters most about the future" ["Creer al corazón. . . . Nunca le desmienta, que suele ser pronóstico de lo que más importa" *Oráculo*, no. 178; 431]). Gracián also provides a matchless example of the authority of self-control. Indeed, Gracián demonstrates what might better be described as an internalization of the control mechanisms that had been inherited from the Counter-Reformation world. In Gracián the privileged place of control is not the Church, but the society of the court; moreover, the authority of control in force at court has been transferred to the subject-self, in such a way that what acquires value in the emergent discourse of the self is the relatively "rationalized" psychology of self-control.

As Maravall notes, the fundamental problem with a mass culture is the heterogeneity of the masses with respect to their origin or estate: "individuals act outside the limits of the traditional group to which they belong, and they are united in functional and impersonal forms of behavior extending beyond differences in profession, age, wealth, and beliefs" (*Culture* 102). In other words, the heterogeneity of the masses represents a problem for society as a whole insofar as it came to generate anxieties about the terms in which social "subjects" might identify themselves and be recognized by others. The protocols of behavior developed at court mirror this problem in myriad ways. On the one hand, the Baroque court incorporates the "naturalistic" principles of social distinction characteristic of a hierarchical society. On the other hand the increasing "psychologization" of behavior, the continual testing of moral psychology against observations drawn from "experience," required principles of differentiation that a hierarchical structure could not easily accommodate. Accordingly, a series of procedures arose designed to control and regulate—on the basis of "psychological" rules—the experience of increasingly heterogeneous subject-selves. Unlike the empirical psychology that later took shape in the writings of Locke and Hume, and that assumed as its object the individual as fully formed, the art of courtly conduct took as its object a self that had not yet come to conceive of itself as detachable from its social effects. Beverley makes a related point when he argues that art and politics in the Baroque were not yet viewed as separate activities.

Because of the central role of courtly society in establishing rules of conduct and consent, the members of the court came to be aligned with an ethical norm. By the identification of "courtly society" with "good society" they perceived themselves on an exclusionary moral basis as "elites," thus adopting in moral terms a principle of social distinction that could find no basis in the "natural" world. Indeed, the "courtization" of society has been seen by cultural historians like Norbert Elias as essential to the civilizing process insofar as it springs from the ascription of an ethical value to the taming of "natural" aggression or, what amounts to the same thing, the sublimation of "subjective" desires and the transformation of the self into an object of psychological self-control:

> In the midst of a large populated area which by and large is free of physical violence, a "good society" is formed. But even if the use of physical violence now recedes from human intercourse, if even duelling is now forbidden, people now exert pressure and force on each other in a wide variety of different ways. (270-271)

Elias's conclusion is that the court is, if not the first, then certainly among the most important centers of systematic societal regulation and control. Insofar as the various modes of this control (which, following Weber, he labels "rationalization") bring an increase in self-discipline, the courtization of society in the Baroque is of a piece with the "psychologization" of the early modern subject-self; "psychological" analysis and observation develop in this context both as techniques of self-mastery and as means of self-discipline. Hence we have Gracián, who transforms *sprezzatura* into the psychology of self-control (e.g., "To play an open game is neither useful nor fun" ["El jugar a juego descubierto ni es de utilidad, ni de gusto" *Oráculo*, no. 3; 359]).

Considered in ethical terms, a writer like Gracián is faced with the task of finding a new standard of conduct for the self where two once-viable models have been rendered unavailable. The first of these is represented by the figure of the common man (*el hombre vulgar*), repeatedly characterized as incapable of self-control and therefore as "base." (See *Oráculo*, no. 28: "In no respect vulgar" ["En nada vulgar" 370]; and also no. 69: "Do not give in to vulgar passions. A great man is one who never subjects himself to transitory impressions" ["No rendirse a un vulgar humor. Hombre grande el que nunca se sujeta a peregrinas impresiones" 387]).[13] The second is the aristocratic individual or "noble soul" whose desire for social recognition (in the form of honor) has been rendered "inessential" or transformed into aristocratic vice. In place of these images, which are regarded as having been eclipsed, Gracián fashions the image of the "prudent" man (*discreto*). The ideals of the *discreto* are characterized first of all by his rational asceticism, otherwise known as self-imposed moderation and restraint. (See *Oráculo*, no. 82: "A wise man reduced all wisdom to moderation in all things" ["A la moderación en todo redujo la sabiduría toda un sabio" 393]; and no. 117: "Never refer to oneself. For one must praise oneself, which is pride, or one must condemn oneself, which is cowardice" ["Nunca hablar de sí. O se ha de alabar, que es desvanecimiento, o se ha de vituperar, que es poquedad" 406]). In his pursuit of self-control, Gracián's *discreto* has learned to reduce (and in this sense, to "rationalize") the contradictory passions experienced by figures like Segismundo and Don Juan. The prudent man embodies the "modern" value of social tact: "Without lying, not to speak all the truths. There is nothing that requires more tact than truth, which is like a bloodletting from the heart. Just as much is required to know how to speak the truth as to know how to silence it" ("Sin mentir, no decir todas las verdades. No hay cosa que requiera más tiento que la verdad, que es un sangrarse del corazón. Tanto es menester para saberla decir como para saberla callar" *Oráculo*, no. 181; 432). In the process, Gracián helps us see how "psychological" observation came to represent something more than a mechanism of control; in his terms it affords a means of self-regulation through self-understanding: "One cannot be master of oneself," Gracián writes, "if one does not first understand oneself. There are mirrors for the face, but not the soul; let prudent self-reflection serve this purpose" ("No puede uno ser señor de sí, si primero no se comprehende. Hay espejos del rostro, no los hay del ánimo: séalo la discreta reflexión sobre sí" *Oráculo*, no. 89; 386). In conceiving of truth in these terms, Gracián provides a framework for the modern subject's vision of itself as "in control."

With the example of Gracián we shift from a concept of "control" as modeled in the discourses of pulpit, confessional, and prayerbook—where the response to authority is by nature always inadequate, where the effects of persuasion can never be sufficiently willed, and where the action of the will remains inscrutable to mortal eyes—to a social discourse in which the ethical basis of relations is social tact, and in which the allegiance to external authority is represented as having been radically reduced. Yet it would be wrong to think that Gracián somehow represents a decisive break with the psychology of control of Counter-Reformation Spain. Indeed, it would be more accurate to say that the increasingly "rational" model of psychology evident in Gracián both incorporates and subsumes the psychological models developed during the Counter-Reformation. In the process, the methods of authoritarian control were transformed into the principles of autoregulation or "self-control" used to govern social relations in the "modern" world. While Gracián's *discreto* may have received his cultural training at court, he was formally "educated" and historically "schooled" in the Counter-Reformation's methods of control. Thus rather than think of the Counter-Reformation as having presented an obstacle to the process of subject formation in early modern Spain, it might be better to reflect on its surprising historical success. For in a writer like Gracián we can see how the Counter-Reformation's teachings came to yield not only a new source of authority, but also a new logic of truth and a personal psychology adequate to a world of appearances.

Notes

1. The point is not lost on Calderón's Segismundo, who says in Act III: "Since my courage now awaits great victories, the greatest one today will be the victory over myself" ("Pues que ya vencer aguarda / mi valor grandes victorias, / hoy ha de ser la más alta / vencerme a mí" [*La vida es sueño* 533a]).

2. Indeed, if Counter-Reformation Spain is in fact a culture of remarkably uniform authoritarian control, then it is not altogether surprising to find that those who may have been most marginalized within it might have been most strongly motivated to find ways of resisting its mechanisms of control.

3. See Cascardi, *The Subject of Modernity*, for a correction to the views expressed in Blumenberg, *Legitimacy*.

4. As Maravall's translator, Terry Cochran, points out, the issue of the *resorte* (mechanism) is of crucial importance. Literally, the term *resorte* refers to the mechanical action of a coil spring, where the act that "moves" the spring is itself already a reaction to the energy reserved in the coil. When taken as a figure for social action, as is the case in Maravall's text, the term *resorte* points equally to the motivations of individuals and to what motivates them. In Cochran's formulation, the spring came to represent the model for all social activity, including the posing of political hegemony and counterhegemony ("The Translating Mechanism," *Culture of the Baroque* xxi-xxxi).

5. I would hasten to add that these questions are in one respect false, for they fail to recognize the covert links between subjectivity and subjection—between the psychology of the free and autonomous "modern" self and the authority of the liberal State—as a recurrent problem of modernity. They would better be exchanged for questions about the particular modes of subjectivity and the particular discourse of legitimation characteristic of Counter-Reformation Spain.

6. Rosaura addresses the prince as "Generoso Segismundo" in Act III, 528a.

7. The passage is worth quoting in full, insofar as it reveals the ways in which the "generous soul" has learned to refashion the asceticism characteristic of the Baroque according to the principles of self-sufficiency of the new rationalism; in this respect, Descartes and Calderón could not be further apart: "Those who are generous . . . are naturally led to do great deeds, and at the same time not to undertake anything of which they do not feel themselves capable. And because they esteem nothing more than doing good to others and disregarding their own self-interest, they are always perfectly courteous, gracious and obliging to everyone. Moreover they have complete command over their passions. In particular, they have mastery over their desires, and over jealousy and envy, because everything they think sufficiently valuable to be worth pursuing is such that its acquisition depends solely on themselves; over hatred of other people, because they have esteem for everyone; over fear, because of the self-assurance which confidence in their own virtue gives them; and finally over anger, because they have very little esteem for everything that depends on others, and so they never give their enemies any advantage by acknowledging that they are injured by them" (*The Passions of the Soul* 156; in *Philosophical Writings of Descartes* I: 385).

8. The "difficulty" of Baroque style, which Beverley associates with an "antifoundationalist" conception of politics and power, may be understood as an attempt to reproduce conditions of alienation in the subject-spectator of the play, organized in such a way, however, that the subject might come eventually to welcome the imposition of order and control.

9. The erosion of strictly "naturalistic" premises about society and the self contributed in fairly direct ways to the political discourse of the Baroque. On the one hand, the antinaturalism of the Baroque reflects a new confidence in the human capacity to transform and supplement the natural world by human artifice; as such, it may be related to a series of hopeful pronouncements about the salutary consequences of human intervention in political affairs. Maravall cites the *Nueva filosofía de la naturaleza del hombre* of Miguel Sabuco (1587), and in particular Sabuco's "Discourse about what improves this world and its republics" (*Culture* 22) as but one example of the new optimism in political affairs, but I think we miss the point unless we see the State as itself the largest "supplement" of nature in the Baroque. Indeed, there were no guarantees that the human supplement of nature would not worsen the existing state of affairs, or that political conditions could not be blamed on the failures of human artifice. As one of Philip IV's advisors, in all probability González de Cellorigo, wrote of the nation's political decline, "The negligence of those who rule is without a doubt the author of misfortune and the door through which enter all the ills and injuries in the republic, and in my mind no republic suffers greater misfortune than ours

because we live with neither suspicion nor fear of catastrophe, trusting in a lack-adaisical confidence" (cited in Maravall, *Culture* 22).

10. Rather than assert masculine identity and power, Clément sees Don Giovanni in danger of losing himself by blending with the hysterical women he seduces; but his hysteria, unlike theirs, reveals the potential emptiness of an unrecognizable desire, the "emptiness of soul behind the cape and cloak" (*Opera* 36).

11. Maravall writes: "Spaniards used the theatre so that, by means of a popular and efficacious tool, they could contribute to the socialization of a system of conventions, over which at that time it was deemed the concrete social order of the nation then in force was to be supported—an order that it was necessary to preserve, in any case, without posing the question of its possible ethical content" ("Los españoles emplearon el teatro para, sirviéndose de instrumento popularmente eficaz, contribuir a socializar un sistema de convenciones, sobre las cuales en ese momento se estimó había de verse apoyado el orden social concreto vigente en el país, orden que había que conservar, en cualquier paso, sin plantear la cuestión de un posible contenido ético" *Teatro y literatura* 32-33).

12. On Maravall's reading in *Culture of the Baroque*, the "traditional" order of society is one that was imposed in the seventeenth century in the interests of maintaining the status quo, in much the same way, and through many of the same techniques, that an orthodox theology was "imposed" by the preachers and moralists of the Baroque.

13. See also no. 206 ("Know that there is vulgarity everywhere" ["Sépase que hay vulgo en todas partes" 442]) and no. 209 ("To free oneself from common foolishness" ["Librarse de las necedades comunes" 443]).

Works Cited

Blumenberg, Hans. *The Legitimacy of the Modern Age*. Trans. Robert M. Wallace. Cambridge: MIT Press, 1983.

Calderón de la Barca. *La vida es sueño*. In *Obras completas*, Vol. 1, Ed. Angel Valbuena Briones. Madrid: Aguilar, 1969.

Cascardi, Anthony J. *The Subject of Modernity*. Cambridge: Cambridge Univ. Press, forthcoming.

Clément, Catherine. *Opera, or The Undoing of Women*. Trans. Betsy Wing. Minneapolis: Univ. of Minnesota Press, 1988.

Cochran, Terry. "The Translating Mechanism." In Maravall, *The Culture of the Baroque*, xxi-xxxi.

Descartes, René. *Philosophical Writings of Descartes*. Trans. John Cottingham, Robert Stoothoff, and Dugald Murdoch. Cambridge: Cambridge Univ. Press, 1985.

Elias, Norbert. *Power and Civility*. Trans. Edmund Jephcott. New York: Pantheon, 1982.

Elliott, J. H. "Concerto Barroco." *The New York Review of Books*. April 9, 1987: 26-29.

Gilman, Stephen. "An Introduction to the Ideology of the Baroque in Spain." *Symposium* 1(1946): 82-107.

Gilson, Etienne. *Etudes sur le rôle de la pensée médiévale dans la formation du système Cartésien*. Paris: J. Vrin, 1951.

Gracián, Baltasar. *Oráculo manual y arte de prudencia*. Ed. Arturo del Hoyo. Barcelona: Plaza y Janés, 1986.

Habermas, Jürgen. *The Philosophical Discourse of Modernity*. Trans. Frederick Lawrence. Cambridge: MIT Press, 1987.

Maravall, José Antonio. *Teatro y literatura en la sociedad Barroca*. Madrid: Seminarios y Ediciones, 1972.

————. *La cultura del barroco*. Barcelona: Ariel, 1975.

————. *Culture of the Baroque: Analysis of a Historical Structure*. Trans. Terry Cochran. Minneapolis: Univ. of Minnesota Press, 1986.

Tirso de Molina. *El burlador de Sevilla y convidado de piedra*. Ed. Joaquín Casalduero. Madrid: Cátedra, 1977.

Vega Carpio, Lope Félix de. "Arte nuevo de hacer comedias en este tiempo." Ed. Juan Manuel Rozas. Madrid: Sociedad General Española de Librería, 1976.

Contributors

Gwendolyn Barnes-Karol. Recently received her Ph.D. in Spanish from the University of Minnesota. An Assistant Professor at St. Olaf College, she is also General Editor of *Hispanic Issues.* Currently, she is preparing a book on religious oratory.

John R. Beverley. Teaches at the University of Pittsburgh, where he is Professor of Hispanic Languages and Literatures. He has written extensively on the politics of Golden Age and Latin American literatures. His publications include *Aspects of Góngora's 'Soledades'* (Amsterdam: John Benjamins, 1980); *Del Lazarillo al Sandinismo: Estudios sobre la función ideológica de la literatura española e hispanoamericana* (Minneapolis: Institute for Ideologies and Literature, 1987); and with Mark Zimmerman, *Literature and Politics in the Central American Revolutions* (Austin: Univ. of Texas Press, 1990). He has also recently coedited *Texto y sociedad: Problemas de historia literaria* (Amsterdam: Ediciones Rodopi, 1990).

Anthony J. Cascardi. Associate Professor of Comparative Literature and Spanish at the University of California, Berkeley. He has recently published *The Bounds of Reason: Cervantes, Dostoevsky, Flaubert* (New York: Columbia Univ. Press, 1986) and, as editor, *Literature and the Question of Philosophy* (Baltimore: Johns Hopkins, 1987), as well as numerous essays on the relations between philosophy and literature.

Jaime Contreras. *Profesor titular* of Early Modern History at the Universidad Autónoma de Madrid. He has published widely on the Spanish Inquisition, including *El Santo Oficio de la Inquisición de Galicia: Poder, sociedad y cultura* (Madrid: Akal, 1982). He is a contributor to *Historia de la Inquisición en España y América*, J. Pérez Villanueva and B. Escandell Bonet, eds. (Madrid: Biblioteca de Autores Cristianos, Centro de Estudios Inquisitoriales, 1984); and *The Inquisition in Early Modern Europe* (DeKalb, Ill.: Northern Illinois Univ. Press, 1986).

Anne J. Cruz. Associate Professor of Spanish at the University of California, Irvine, where she teaches in the Department of Spanish and Portuguese and the Comparative Literature Program. She has written numerous articles on Golden Age poetry, prose, and theater, focusing especially on cultural and gender studies. She has published *Imitación y transformación: El petrarquismo en la poesía de Boscán y Garcilaso de la Vega* (Amsterdam: John Benjamins, 1988). Her coeditions include *Renaissance Rereadings: Intertext and Context* (Urbana: Univ. of Illinois Press, 1988); and, with Mary Elizabeth Perry, *Cultural Encounters: The Impact of the Inquisition in Spain and the New World* (Los Angeles: Univ. of California Press, 1991).

Jean Pierre Dedieu. Member of the Centre National de la Recherche Scientifique, Université de Bordeaux III, where he researches at the Maison de Pays Iberiques. He has written many important studies on the Spanish Inquisition, including "Les quatre temps de l'Inquisition," in B. Bennassar, *L'Inquisition Espagnole, XVI-XIX siècles* (Paris: Hachette, 1979); with Jaime Contreras, "Geografía de la Inquisición española. La formación de los distritos (1480-1820)," in *Hispania* 40 (1980): 37-93; and *L'Administration de la Foi* (Madrid: Biblioteca de la Casa de Velázquez, 1989). He is also a contributor to *Historia de la Inquisición en España y América*, J. Pérez Villanueva and B. Escandell Bonet, eds.

Sara T. Nalle. Received her Ph.D. in Spanish History from The Johns Hopkins University and is currently Assistant Professor of History at William Paterson College. Among her articles are "Inquisitors, Priests, and the People during the Catholic Reformation in Spain," which won the 1988 Harold J. Grimm Prize of the Sixteenth Century Studies Conference and appeared in the *Sixteenth Century Journal* 18 (1987): 557-587; and "Literacy and Culture in Early Modern Castile," *Past and Present* 125 (1989): 65-96. She has recently authored *God in La Mancha: Religious Reform and the People of Cuenca, 1500-1650.*

Mary Elizabeth Perry. Research Associate at the UCLA Center for Medieval and Renaissance Studies, and Adjunct Professor of History at Occidental College. A social historian, she has published articles on issues of gender and deviance. Her books include *Crime and Society in Early Modern Seville* (Hanover, N.H.: Univ. Press of New England, 1980); and *Gender and Disorder in Early Modern Seville* (Princeton: Princeton Univ. Press, 1990). She has coedited, with Anne J. Cruz, *Cultural Encounters: The Impact of the Inquisition in Spain and the New World.*

María Helena Sánchez Ortega. *Profesora titular* of Medieval and Early Modern History at the Universidad Nacional de Educación a Distancia, Madrid. Her pioneering studies on the Spanish gypsies and sexuality in Spain include *Los gitanos españoles, El período borbónico* (Madrid: Castellote, 1977); *La Inquisición y los gitanos* (Madrid: Taurus, 1988); and *La mujer y la sexualidad en el Antiguo Régimen: La perspectiva inquisitorial* (Madrid: Akal, 1991).

Bernard Vincent. Agrégé d'Histoire, he is Directeur d'Etudes of the Ecole des Hautes Etudes en Sciences Sociales, Paris. He has been General Secretary and Scientific Member of the Casa de Velázquez, Madrid, and currently directs research on marginality and minorities in Early Modern Spain at the Université de Toulouse and the Centre Nationale de Recherche Scientifique, Toulouse. Author of numerous articles, he has published, with Antonio Domínguez Ortiz, *Historia de los moriscos: Tragedia de una minoría* (Madrid: Revista de Occidente, 1978).

Alison Weber. Associate Professor of Spanish at the University of Virginia, she has written essays on Golden Age literature, and is guest editor of the "Feminist Topics" issue of *Journal of Hispanic Philology* 13 (Spring 1989). She has recently published *Teresa of Avila and the Rhetoric of Femininity* (Princeton: Princeton Univ. Press, 1990).

Index